Wheeling

OHIO

Ohio R.

Harpers
Ferry

Grafton

W.VIRGINIA

Kanawha R.

Charleston

exington

CKY OHIO

Cumberland
Gap

Knoxville

NORTH C

SOUTH CA

APPALACHIAN MOUNTAINS

Atlanta

GEORGIA

Andersonville

Oluster

Tallahassee

edar Keys

Washington

Shenandoah R.

VIRGINIA

Richmond

James River

Roanoke

Roanoke R.

Chesapeake Bay

Norfolk

Plymouth

ROANOKE I

Plymouth

FV

E

cy

Jefferson

Lincoln's Loyalists

L I N C O L N ' S

They were most efficient defenders of the Republic
whose loyalty was almost martyrdom.
History will do them justice,
when it shall come to be fairly & fully written.

—Charles H. Foster   February 28, 1866

LOYALISTS

Union Soldiers from the Confederacy

Richard Nelson Current

Northeastern University Press BOSTON

Northeastern University Press

Library of Congress Cataloging-in-Publication Data
Current, Richard Nelson.
   Lincoln's loyalists : Union soldiers from the Confederacy /
Richard Nelson Current.
      p.   cm.
   Includes bibliographical reference and index.
   ISBN 1-55553-124-5 (cloth)
      1. United States. Army—History—Civil War, 1861–1865. 2. United
States. Army—Recruiting, enlistment, etc.—Civil War, 1861–1865.
3. United States—History—Civil War, 1861–1865. 4. Lincoln,
Abraham, 1809–1865.   I. Title.
E491.C94   1992
973.7′41—dc20   91-47876

Designed by David Ford

Composed in Sabon by Graphic Composition, Inc., Athens, Georgia. Printed and bound by Princeton University Press, Lawrenceville, New Jersey. The paper is Glatfelter Writer's Offset, an acid-free sheet.

MANUFACTURED IN THE UNITED STATES OF AMERICA
97 96 95 94 93 92   5 4 3 2 1

TO MARCIA *a Lincolnite from Texas*

Contents

Preface

*V*ERY LITTLE has been written about white Southerners who fought for the Union in the Civil War, and nothing has heretofore been published about the group as a whole. This book, then, has necessarily been based almost entirely on primary sources, mainly those in the *Official Records* of the war. Quite a few authors, however, have helped to fill out the story, especially by providing background information. I acknowledge their work in the bibliography and endnotes of the book.

Several other people have given assistance of a more personal kind, and I wish to thank them here. Frank J. Williams allowed me free access to the wonderful Frank and Virginia Williams Collection of Lincolniana. Clark W. Evans made my research in the Library of Congress a pleasure instead of a chore. Arthur Bergeron and William C. Davis furnished copies of materials that I otherwise would never have found. Fred H. Harrington (more than thirty years ago) donated his set of the *Official Records,* which enabled me to do most of my note taking in the comfort of home. Kenneth M. Stampp gave the manuscript the benefit of his expert and critical reading. William A. Frohlich coauthored the title of the book and provided the enthusiasm and encouragement that kept me going.

R. N. C.

South Natick, Massachusetts

Lincoln's Loyalists

Virginia Volunteers

*W*HEN A GROUP of Southerners fired on the American flag, the President had to act, and he hoped for the support of a majority of the people, even in the South.

The country appeared to be breaking up. Seven states of the lower South claimed that they had seceded from the Union and that they had formed a new nation, the Confederate States of America. The Confederates had taken over forts, mints, customhouses, post offices, and other properties belonging to the United States. Most recently they had seized Fort Sumter in Charleston harbor after bombarding the fort and compelling its garrison of U.S. troops to haul down the Stars and Stripes.

Eight other slave states, those of the upper South and the border, remained in the Union for the time being. They stood in a precarious balance between the free states of the North and the slave states of the lower South.

On April 15, 1861, two days after the fall of Fort Sumter, President Abraham Lincoln acted. He found authority in a 1795 statute for "calling forth the militia to execute the laws of the Union" whenever these were resisted by "combinations too powerful to be suppressed by the ordinary course of judicial proceedings." The laws of the Union, he pointed out in a proclamation, were now being resisted by such combinations in South Carolina, Georgia, Alabama, Florida, Mississippi, Louisiana, and Texas. He therefore called upon the rest of the states for a total of 75,000 militiamen to put down the combinations and enforce the laws.

The call went by telegraph to the governors of these other states, and sooner or later a reply came by telegraph from each of them. All the replies from the free states were prompt and patriotic. Even before receiving the appeal from Washington, the governor of Minnesota had offered a thousand troops, a number larger than his state's quota would be.

But a stern refusal came from all four governors of the upper South. From John Letcher of Virginia: "The militia of Virginia will not be furnished to the powers at Washington for any such use or purpose as they have in view." From John W. Ellis of North Carolina: "You can get no troops from North Carolina." From Isham G. Harris of Tennessee: "Tennessee will not furnish a single man for [the] purpose of coercion." "In such unholy crusade no gallant son of Tennessee will ever draw his sword." And from Henry M. Rector of Arkansas: "In answer to your requisition of troops from Arkansas to subjugate the Southern States, I have to say that none will be furnished." [1]

Instead of coming to the support of Lincoln and the Union, the governors of Virginia, North Carolina, Tennessee, and Arkansas now began to give aid and comfort to his enemies. All four states of the upper South adopted ordinances of secession and joined the Confederacy.

The governors of Kentucky and Missouri, likewise denying Lincoln troops, would have preferred to lead their states into the Confederacy also. With Unionists dominating the legislature, however, Kentucky declared its neutrality, which it managed to maintain for several months. Missouri suffered the bloodletting of a war among its own people, a war the Unionists finally won. Kentucky and Missouri stayed in the Union, though secessionists claimed both states for the Confederacy. The people of the border were badly divided but, on balance, pro-Union. Three times as many (white) Missourians would fight for the Union as for the Confederacy, twice as many Marylanders, and half again as many Kentuckians. [2]

Originally, Lincoln inclined to the view that, at heart, the people of the South as a whole were mostly opposed to secession. "It may well be questioned whether there is, to-day, a majority of the legally qualified voters of any State, except perhaps South Carolina, in favor of disunion," he said in his message to Congress on July 4, 1861. "There is much reason to believe that the Union men are the majority in many, if not in every other one, of the so-called seceded States."

True, in Virginia, Tennessee, and elsewhere a majority of the voters endorsed secession when the question was put to a referendum. But by that time secession was a fait accompli, and the states of the upper

South, as well as those of the lower South, were in arms against the Lincoln government. As the President observed, "the result of an election, held in military camps, where the bayonets are all on one side of the question voted upon, can scarcely be considered as demonstrating popular sentiment. At such an election, all that large class who are, at once, *for* the Union, and *against* coercion, would be coerced to vote against the Union." [3]

Unionists in the Confederacy could also be coerced to *fight* against the Union. As the war began, Lincoln nevertheless seemed confident that a great many of them could be enlisted on the Union side. As the war dragged on and he had to call for more and more troops, he continued to look to the South to supply its share of them. He did not get as many as he hoped for, but the number he got was vastly larger than what the governors of the upper South had sworn he could ever get— which was zero. Indeed, every Confederate state except South Carolina provided at least a battalion of white soldiers for the Union army, and individual South Carolinians joined Union regiments from other states. These soldiers, known to their friends as "loyalists" and to their enemies as "tories," are the forgotten men of the Civil War.

No sooner had the Richmond convention, on April 17, 1861, voted (85–55) for secession than pro-Confederate Virginians took the offensive. Within a few days they seized the U.S. arsenal at Harpers Ferry and the navy yard at Norfolk. Governor Letcher promised military support for Maryland secessionists, who were burning railroad bridges, cutting telegraph lines, and doing all they could to prevent Northerners from coming to the defense of the nation's capital.

But Letcher had yet to gain control over the northwestern counties of his own state. Most of the people in that mountainous area had more in common with the neighboring Ohioans, Pennsylvanians, and Marylanders than with the secessionist Virginians. Yet in some of the northwestern counties the secessionists constituted a majority, and in others a large minority. Thus the stage was set for an internecine conflict between secessionists and Unionists.

Robert E. Lee, who commanded the Richmond state government's armed forces, looked to northwestern Virginia with a plan for the Confederates to extend their sway. He intended, in particular, to get control of the Baltimore and Ohio Railroad or, at least, to deprive the

United States of its use. This railroad ran from Baltimore over and through the mountains of western Maryland and northwestern Virginia to the Ohio River towns of Wheeling and Parkersburg. It was a lifeline of the Union.

To help carry out Lee's strategy, Letcher on May 3, 1861, ordered the militia of nineteen northwestern counties to rendezvous at Parkersburg and Grafton. The junction of the Baltimore and Ohio's Parkersburg and Wheeling branches, Grafton was a strategic point for the mastery of the railroad.[4] A Grafton Unionist wrote to Lincoln's secretary of war, Simon Cameron:

> You will see by Governor Letcher's late proclamation that Grafton is made a point for the concentration of the State's volunteers. This has been arranged by the secession leaders in order to intimidate us, as this is one of the strongest Union towns in this section of the State. There is no avowed secessionist in our town, and our people are very indignant at the proclamation of the governor, and are rapidly preparing to resist the entrance of troops unloyal to the Star-Spangled Banner into our town. . . . We are now enrolling men and drilling every day, collecting such arms as may be had, and preparing for a fight if Governor Letcher's troops attempt to enter our town.[5]

If there was no avowed secessionist in Grafton, there must have been some unavowed ones there. One of them confided to General Lee that, from the Confederate point of view, the situation was indeed disheartening. "The feeling in nearly all our counties is very bitter," this Grafton man wrote, "and nothing is left undone by the adherents of the old Union to discourage those who are disposed to enlist in the service of the State. I find that organizations exist in most of the counties pledged to the support of what they term the Union." There were, the man added, "various rumors about forces being sent from Ohio and Pennsylvania for the purpose of holding the Baltimore and Ohio Railroad at Grafton." The prospects for the Confederacy were poor; this part of the state was verging on "actual rebellion"—against the rebellion.[6]

Colonel George A. Porterfield got the same impression when he arrived at Grafton with his (pro-Confederate) Virginia Volunteers. There is "much bitterness of feeling among the people of this region," he reported. "They are apparently upon the verge of civil war." A "few bad men" (Unionists) had been "stirring up rebellion among the people" and intimidating the "law-abiding" citizens. "Many good citizens have been dispirited, while traitors have seized the guns and ammunition of the State, to be used against its authority. Arms in the hands of disbanded volunteer companies have been retained for the same avowed purpose." [7]

Secessionists as well as Unionists were practicing intimidation. A major of the militia in Berkeley County, which borders on the upper Potomac, fled across the river "because three companies of Confederate troops arrived there for the purpose of impressing into service all the militia." The major said that two regiments had already been impressed in Berkeley County—"most of them strong Union men who are determined to shoot their officers and go over to the Government troops the first opportunity." [8] (Compulsory military service in the Confederacy did not wait for the passage of the first conscription act on April 16, 1862. Men were "impressed" into state militias and compelled to serve as Confederate soldiers from the very beginning of the war.)

In quite a few localities the secessionists were on the attack. A band of mounted men rode from Charleston to Point Pleasant, where the Kanawha River joins the Ohio, "and took some of the most prominent Union men there prisoners and marched them off." Ohio troops from Gallipolis crossed the Ohio River and took thirty prominent secessionists as hostages for the safety of the Union men. Virginia Unionists sought refuge across the Ohio as well as across the Potomac. There were "many of the Union men with their families driven into Ohio from Jackson County—from Ravenswood and that vicinity." [9]

Pro-Confederate saboteurs had their eyes on the Baltimore and Ohio Railroad, which was especially vulnerable to sabotage, running as it did through a wild and rugged country, with many wooden trestles. Bridge burners succeeded in destroying two trestles near Fairmount and threatened "greater injury to the road" if any effort were made to repair them.

General George B. McClellan, commanding the Department of the Ohio, ordered an immediate advance to Grafton on May 26, 1861. "The principal reason for this order," he explained at the time, "was the burning of the bridges, which caused me to anticipate, by some two or three days, the more carefully prepared measures I had contemplated, with the intention of not only securing the Baltimore and Ohio Railroad, but also of driving all the armed secessionists out of Western Virginia." Though McClellan did not succeed in driving out all the armed secessionists, he managed to take Grafton and to secure the railroad for the time being.[10]

Then General Jacob D. Cox, with another U.S. force, moved up the Kanawha toward Charleston, which General Henry A. Wise held with Confederate troops, including men who had been recruited locally. General Wise, an ex-governor of Virginia and a rabid secessionist, felt that he was surrounded by a hostile people. They "invite the enemy, feed him, and he arms and drills them," he complained to Lee. "A spy is on every hill top, at every cabin, and from Charleston to Point Pleasant they swarm." As Wise retreated from Charleston, he attributed his defeat to the popular hostility. On the retreat "the State volunteers under my command lost from three to five hundred men by desertion," he reported to Lee. "The Kanawha Valley is wholly disaffected and traitorous."[11] (The Kanawha Valley was the home country of Lee's later right-hand man, the Confederate war hero Thomas J. "Stonewall" Jackson.)

By midsummer 1861 the U.S. army had gained control of a large part of northwestern Virginia. The army's victories, which the local Unionism made possible, encouraged further displays of Unionism in the area. A larger and larger number of Virginians became willing to fight for the United States.

All along, President Lincoln had been seeing to the recruitment of as many Virginians as possible. Normally, the governor would take the initiative in recruiting in a state, and he would commission the regimental and company officers. In a state where the governor refused to cooperate, however, Lincoln would have to proceed on his own.

He found a way to proceed when, in response to the April 15th call, the governor of Delaware, William Burton, said the laws of his state gave him "no authority whatever" to order militia into the U.S. service. Learning of Burton's uncooperativeness, Robert Patterson offered to help. Patterson, a nearly seventy-year-old veteran of the War of 1812 and the Mexican War, was now commanding the Pennsylvania troops. He requested and received permission "to muster into the service of the United States one or more regiments of loyal Delawareans, and to transmit the names of officers, to be selected by themselves, to the [War] Department for approval." Thus Delaware met its quota of a single regiment.[12]

The procedure used in Delaware could also be used in Virginia. On May 2 Lincoln's secretary of state, William H. Seward, recommended Colonel Frederick W. Lander as a good man to raise a Virginia regiment. Lander had just returned from a secret mission, on behalf of the Lincoln administration, to the Unionist governor of Texas, Sam Houston. Lincoln sent Seward's note of recommendation to General-in-Chief Winfield Scott (himself a Virginian) with this endorsement: "Col. Lander is a valuable man to us. Will Genl. Scott see him a few minutes, and consider the feasability of his plan?"[13]

With an assignment as General McClellan's aide-de-camp, Lander proceeded to Wheeling, Virginia. There his subordinate, Major James Oakes, took charge of recruiting. By mid-May there were, as a Confederate sympathizer indignantly reported, "between three and four hundred Federal troops stationed upon the fair grounds on Wheeling Island" in the Ohio River. They had been "regularly sworn into the service of the U.S. Government" and had been "furnished with arms by the U.S. Government" for the "express purpose of resisting the authorities of the State of Virginia."[14]

Nine of the ten companies of the First Regiment of Virginia Infantry were recruited in and around Wheeling. Company D was organized on the other side of the river, in Steubenville, Ohio; it contained refugee Virginians as well as Ohioans. The regiment completed its organization on May 23 and left for Grafton with McClellan's army a few days later. These 779 men, like the militia from other states responding to Lincoln's April 15th call, would serve for only three months.[15]

Lincoln had already realized that he would need soldiers for a longer term than that. In a proclamation of May 3, 1861, he said that "the suppression of the insurrectionary combinations now existing in several states for opposing the laws of the Union" would require "a military force in addition to that called forth" by his proclamation of April 15. He must now "call into the service of the United States" a total of 42,034 volunteers to serve for three years, "unless sooner discharged." He was doing this in his capacity as commander in chief of the army and navy "and of the Militia of the several States, when called into actual service." At the same time, he directed that the regular army be increased by 22,000 and the navy by 18,000.[16]

Lincoln thus began to construct a volunteer army while enlarging the regular army. Both of these steps were of doubtful constitutionality, since the Constitution gives Congress, not the president, the power to raise and support armies. When Lincoln referred again to "combinations" that were "opposing the laws of the Union"—and when he referred to himself as commander in chief of the "Militia of the several States"—he obviously was trying to justify his May 3rd call for volunteers on the basis of the same 1795 act he had used to justify his April 15th call for militiamen.

Lincoln now empowered Colonel Robert Anderson, the Kentuckian who had been in command at Fort Sumter when it fell, "to receive into the service of the United States as many regiments of volunteer troops from the State of Kentucky and from the Western part of the State of Virginia" as would be willing to serve for three years. These troops would be "on the same footing in every respect" as others enlisting under the May 3rd call—"except that the officers thereof" would be "commissioned by the United States" (and not by the individual states, whose governors would normally have commissioned the regimental and company officers).[17]

Anderson was soon preoccupied with his duties as commander of the Department of Kentucky, and responsibility for recruiting in western Virginia fell to the local Unionist John S. Carlile, who had led the opposition to secession at the Richmond convention and who now was acting as a special agent for the Lincoln administration. During McClellan's advance toward Grafton, Carlile urged the importance of gathering recruits along the way. "Recent developments show that it is absolutely necessary to muster in Virginia troops between Grafton and Parkersburg for service in that State," McClellan informed General-in-Chief Winfield Scott. "I am so earnestly solicited by Carlile and other reliable Unionists that I feel forced to do so." Carlile sought arms and other equipment from the War Department. "May I beg you to forward them at once," he wrote to Secretary of War Cameron, "as delay in getting them tends to discourage enlistments, while the men armed and well equipped and drilled have the opposite effect."[18]

Another factor that stimulated enlistments was the presence of the U.S. army. "There is a strong Union feeling along the route," McClellan observed during his advance, "especially in Hampshire and Morgan Counties, which only awaits protection to practically develop itself, companies in that vicinity being prepared to muster into ser-vice." (Actually, Hampshire County, on the upper Potomac, was to provide only one company for the U.S. army.) From Martinsburg, while a Union force occupied the place, General Patterson wrote: "The Union sentiment here is apparently very strong, but many fear a reverse, and that this force will retire, either voluntarily or forcibly. The people cannot be made use of to raise a force for self-defense unless supported by a strong force of U.S. troops." [19]

Lincoln was fortunate in gaining a specially authorized personal agent to assist him in his effort to recruit northwestern Virginians. This was his "particular friend" from Illinois, Ward Hill Lamon, whom he had appointed as U.S. marshal for the District of Columbia. Lamon was a native of the Shenandoah Valley, and his mother and three brothers were still living there. He feared that his brothers, as members of the local militia, would be called upon to fight for the Confederacy. So he begged his mother to remind them of the lesson she had taught all of them as children—that they should always obey their country's laws. He was now asking them "not to defend a Re-publican President" but "to defend their *Country.*" [20]

The more Lamon thought about his friends and relatives in the old homeland, the more he felt an urge to do something for them and with them. Finally, on May 27, 1861, he sat down in the U.S. marshal's office in Washington and composed a letter to his friend the President:

I was born in Frederick County, Virginia, within twenty miles from Harper's Ferry, and I lived in that section of country until I was twenty one years of age. Since that time I have associated intimately with those that I knew there in my boyhood, and I know that there are thousands of men who are at heart loyal to the Union and to the Government. Their voices are now silenced by the reign of ter-ror and violence to which they are subject, but give them an oppor-tunity and they will at once manifest their real sentiments. I desire to serve this Government to the best of my humble ability, and in so doing it would be peculiarly gratifying to me to be instrumental in relieving my early associates from their present thraldom, and to rejoice with them in seeing our standard again wave over their heads. With these ends in view, I propose to raise a regiment of one thousand men from the Valley of Virginia for and during the war, of which regiment I propose to take the command. I desire the Government to accept the regiment when raised, and should your Excellency signify your willingness to do so, I hereby tender my resignation of the office of U.S. Marshal of the District of Columbia.

Lincoln agreed to accept Lamon's regiment but declined to accept his resignation (the duties of the marshal's office fell temporarily to a deputy).

Lincoln provided a testimonial—"The bearer of this, W. H. Lamon, is entirely reliable and trustworthy"—and with it Lamon proceeded up the Maryland side of the Potomac to Williamsport, where he set up a staging area that became known as Camp Lamon. He issued a handbill to be "posted in various parts of Virginia"; it advised loyal Virginians to present themselves at Williamsport if they desired to enlist. Many loyal Virginians had already sought refuge in Maryland, and several companies of them quickly began to take form at the encampment.[21]

The companies proved slow to fill up, however, and Lamon heard from his quartermaster that according to army regulations a company could not be mustered in and be supplied by the U.S. government until it had a minimum of eighty-five men. He had expected to cross the river and find rich recruiting in the vicinity of his old Virginia home, but he was disappointed to learn that the Union forces had abandoned that vicinity and the Confederates had retaken it. The enemy had "5000 men 27 miles from Martinsburg at Mill Creek (where my folks live)," Lamon reported to Lincoln after a couple of weeks at Williamsport.

> The refugees are still coming from the "sacred soil" (that formerly flowed with milk & honey). I wish you would see Mr. Cameron and get him to authorize me to have those Virginians mustered into service as they come without reference to the minimum number for each particular company (and let us fill up the Cos. as they come in). I fear our inability to go into Va at once will entail upon me an enormous expense individually in provisioning the men as they come—as I put them on rations at once as they enrol themselves.

Lincoln was willing to make an exception for his particular friend. He replied (June 25, 1861): "I spoke to the Secretary of War yesterday, and he consents, & so do I, that as fast as you get companies, you may procure a U.S. officer, and have them mustered in. Have this done quietly; because we cannot do the labor of adopting it as a general practice." Thus Lamon would be spared the expense of provisioning unfilled companies out of his own pocket.

Union troops reoccupied Martinsburg in time for Lamon to join in celebrating the Fourth of July there. "The Flag is now waving over the Court house, and in different parts of the town," he wrote to Lincoln in the midst of the celebration. "Bands are playing 'Hail Columbia' & 'Star Spangled Banner' and there is a general jollification here." But later in the summer the rebels were back, and Lamon was eager to accumulate enough troops at Williamsport to recross the river and "try to clean out Martinsburg." [22]

By September 1861 Lamon could boast that he had raised more than twice as many troops as he had originally asked permission to raise. His "command" now consisted of two regiments, one of them a mixture of cavalry, infantry, and artillery, and the other exclusively cavalry. He had begun to form two infantry regiments besides. Still, he was not satisfied. No longer content to talk of "Lamon's Regiment," he aspired to become the leader of "Lamon's Brigade." In his correspondence (except with Lincoln) he called himself "Colonel" or, in his more expansive moods, "General," though he held no official rank except as a colonel in the Illinois militia.

Lamon found it harder and harder to get recruits in Virginia and Maryland for his projected infantry regiments, so he turned to other states. When he tried to take men from Pennsylvania, both General McClellan and Governor Andrew G. Curtin objected. Lamon then went to Illinois to recruit. Apparently he went with at least the tacit approval of Lincoln and Cameron, but eventually he received notice from the U.S. adjutant general that he had "no authority to recruit men outside of the State of Maryland."

Frustrated as he was, Lamon now gave up his anticipation of a military career. Still, he wanted to see Lamon's Brigade kept together as a monument to his labors, and he wanted to see Leonard Swett put in command of it. Swett was an old friend and fellow lawyer who had traveled the Illinois circuit with Lincoln and Lamon. Trying to persuade Lincoln to give the command to Swett, Lamon urged: "He would like it, my men would like it, and there is no one thing I would like so much. But by no means let my Brigade be broken up, or its name be changed. It will cause great disappointment among my men. They are attached to me and I am to them."

Fond of Lamon and eager for soldiers from Virginia, Lincoln had given him a fairly free rein in his unorthodox recruiting efforts. These efforts brought a bit of embarrassment to Lincoln when Lamon tried to detach an Illinois regiment from John C. Frémont's St. Louis command and add it to his own Virginia brigade. After investigating the matter, a congressional committee reported: "He seems to have made use of his official position as marshal for the District of Columbia, and his assumed position as a brigadier general, to secure his object of removing the regiment, and in travelling in special trains at public expense." The committee thought that, at the very least, "he should be called upon to refund the amount paid for the special train which took him and his friends from St. Louis to Springfield." But Lamon insisted he was the creditor rather than the debtor of the government; he claimed he had spent thousands of dollars of his own money and had never asked for a penny in reimbursement.

Lincoln apparently did not reprove Lamon for his offenses—the most serious of which was impersonating an officer—but neither did Lincoln gratify him by yielding to his plea that the Lamon Brigade be allowed to keep its identity. The brigade was broken up, and its companies were distributed among other than Virginia units. The cavalry companies of what had been the First Virginia Union Volunteers became parts of the First Maryland Cavalry; the infantry companies, parts of the Third Maryland Infantry; and the artillery units, batteries of the Pennsylvania Light Artillery. In raising these and other troops, which served throughout the war, Lamon had done well by his country.[23]

By the time Lamon returned to his duties as U.S. marshal, in November 1861, Lincoln had long ceased to need special agents such as Lamon and Carlile for raising Virginia troops. For several months there had been a loyal governor of Virginia, one who cooperated in recruitment as willingly and as effectively as the governor of any Northern state.

Unionists in northwestern Virginia hoped the people of the state would reject the secession ordinance when it was put to a vote on May

23, 1861. After the ordinance won approval, the Unionists were ready to secede from secession and create a loyal government either for Virginia or for a new and separate state. In June, delegates to a convention in Wheeling set up a "restored" government for the entire commonwealth, while they began to take steps toward establishing the separate state of West Virginia, which would not be admitted to the Union until two years later. Meanwhile, Virginia had two governments and two capitals, one at Richmond and the other at Wheeling.

The Wheeling governor took office on June 20, 1861. He was Francis H. Peirpoint (he later changed the spelling of his name to Pierpont), a forty-seven-year-old native of northwestern Virginia who had spent his entire life in the state, gaining a fortune as a lawyer and merchant. His Northern-born wife was something of an abolitionist, and he himself, unlike most Virginia Unionists, had antislavery leanings. The reorganization of the Virginia government, as he saw it, was the "brightest scheme for putting down the rebellion." He looked on reorganization as a model that Unionists in East Tennessee and other parts of the South could follow in bringing about a restoration of the Union.[24]

On the day after his inauguration, Governor Peirpoint appealed to President Lincoln. There were "evil-minded persons" in Virginia who intended to overthrow the government, and "like-minded persons from other States" who had "invaded this Commonwealth," Peirpoint declared. "They are making war on the loyal people of the State. They are pressing citizens against their consent into their military organizations and seizing and appropriating their property to aid in the rebellion." The governor therefore felt it was his duty "to call on the Government of the United States for aid to suppress such rebellion and violence."

Lincoln responded through his secretary of war, no doubt composing the letter that Cameron signed, telling Peirpoint: "the President directs me to say that a large additional force will soon be sent to your relief." Lincoln took advantage of the occasion to give the Peirpoint government implied recognition and an implied apology.

The President [Cameron went on] . . . never supposed that a brave and free people, though surprised and unarmed, could long be subjugated by a class of political adventurers always adverse to them, and the fact that they have already rallied, reorganized their government, and checked the march of these invaders demonstrates how justly he appreciated them. The failure hitherto of the State authorities . . . to organize its quota of troops called for by the President, imposed upon him the necessity of providing himself for their organization, and this has been done to some extent; but instructions have now been given to the agent of the Federal Government to proceed hereafter under your directions, and the company and field officers will be commissioned by you.[25]

Cameron then informed Carlile: "As the President has now been appealed to by his excellency Governor Peirpoint, . . . you are requested to take your instructions from him in organizing forces in Virginia."[26] Having acted as an agent of the Federal government and having played a leading role at the Wheeling convention in the creation of the new state government, Carlile was a congressman-elect from loyal Virginia and would soon become a U.S. senator from that state.

Lincoln soon made his recognition of the Peirpoint regime quite explicit. The U.S. government, he told Congress on July 4, 1861, had to deal with the "giant insurrection" wherever it found it, and Virginians had allowed it to "make its nest" among them. "And it [the U.S. government] has the less regret, as the loyal citizens have, in due form, claimed its protection. These loyal citizens, this government is bound to recognize, and protect, as being Virginia."[27]

Peirpoint and Carlile labored hard with recruiting and organizing troops, but they kept running into difficulty because of a lack of supplies. Carlile, in Washington for the special session of Congress, wrote again and again to Cameron and tried repeatedly to see him, without success. Finally he turned to Lincoln. "By great exertions we have got up a spirit of enlistment in the volunteer service of the United States," he wrote. "Our men who have enlisted have been lying out without even a blanket, destitute of tents and camp equipage, destitute of arms and ammunition, for weeks and weeks." Lincoln immediately sent a note to Cameron: "Please lose no time, in giving an interview to Adjt. Genl. Wheat of Western Virginia, and furnish him, if possible, with what arms, equipage &c. &c. he needs."

But supplies still failed to keep up with enlistments, and Peirpoint dispatched two members of his council, Daniel Lamb and James W.

Paxton, to Washington. Carlile, now in the Senate, gave Peirpoint's men an introduction to Lincoln, who handed them a note to take to Cameron: "If it is possible to furnish 5000 stand of Arms to the State Govt. at Wheeling, without endangering other points too much, let it be done." The War Department complied to the extent of providing 2,000 arms and 200,000 cartridges.[28]

When the Union suffered a disastrous defeat at Bull Run on July 21, 1861, it became apparent that Lincoln was going to need a larger army than Congress had authorized. The next day Congress passed a bill allowing the President to raise as many as a half-million volunteers. Congress thus approved, retroactively, Lincoln's May 3rd call for troops and his subsequent recruitment policy. (At the special session Congress also endorsed Lincoln's action in enlarging the regular army.)[29]

The Peirpoint government was eager to furnish Virginia's share of the needed volunteers. "I have received no call from the President for any definite number of troops," Peirpoint telegraphed to Carlile. "I want you to procure an order from the War Department on the Executive of Virginia for eight regiments of infantry and two of cavalry. Act immediately." The War Department authorized Peirpoint to raise the ten regiments.[30]

Peirpoint also needed state militia for duty as home guards to protect Unionist civilians. Cameron informed General William S. Rosecrans, McClellan's successor in the western Virginia command, that he might muster some of the militia into the U.S. service to guard railroad bridges. When Cameron became concerned for the safety of Washington, he inquired of Peirpoint (and the rest of the loyal governors) whether calling home guards into temporary U.S. service "would seriously retard or embarrass the enrollment and organization of the volunteer forces now being enrolled for three years, or during the war." Peirpoint replied that he had no more than 1,500 home guards and they were "scattered in single companies," most of them busy "watching organized bands of secessionists in their respective neighborhoods."[31]

Instead of lending his militia to the U.S. army, Peirpoint wanted the army to help his militia. He sent an urgent appeal to Rosecrans: "I learn that the rebels in Calhoun and Wirt [counties] have assembled 200 strong, and have killed 7 Union men last week, and are burning property daily. They [the Union men] call for help." An army officer serving in Logan County, southwest of Charleston, had reported to Peirpoint that at one time he had "had upward of 100 Union citizens in that section with him, and mostly armed," who were willing to "turn out against the rebels" but lacked self-confidence. "With 20 regular volunteers they would go almost anywhere, but would not go by themselves." [32]

Peirpoint needed weapons for his militiamen, and he learned that there were 4,000 muskets belonging to the U.S. government in Bellaire, Ohio, just across the river. "They would serve for our home guards, and are useless for any other service," he urged the War Department. "Can't you let us have them?" The chief of the ordnance bureau refused, explaining: "Our supply of arms will not admit of furnishing at this time other troops than those mustered into the U.S. service." And the men for whom Peirpoint wanted the guns were only state troops, not U.S. soldiers.

Despite this rebuff, Peirpoint remained eager to recruit for the U.S. army. When he heard that Rosecrans needed artillery, he asked Cameron for authority to raise a regiment. "You may raise and organize five batteries of artillery of six guns each," Cameron answered. "We prefer independent batteries to regiments of artillery." [33]

On October 26, 1861, Peirpoint's state adjutant general promised Cameron that by December 1 Virginia would have furnished (in addition to the regiment of three-month volunteers) ten regiments of infantry, two of cavalry, and a battalion of artillery, all to serve for three years. Peirpoint failed to meet his self-imposed December 1st deadline, but by March 20, 1862, he could boast to Edwin M. Stanton, the new secretary of war: "Mustered and ready for muster eleven regiments of infantry, two regiments and one battalion cavalry, three batteries artillery." As of June 30, 1862, according to the U.S. adjutant general's report, a total of 11,428 volunteers from "Virginia (Western)" were in the Federal service. This was a larger number than was credited at that time to New Hampshire, Vermont, Rhode Island, Connecticut, or New Jersey. [34]

Not all the men credited to Virginia were Virginians. One company of the First Virginia Regiment (the three-month volunteers) came partly from Ohio, as was pointed out earlier. The Second Infantry (the first three-year regiment) contained recruits from three states. Company A, originally the Washington Rifle Guards, had got together in Pittsburgh in response to Lincoln's first call, only to find the Pennsylvania quota already filled. They chartered a steamboat and went downriver to Wheeling, where they were mustered in. Companies D, F, G, and I also came from Pennsylvania; company H from Ohio; and companies E and K came from both sides of the Ohio River. Only companies B and C were recruited entirely in Virginia.[35]

Ohioans formed the whole of what became the Second Regiment of Loyal Virginia Infantry. The Ohio governor refused to accept the regiment, since the War Department had instructed him to raise no more cavalry for the time being. So the regiment's colonel applied to Peirpoint, who obtained Cameron's approval and accepted the organization. One of its veterans wrote long after the war: "Many of us have always regretted that we were not allowed to be mustered in as the 4th Ohio Cavalry, where we properly belonged." Several companies of the Fourth Virginia Infantry also were recruited in Ohio.[36]

These and other early recruits were volunteers in the truest sense, for they enlisted without the stimulus of a possible draft. When Congress provided for a limited draft in a new conscription act of July 17, 1862, it required the states to conscript "able-bodied male citizens between the ages of eighteen and forty-five" when necessary to fill the states' quotas of militia called into the U.S. service for periods not to exceed nine months. Meanwhile the War Department continued to depend mainly on three-year volunteers.[37]

After having temporarily declined Peirpoint's offers to provide more troops, the War Department asked for another three-year regiment from Virginia. Peirpoint replied that, since the Federal government had "discouraged all idea of further volunteering among the people," they had "engaged in other pursuits" for the summer. "I fear I cannot raise a regiment in any reasonable time." He was beginning to think that, anyhow, three years was too long to require Virginians to serve. "My decided impression is that the new levies asked for from this State should be for one-year troops," he advised Secretary Stanton. "If the rebellion cannot be put down in one year, it cannot be at all." After more than a year of strenuous exertion to raise troops, Peirpoint was losing some of his eagerness and enthusiasm. He was inclined to think that he and his Virginians had done enough.

On August 4, 1862, Lincoln issued a call for nine-month troops under the new conscription act—any "deficiency" to be made up by special draft from the militia. The quota for "Virginia (Western)" was 4,650. This quota was never filled; no men at all were furnished in response to the call. Yet the draft did not go into effect in Virginia. The 4,650 nine-month men called for would have been equivalent to one-fourth as many three-year men, or 1,163 of them, and, as Peirpoint argued, reasonably and persuasively, Virginia had already exceeded its share of three-year recruits by that many and more.[38]

The U.S. Constitution provides that "no new state shall be formed or erected within the jurisdiction of any other state" without the consent of both the other state and Congress. The Virginia legislature in Wheeling gave its consent to the formation of West Virginia, and Congress did the same.

When the statehood bill came before Lincoln, he nevertheless had some doubts about its constitutionality. After all, the legislature giving consent had been, as he noted, "chosen at elections, in which a majority of the qualified voters of Virginia did not participate." But Peirpoint kept insisting that a veto "would be disastrous to the Union cause in Western Virginia."

Lincoln finally decided that the measure was both constitutional and expedient. It was "made expedient by a war" and was "no precedent for times of peace." If, as some said, it was "our secession," there was a real difference "between secession against the constitution and secession in favor of the constitution." (Surely they strain at a gnat and swallow a camel—those contemporaries and those historians who have strained at the admission of West Virginia and swallowed the secession of Confederate Virginia.)

Lincoln signed the bill on December 31, 1862, but he would not proclaim West Virginia a state until June 20, 1863. The bill had to be ratified by West Virginia voters, and it contained a controversial amendment requiring gradual emancipation in the new state. This amendment so disgusted Carlile, the original sponsor of the bill, that he had tried to defeat the bill by enlarging the proposed boundaries so as to include counties that were proslavery and pro-Confederate. Hence there was a half-year's delay.[39]

By the time West Virginia finally was admitted, the procedure for recruiting had been drastically changed. The enrollment act of March 3, 1863, provided for Federal officials to enroll able-bodied men and to conscript them, as needed, for as long as three years. The bounty for three-year enlistees was increased from $100 to $300. Conscription was to go into effect only in those states that failed to fill their quotas through volunteering. State officials would still have the responsibility for recruiting volunteers and the possibility of thus enabling their state to avoid the draft.[40]

Both Peirpoint and the prospective governor of West Virginia, Arthur I. Boreman, protested against the steps the U.S. government began to take to carry out the enrollment act. The Wheeling adjutant general listed seven cogent reasons why the act should not be enforced in West Virginia:

First. West Virginia has contributed some four or five regiments more than her quota under the previous calls of the President.

Second. This contribution has been heavier on her loyal men because of the disloyal element therein, all of whom were included in the basis estimate on which the calls were made.

Third. Full 50 percent. of her fighting men are now in defense of the Government either as U.S. volunteers or [as] State companies.

Fourth. A conscription would result in adding to the Confederate forces as many persons as our Army would gain in West Virginia.

Fifth. The male population of West Virginia if further withdrawn from agricultural pursuits, will prevent subsistence from being raised therein for the inhabitants, the production having already reached the minimum necessary for that purpose.

Sixth. The roving bands of guerrillas, thieves, and plunderers would be able to carry on their business more successfully in the same ratio that the owners of property are withdrawn from its protection.

Seventh. The share of West Virginia can be raised by volunteers if they are permitted by the terms of their enlistment to remain in the State while the war is waged therein.

Provost-Marshal-General James B. Fry was not inclined to exempt the whole state from the possibility of conscription. "The organization of the State under the enrollment act and the enrollment (which is taking the census of the fighting men) does not provide that a draft will be made," Fry explained. "It is certain no draft will be made without giving every State due credit for all the men it has furnished." [41]

When Federal officials nevertheless began the conscription procedure in West Virginia early in 1864, Governor Boreman telegraphed to Fry: "I cannot understand this, as this State has furnished more than [its] quota of volunteers." Fry immediately issued an order suspending the West Virginia draft.

Boreman continued to seek recruits without regard to specific calls from the President. "Will you authorize me to raise one or two regiments?" he asked Stanton in July 1864. He got permission to raise only one. [42]

When Lincoln issued a new call later that year, however, Boreman had difficulty in filling the state's quota. "Counties are paying large local bounties and recruits are beginning to come in rapidly," he informed Fry in February 1865, "but without an extension of time it will be impossible to furnish the men required by voluntary enlistments." Boreman complained that the War Department had misled and confused West Virginians. According to the Department's original announcement, the quota for the First Congressional District was only *four* men. When this number quickly enlisted, the people of the district relaxed. Then there came a revised quota of nearly 1,600!

Boreman sent Lincoln a copy of the legislature's resolutions requesting the President to "exempt from draft such of the State troops as may actually be employed by the Governor in defense of the border counties . . . and to cause a credit to be given to this State upon her quota . . . for the full number of troops so employed." Boreman enclosed a list of "independent companies of scouts in the service of the State," showing 24 companies and a total of 865 men. Lincoln referred the resolutions to Stanton, and apparently West Virginia obtained both a credit for the scouts and an extension of time for volunteering. [43]

After the admission of West Virginia, Peirpoint left Wheeling, which became the capital of the new state, and moved his Virginia government to Alexandria, across the Potomac from Washington. Henceforth he actually governed only the Eastern Shore, the Norfolk area, and the counties of Alexandria, Fairfax, and Loudoun. The "insignif-

icance of the parts which are outside of the rebel lines, and consequently within his reach, certainly gives a somewhat farcical air to his
dominion," Lincoln conceded. Still, the President believed that "in organizing and furnishing troops," Peirpoint had been "as earnest, hon-
est, and efficient to the extent of his means, as any other loyal governor." [44]

Peirpoint continued to encourage recruiting, to the extent of his
means, in those parts of the state that were within his reach. From the
beginning, Lincoln had hoped to raise troops in eastern as well as
western Virginia, but the results in the east had been and remained
disappointing.

As early as June 23, 1861, General Irvin McDowell, commanding
the Department of Northeastern Virginia, obtained permission from
the War Department to "receive and muster into the service of the
United States such citizens of the State of Virginia as may offer their
services as cavalry soldiers." That was about a month before Mc-
Dowell's ill-fated Bull Run campaign, in the course of which he did
not recruit a great many Virginia cavalrymen (in fact, none at all). [45]

In November 1861, with McClellan in command of the Army of the
Potomac, Lincoln again expected that Union troops would advance
from Washington to Richmond, and he renewed the idea of recruiting
along the way. He talked with Treasury Department official John C.
Underwood about it in the White House. Underwood, a New Yorker
by birth, a Virginian by residence, had been compelled to leave his
Virginia home after supporting the Republican party and thus incur-
ring the hostility of his neighbors. He then undertook to colonize
Northerners in Virginia and thereby convert it into a free state. He
and Lincoln then agreed on a project for "the collection of our Eastern
Va Refugees into an organization first of a Regiment & on the advance
of the Army so that we could reach the Union men of the northern
counties . . . a Brigade of loyal Eastern Virginians." Both men thought
"the moral influence of such an organization would be very favorable
to the Union cause." Thus Lincoln suggested that Underwood go and
see Cameron.

Cameron was enthusiastic about the idea, and so was Peirpoint. The
governor commissioned Colonel William Wall to start by raising a
regiment. Months passed, however, and McClellan made no movement toward Richmond. In February 1862 Underwood wrote Lin-

coln: "[Colonel Wall] has given much time and money to the enterprise but in consequence of the failure of our army to open Va as was expected last fall he has only obtained about two companies of these refugees as yet though he feels confident as soon as an advance is made he can make up a Regiment of loyal men in Eastern Va." Stanton having recently replaced Cameron as secretary of war, Underwood told Lincoln: "Col Wall is apprehensive that the new secretary may not look upon his efforts with the same favor that Genl Cameron did." Wall needed "a good word" from Lincoln.

Lincoln forwarded Underwood's letter to Stanton after endorsing it: "This being a Virginia case, ought to be dealt with as favorably as possible." It was too late. Stanton had already directed his adjutant general to inform Underwood: "the authority heretofore granted you by the Secretary of War to raise a brigade of volunteers, to be known as the Eastern Virginia Brigade, is hereby revoked. Such companies as are already formed will be attached to other organizations." Attached to organizations from outside the state, these companies would lose their identity as Virginia troops.[46]

Stanton was more interested in recruiting in another part of Virginia—in Loudoun County, along the Potomac River above Washington. Soon after taking over the War Department he invited Samuel C. Means to come and see him. Means was a prominent citizen and a successful businessman of Loudoun County. He owned and operated a large flour mill there and, with his brother, a mercantile firm across the river at Point of Rocks, Maryland, where he also acted as station agent for the Baltimore and Ohio Railroad. Rebels had threatened to confiscate his property unless he sided with them. Instead of doing so, he served as a guide for New York and Pennsylvania troops raiding in Virginia. Stanton commissioned him as captain and directed him to organize an independent company of partisans or rangers.

Recruiting in Loudoun County, Means had no difficulty in filling his command. His Loudoun Rangers were mustered into the U.S. service at Lovettsville, Virginia, on June 20, 1862. A total of 120 men sooner or later enlisted. Most of them were of German or English ancestry, but, according to the company's historian, "there was quite a sprinkling of other nationalities, principally Scotch-Irish."[47]

Union recruiters made one more serious effort to enlist troops in eastern Virginia, this time in the Norfolk vicinity, which the Confederates had abandoned during McClellan's Peninsular campaign in May 1862. In December 1862 Hazard Stevens was relieved from duty as assistant adjutant general on the staff of General George W. Getty so that he could raise troops and serve as acting colonel of the "1st Regt Loyal East Virginians," with his headquarters at Portsmouth. Born in Rhode Island, Stevens had spent some time in the Pacific Northwest, where his father, Isaac Stevens, was an explorer, a negotiator with the Indians, and a governor of Washington Territory. Hazard Stevens was wounded and his father was killed in the second battle of Bull Run.[48]

Stevens launched his recruitment campaign by having the following "Notice" printed and circulated:

> The undersigned having been appointed to raise a regiment of loyal Virginians, calls upon all those desirous of proving their loyalty, to come forward and enter the regiment. Those who wish to see this unhappy war at an end; those who wish to put down the system of roadside murder now so prevalent; those who wish to remove the stigma of past disloyalty, should enter this regiment.
>
> To every man who enlists the Government offers a bounty of ONE HUNDRED DOLLARS, twenty-five dollars down, the remainder at the expiration of the term of service, and one month's pay in advance. To every man who brings in a recruit two dollars will be paid. Where the recruit comes himself, the two dollars will be paid to him.
>
> The following Recruiting Stations will be opened: BERNARD MILLS, near Suffolk, Va.; COINJACK BRIDGE, North Carolina; PORTSMOUTH, Va.; EASTERN SHORE, Va.; DEEP CREEK, Va.

Optimistically, Stevens ordered "a full supply of regimental and company books, infantry tactics and military regulations" for his prospective regiment. But he ran into resistance. Someone signing himself "Virginia" denounced the project in a letter to the Norfolk *Old Dominion*. The writer objected on two grounds: first, the bounty offered was only a hundred dollars, whereas recruits in other states were getting three or four times as much; second, the officers who joined up would all be outsiders, not Virginians. (In fact, all the proposed regimental officers were from New York, Pennsylvania, New Hampshire, Connecticut, and Rhode Island.)

Indignantly, Stevens penned a reply: "The U.S. bounty is the same here as elsewhere. In other states large bounties are paid by the State, but here not a cent. The low bounty therefore is not the fault of the Govt. nor of those engaged in raising the Regt, but of the state authorities, who with all their vaunted loyalty refuse to give one cent of bounty to those brave and loyal men who vindicate their loyalty by the sword, and not by words merely." As for the statement that no Virginian could become an officer, Stevens asserted: "This is false. True, some of the officers are taken from those who have proved their competence to command by service in the field," but any Virginian who could pass the appropriate examination could become a captain by enlisting a company, a first lieutenant by enlisting forty men, or a second lieutenant by enlisting thirty.

"But there are several advantages given to this Regt. over all others," Stevens went on, "which advantages 'Virginia' says nothing about." For one thing, the recruits could stay fairly close to home; they would "not be taken beyond the limits" of the military department of Virginia and North Carolina. For another thing, their families would be "subsisted by the Govt"; the families of men recruited in Portsmouth were already "drawing rations." So by misrepresenting the facts, "Virginia" was discouraging enlistments. Such activity, Stevens hinted, could be punished as treasonable.[49]

Stevens interrupted his recruiting efforts to serve on General Getty's staff during the battle of Fredericksburg. In January 1863, after he got back to Portsmouth, he received disheartening news from Joseph F. Throckmorton, who signed himself "Lieut. and Recruiting Officer, 1st Loyal Eastern Virginians." "I have used every effort to obtain recruits during your absence without any success whatever," Throckmorton had written from Great Bridge, Virginia. "I have kept the three recruits I have with me constantly employed, visiting their acquaintances around this vicinity, and also among the citizens passing in and out of Norfolk; the Sergeant and myself have also exerted ourselves to the utmost but to no avail."[50]

All together, the efforts of Stevens and his subordinates netted only enough men to fill one company of the First Loyal East Virginia Infantry. As of January 1865, Company A consisted of two commissioned officers and eighty-two enlisted men. They were at that time stationed in small squads on the Eastern Shore, where they patrolled the telegraph line. Other eastern Virginians, along the Potomac below Alexandria, belonged to the Accotink Home Guards.[51]

At the end of the war the U.S. provost marshal general credited West Virginia with a total of 31,872 white enlistments. He did not credit *Virginia* with a single one.

The figure 31,872 included all the troops from the northwestern counties of Virginia that eventually were incorporated in the new state. But a majority of these men had enlisted before the new state came into existence. Organized before 1863, while the area was still a part of Virginia, were three of seven cavalry regiments, five of eight artillery batteries, and seventeen of eighteen infantry regiments, as well as an independent battalion of infantry.

From the Confederate point of view, the northwestern counties never ceased to belong to (Confederate) Virginia. They constituted *terra irredenta* that needed to be restored before there could ever be peace. The Confederate Congress had resolved to maintain Virginia's integrity "to the uttermost limits of her ancient boundaries, at any and every cost."[52] It would seem reasonable, therefore, to count the white recruits from both West Virginia and Virginia as Union soldiers from the Confederacy. Certainly it is anachronistic to pretend that the state of West Virginia furnished soldiers at a time when the state did not exist.

The figure 31,872 included men who were credited to West Virginia but who actually came from Pennsylvania or Ohio. It did not, however, include those Virginians whom Lamon recruited but who were distributed among units from Maryland and Pennsylvania and were credited to those states. Nor did it include the Virginians who came from counties that were not incorporated in the state of West Virginia—the men who composed the Loudoun Rangers, Colonel Wall's two companies, and Company A of the First Loyal East Virginia Infantry. Also omitted from the official report were uncounted units of home guards or state militia that bore arms for the Union but were never mustered into the U.S. service.[53]

2   Tennessee Troops

*W*HEN SECESSION was put to the voters of Tennessee, on June 8, 1861, those in the eastern third of the state rejected it by more than two to one (32,923 to 14,780). Several days later a convention of Unionists met in Greeneville and resolved that secession was unconstitutional and that East Tennessee should become a separate state.[1] If this region, which contained in common with West Virginia the Appalachian Mountain chain, had been as readily accessible to Union forces, it too would doubtless have achieved separate statehood (perhaps with added fringes from western North Carolina and northern Georgia and Alabama).

President Lincoln looked to East Tennessee with great interest. Not only did the region offer the prospect of statehood and thus a step toward the restoration of the Union; it also had strategic importance, for across it ran railroads that formed links in the main line from Norfolk on the Atlantic Coast to Memphis on the Mississippi River. These railroad links—between East Tennessee and Virginia and between East Tennessee and Georgia—were as essential to the Confederacy as the Baltimore and Ohio Railroad was to the Union.

There was yet another reason for Lincoln's preoccupation with East Tennessee: the area had tremendous potential for recruiting. Its Unionists would add a great deal to the strength of his army if they could be reached, armed, equipped, and organized. He and his secretary of war, Simon Cameron, agreed that the government should promptly undertake to tap this source of military manpower. Lincoln endorsed Cameron's order of June 27, 1861, directing General-in-Chief Winfield Scott to "send an officer to Tennessee to muster into the service of the United States 10,000 men."[2]

For this duty, Lincoln chose the Kentuckian William ("Bull") Nelson, a brother of one of Lincoln's friends. Nelson, a muscular giant, was an Annapolis graduate, a Mexican War veteran, and a naval lieutenant. He had run errands for Lincoln in the past, helping to organize Kentucky home guards and distributing arms he had persuaded Lincoln to provide. He had also been in charge of gunboats on the Ohio River.[3]

Nelson, in Cincinnati, received orders from the War Department on July 1, 1861, to muster in five regiments of infantry and one regiment of cavalry in East Tennessee and one regiment of infantry in West Tennessee. The department would forward ten thousand stands of arms and accouterments to Cincinnati, "to be carried thence through Kentucky into East Tennessee" for distribution among the men to be mustered in there. Nelson was also to see to the raising of three infantry regiments in Kentucky, these to assist in the Tennessee operation.

Nelson proceeded at once to enlist Kentuckians and to make logistical plans. "The transportation of 13,000 stands of arms, with ammunition, accouterments, artillery with its ammunition, &c., also supplies and camp equipage from Cincinnati beyond the Cumberland Gap, a distance of 240 miles, is an undertaking of no little labor," he found. "To Nicholasville, Ky., 110 miles, I shall forward them by railroad; thence to Crab Orchard, 34 miles, is a good turnpike road; thence to the Gap, 96 miles, is a tolerable dirt road." On such a road, a wagon could haul no more than a ton; there would be 350 wagonloads.

> The gaps in the mountains are all guarded by rebel troops, but not in sufficient numbers to prevent my going through whichever gap I may select, there being seven. The one that affords the most easy access I will of course choose. I want 100 "broken mules" for pack-mules, with proper pack-saddles. Without them I will be confined in my movements to roads that are passable for wagons. With them I can move 1,000 men by a bridle-path through the mountains any reasonable distance.

Despite the difficulties and dangers, Nelson was quite optimistic— much more optimistic than the realities warranted.[4]

Others besides him were undertaking to enable East Tennesseans to fight against the secessionists. No East Tennessean was more active in the cause than Andrew Johnson, formerly governor and then U.S.

senator, the only senator who stayed in office when his state seceded. Before the Tennessee vote on secession, Johnson had campaigned vigorously against the proposition in the eastern counties. After the vote he made his way back to Washington, accompanied by another East Tennesseean who also had campaigned against secession—James P. T. Carter, a former iron manufacturer and one of three prominent Unionist brothers who were natives of the state.

In Washington, Andrew Johnson sent James Carter to the War Department with a note for Secretary of War Cameron, in which the two requested rifles for their people. Cameron referred Johnson to Nelson, who had "the requisite authority to act in the premises," so Johnson sent James Carter to Cincinnati to confer with Nelson. Carter was then to go back to East Tennessee to spy out the land and see what resistance could be expected from the Confederates. "I learn that the Secessionists of Tennessee are on the lookout for Carter," Nelson reported to Johnson, "and I fear that he will find some serious difficulty in getting through."

After Carter had left Cincinnati, Nelson heard that Carter had been talking about the proposed expedition in the presence of people who ought not know about it. According to Nelson, the "chatterbox" had put the enterprise at risk: "Strong guards are now necessary to guard the stores in their transit through Kentucky." Nelson continued to get reports of Carter's "blabbing," which he thought caused more mischief than five thousand secessionists could have done. "I am so provoked that I half wish they would catch and hang him." But Carter blamed Nelson for exposing the materiel to capture: "I think his plan a very bad one for getting through with our arms." The program was making an inauspicious start.

Traveling at night, Carter arrived before dawn on July 15 at the house of Unionist friends in Barbourville, Kentucky, thirty-three miles from Cumberland Gap. He stayed all day—"without any of the traitors in our midst suspecting he was here"—and left after dark with a local man as a guide. After a week, the guide returned with the news "that the friends about Knoxville were of the opinion if arms came on to the Gap for E Tennessee they would send any number of rebels up there and crush them out." [5]

After another week Carter himself returned and, in southeastern Kentucky, chanced to meet his older brother, Samuel Powhatan Carter. This Carter, like Nelson, was an Annapolis graduate and a naval lieutenant. He had been stationed in Brazil when the war broke out. As soon as he could, he got to Washington to offer his services for the Union cause in his home state. The navy detailed him to the War Department, which assigned him to special duty in East Tennessee, where he was to drill the troops that were to be raised there. (Eventually he would become the only American ever to hold the ranks of both rear admiral and major general.)

James Carter advised his brother Samuel "not to attempt to enter E. Tenn.," for "nearly every pass in the Cumberland mountains was even then guarded by rebels." Anyhow, "the undertaking was unnecessary, inasmuch as he [James] had made all needful arrangements for the union men to rendezvous in South Eastern Ky. where they could be organized, armed & drilled." So, while James went on to Washington—to report to Johnson, Cameron, and Lincoln—Samuel stayed in Barbourville, where he drilled Kentuckians and waited for Tennesseeans. "Many E. Tennesseeans are [due her]e in a few days, & it shall be my special business to look out for them," he informed Johnson. "If I had authority to muster them into service here & could place arms in their hands, they might be organized & be made in a very short time efficient."

Early in August the fugitives from the Confederacy began to reach Kentucky. "On the 5th, a considerable body came in, carrying the U.S. flag at their head, some armed with long hunting rifles, & many with a rough style of bowie knife, manufactured by country blacksmiths," Lieutenant Samuel Carter later recalled. "All were foot sore, travel stained & bore in their torn garments evidence of the roughness of the way over which they had made their escape from the tyranny of rebel rule; but they were overflowing with enthusiasm." [6]

"The East Tennesseeans are trying to get to Kentucky by thousands," one of the refugees wrote to Johnson, "for the purpose of arming and organizing—and then going back to relieve those we have left behind us." Not all of them managed to get safely through the mountain passes. A New Market physician and Mexican War veteran, John W. Thornburgh, organized a cavalry company

and started to Barbourville Ky. to be mustered into the service and get arms for his Co. And on the 8th of August & at night the Company got together and started and traveled all night, getting near the Cumberland Mountain 19 miles from Cumberland Gap, and stopped and rested their horses & got a cup of coffee, and then resumed their journey. As the Company got to the top of the Cumberland Mountain at the Baptist Gap, the Rebels dashed in & cut off about half of the Co. driving them back into Tennessee, taking Capt. Thornburgh prisoner & eight of his men.

Only about a third of Thornburgh's men made it to Barbourville.

At Camp Dick Robinson, near Lexington, Samuel Carter proceeded to organize escaping Tennesseeans into a regiment, of which his brother James became colonel. Robert K. Byrd, a well-to-do Roane County farmer and trader and a Mexican War veteran, organized and commanded another regiment, consisting largely of men he had brought to the camp from his home county. Byrd received his commission on September 1; Carter did not get his until September 28. So Byrd's regiment was designated the First East Tennessee and Carter's the Second.[7]

On September 30 Johnson sent a note to Lincoln's secretary of the navy, Gideon Welles: "There are now two thousand fugitives from East Tennessee under arms in Ky and impatient to march back upon their oppressors." But Virginian George H. Thomas, the officer in command at Camp Dick Robinson (who had taken over for Kentuckian William Nelson of the U.S. navy), was not ready for the men to march back. Kentucky was no longer neutral, having declared for the Union after Confederates invaded the state. General Thomas was not thinking of an early advance into East Tennessee; instead, he was worrying about the possibility of a rebel attack from that direction.[8]

Little had come of the Lincoln administration's grand scheme that Nelson was originally supposed to put into effect—the scheme for raising and arming a loyal legion in the mountains of East Tennessee.

Lincoln soon had another plan, thanks to yet another Carter brother. Even more daring and more promising, this plan was intended to bring about a revolt on the part of the Unionists in East Tennessee. Local Unionists would either seize or sabotage the railroad that ran across the eastern end of the state, and at the critical moment, the U.S. troops waiting in Kentucky would make their way through the mountain passes. The Confederates, deprived of their key rail line, would be unable to bring up reinforcements fast enough to resist the combined strength of U.S. troops and local Unionists. East Tennessee would be liberated, and a valuable source of military manpower would be made available to the Union.

The Carter brother who proposed this operation and offered to start it off was William Blount Carter, who had been a Presbyterian preacher until he resigned from the ministry on account of poor health. After the secession of Tennessee he left his East Tennessee home to give Union speeches in Kentucky and Ohio. He was in Washington when fugitive Tennesseeans began to join the U.S. army in Kentucky. On their behalf he and Johnson addressed a joint letter to Lincoln on August 6, 1861: "Although they are encompassed with enemies, our brave men are daily organizing, and are only waiting for you to place arms in their hands with which they may strike in defence of themselves & their Country." [9]

After returning to Kentucky, William Carter broached the idea of railroad sabotage to General Thomas at Camp Dick Robinson, on September 30, 1861. Thomas was enthusiastic. He immediately telegraphed to George B. McClellan, now the commander of the Army of the Potomac and the general in chief of all the Union armies, with his headquarters in Washington:

> I have just had a conversation with Mr. W. B. Carter, of Tennessee, on the subject of the destruction of the Grand Trunk Railroad through that State. He assures me that he can have it done if the Government will intrust him with a small sum of money to give confidence to the persons to be employed to do it. It would be one of the most important services that could be done for the country, and I most earnestly hope you will use your influence with the authorities in furtherance of his plans, which he will submit to you, together with the reasons for doing the work.

In Washington again, William Carter spoke with McClellan, Cameron, and Lincoln. McClellan was particularly impressed; indeed, he thought the occupation of East Tennessee a necessary precondition for his movement of the Army of the Potomac from Washington to Richmond. After the conference with Carter, Cameron urged upon William T. Sherman, commanding the Department of the Cumberland, in Louisville, "the necessity of an outward movement on our part to seize the Cumberland Gap and afford protection to our friends in East Tennessee." Later Cameron visited Sherman in Louisville and told him he "desired that the Cumberland Ford and Gap should be seized, and the East Tennessee and Virginia Railroad taken possession of, and the artery that supplied the rebellion cut." Sherman was "gloomy" and unresponsive.[10]

Leaving Washington with $2,500 to finance his undertaking, William Carter met again with General Thomas at Camp Dick Robinson. He and Thomas discussed the plan, and Thomas detailed Captain David Fry of Company E, Second Regiment East Tennessee Volunteers, to accompany him for "special service." When Carter, along with Fry, set out from the camp, he thought he and Thomas had an understanding as to what Thomas's role in the enterprise would be. Before long Carter would realize that he had been overoptimistic.

William Carter reached Morgan County, Tennessee, on October 22, to find "our Union people in this part of the State firm and unwavering in their devotion to our Government and anxious to have an opportunity to assist in saving it. The rebels continue to arrest and imprison our people." Carter engaged some loyal Tennesseeans to carry a message to Thomas and bring back lead, powder, and caps. The main point of the message was "Hasten to our aid."

Five days later Carter was in Roane County, "within a few miles of our railroad." Again he dispatched couriers with a letter for Thomas:

I have not yet had time to obtain all the information I must have before I decide on the best course for me to adopt. If I can get half a dozen brave men to "take the bull by the horns," we can whip them completely and save the railroad. If I cannot get such leaders, we will make a desperate attempt to destroy all the bridges, and I firmly believe I will be successful. . . .

I beg you to hasten to our help, as we are about to create a great diversion in General McClellan's favor. . . .

I know you will excuse a civilian for making suggestions to a military man, when you remember that I am risking my life and that I am about to ask my people to do the same. . . .

Perhaps it would be well for you to let General McClellan know that I have reached East Tennessee, as I know he is very anxious for my success.

By November 8, William Carter was ready with his part of the operation. He had arranged for armed men to station themselves near each of the main bridges on the railroad between the Virginia border and the Georgia border, a distance of more than 150 miles. That night the men were to overpower the guards at the bridges and set fire to the wooden structures. This would be the signal for loyalists throughout the area to rise and assist in their own liberation. It would only remain for Thomas's troops to arrive from Kentucky and help to rout the rebels.[11]

McClellan was indeed anxious for Carter's success. He had just sent instructions to Don Carlos Buell, who was replacing Sherman in what was now the Department of the Ohio. Sharing Lincoln's view of the matter, McClellan advised Buell:

Were the population among which you are to operate wholly or generally hostile, it is probable that Nashville should be your first and principal objective point. It so happens that a large majority of the inhabitants of Eastern Tennessee are in favor of the Union. It therefore seems proper that you should remain on the defensive on the line from Louisville to Nashville, while you throw the mass of your forces by rapid marches, by Cumberland Gap or Walker's Gap, on Knoxville, in order to occupy the railroad at that point, and thus enable the loyal citizens of Eastern Tennessee to rise, while you at the same time cut off the railway communication between Eastern Virginia and the Mississippi.

Buell was not particularly eager for an early movement toward East Tennessee, and Thomas was still less so. Thomas, now a divisional commander under Buell, thought he needed at least four additional regiments before he dared to advance. He was offended when Johnson urged him to go at once to the rescue of the East Tennesseans. "It is time that discontented persons should be silenced both in and out of the service," Thomas expostulated in private. To Johnson he said: "If the Tennesseans are not content and must go, then the risk of disaster will remain with them."[12]

On November 16 William Carter, without Captain Fry, completed the hazardous journey from East Tennessee back to Kentucky, where, at Camp Calvert, his brother Samuel was now commanding the Twelfth Brigade of Thomas's division, a brigade consisting of the First and Second Tennessee, the Sixth Kentucky, and the Thirty-first Ohio. William's news about his mission seemed so important that Samuel immediately dispatched a special messenger to convey it to General Thomas at Crab Orchard, Kentucky. "He [William] reports that on Friday night, 8th instant, of last week, he succeeded in having burned at least six, and perhaps eight, bridges on the railroad," the message read. "General . . . let us advance into East Tennessee; now is the time." [13]

In East Tennessee the Confederate authorities and sympathizers were reacting with consternation to the "atrocious rebellion" in their midst, even though they had long had reason to expect such a thing. As early as July 6 one East Tennessee secessionist had warned the Confederate secretary of war, Leroy P. Walker: "there are organized now of Union men, as they call themselves, at least ten regiments, which, if in anywise assured of aid from Lincoln and Johnson, would rise and rush into rebellion." Governor Isham G. Harris, who earlier had declared that Lincoln would never get a single soldier from Tennessee, took alarm when, in August, Tennesseeans began to cross over into Kentucky to enlist in the U.S. army. "I am satisfied from the movements of the Union men of East Tennessee that more troops should be stationed in that division of the State," he wrote Walker. "We can temporize with the rebellious spirit of that people no longer."

The events of November 8 confirmed the governor's worst fears. "The burning of railroad bridges in East Tennessee shows a deep-seated spirit of rebellion in that section," Harris advised Jefferson Davis. "Union men are organizing. This rebellion must be crushed out instantly, the leaders arrested, and summarily punished." [14]

Confederate troops began to track down the rebellious "Lincolnites," who were not easy to catch. Hearing that some of them had gathered in the vicinity of Newport, the Maine-born Confederate Colonel D. Leadbetter ordered his troops to converge there from different directions. "That country consists of a tumultuous mass of steep hills, wooded to the top, with execrable roads winding through the ravines and often occupying the beds of water-courses," he discovered. "At the farm houses along the more open valleys no men were to be seen, and it is believed that nearly the whole male population of the country were lurking in the hills on account of disaffection or fear. The women in some cases were greatly alarmed, throwing themselves on the ground and wailing like savages."

Despite the difficulty, hundreds of suspects were rounded up. Among them were prominent men, including Johnson's son-in-law Judge David T. Patterson and several members of the state legislature. (The Unionist Congressman Thomas A. R. Nelson had been arrested earlier.) "The influence of their wealth, position, and connections has been exerted in favor of the Lincoln Government, and they are the parties most to blame for the troubles in East Tennessee. They really deserve the gallows," Colonel W. B. Wood, commanding at Knoxville, informed Judah P. Benjamin, the new Confederate secretary of war. "The [other] prisoners we have tell us that they had every assurance that the [Union] army was already in the State, and would join them in a very few days; that the property of Southern men was to be confiscated and divided amongst those who would take up arms for Lincoln."

To Colonel Wood and to other commanders in East Tennessee, Confederate Secretary of War Benjamin sent the following instructions for dealing with the "traitors":

> 1st. All such as can be identified as having been engaged in bridge-burning are to be tried summarily by drum-head court-martial, and, if found guilty, executed on the spot by hanging. It would be well to leave their bodies hanging in the vicinity of the burned bridges.
>
> 2d. All such as have not been so engaged are to be treated as prisoners of war, and sent with an armed guard to Tuscaloosa, Ala., there to be kept imprisoned . . . till the end of the war. . . .
>
> P.S.—Judge Patterson, Colonel Pickens, and other ringleaders of the same class must be sent at once to Tuscaloosa to jail as prisoners of war.

Several prisoners were hanged and left hanging in accordance with Benjamin's instructions. Two were strung up on "the same limb of an oak-tree over or close by the railroad-track" in Johnson's hometown of Greeneville. Colonel Leadbetter "tied the knots with his own hands" and "ordered these two men to hang four days and nights, and the trains to pass by them slowly, so that the passengers could see, and kick, and strike with canes the dead bodies, from the front and rear platforms of the cars, as they passed,—which was actually done." But, "as the weather was somewhat warm and the corpses were becoming somewhat offensive," he "ordered them to be cut down at the expiration of some thirty-six hours." So the thoroughgoing Unionist William G. ("Parson") Brownlow heard from fellow inmates of the Knoxville jail, who were awaiting transfer to a Tuscaloosa prison. About four hundred were thus arrested and incarcerated without trial.[15]

(Maryland secessionists had previously burned bridges on the railroad between Washington and Philadelphia, and Virginia secessionists had done the same on the Baltimore and Ohio Railroad. Lincoln had authorized his army to arrest and temporarily hold without trial the Maryland bridge burners, among them John Merryman. In the Merryman case and in similar cases, Lincoln asked for no executions and no war-long imprisonment. Yet sympathizers with Merryman have denounced Lincoln for dictatorial interference with civil liberties.)

To justify the treatment of East Tennessee "traitors," the Confederates referred to Jefferson Davis's August proclamation "stating that all those who did not fully recognize their allegiance to the [Confederate] Government should . . . remove from its limits, with their effects, before October, 1861. Those persons who remained tacitly recognized the Government and are amenable to the laws." Actually, the Confederates before October 1861 had attempted to prevent, and at times had succeeded in preventing, Tennessee Unionists from leaving the Confederacy. After the November 8th bridge burning, the Davis government intensified its efforts to keep the disaffected from getting away. Those who failed to get away faced persecution. Colonel Leadbetter ordered his troops

to impress horses from Union men and be active in seizing troublesome men in all directions. They [the troops] will impress provisions, giving certificates therefor, with assurance that the amounts will be paid if the future loyalty of the sufferers shall justify the clemency of the Government. The whole country is given to understand that this course will be pursued until quiet shall be restored to these disaffected counties, and they can rely upon it that no prisoner will be pardoned so long as any Union men shall remain in arms.

Some Confederate officers thought this draconian policy unwise, for it would make their recruiting more difficult and, incidentally, would cause the innocent to suffer. "The greatest distress prevails throughout the entire country in consequence of the various arrests that have been made, together with the facts that the horses and other property of the parties that have been arrested have been seized by the soldiers, and in many cases appropriated to personal use or wantonly destroyed," wrote one officer in appealing to the Davis government for a little clemency. "Old political animosities and private grudges have been revived, and bad men among our friends are availing themselves of the opportunity afforded them by bringing Southern men to hunt down with the ferocity of bloodhounds all those against whom they entertain any feeling of dislike." [16]

The Confederate campaign of repression yielded no more than a superficial calm. "The rebellion in East Tennessee is nearly smothered," a Confederate official in Knoxville reported to Secretary Benjamin at the end of November, "but is far from being extinguished, and would burst forth with increased intensity had the enemy a commissioned Lincoln commander, quartermaster, and paymaster within our borders to form a nucleus around which our malcontents and disloyal people could rally." Men continued to escape and make their way through the mountains to the Union camps in Kentucky. "They are passing daily, almost hourly," observed a pro-Confederate citizen living on one of the routes. "If this gap could be stopped it would check a host from joining the Lincoln Army."

As late as Christmas Eve 1861 Colonel Leadbetter still had doubts about the effectiveness of all the hanging, imprisoning, and confiscating. "Notwithstanding the favorable aspect of things generally in East Tennessee," he believed, "the country is held by a slight tenure, and the approach of an enemy would lead to prompt insurrection of an aggravated character." [17]

All along, Lincoln had been hoping for Union troops to make just such an approach. So had the Carters and Johnson and Johnson's colleague and fellow East Tennesseean Horace Maynard, who remained in the U.S. House of Representatives. McClellan, too, was eager for an early advance, but Buell and Thomas still held back.

After the bridge burning, Samuel Carter repeatedly begged Thomas to get going. "Recruits are arriving almost every day from East Tennessee," Carter wrote from his Kentucky camp. "The Union men coming to us represent the people in East Tennessee as waiting with the utmost anxiety [for] the arrival of the Federal forces," and again, "if the loyal people who love and cling to the Government are not soon relieved they will be lost." [18]

When Thomas failed to respond, Carter addressed two long letters to Representative Maynard. "Will help never come?" "Can you not get those in power to give us a few more men and permission to make at least an effort to save our people?" Maynard took the letters to Lincoln, and Lincoln referred them to McClellan after endorsing each one: "Please read and consider this letter." McClellan in turn forwarded them to Buell along with a letter of his own to "urge the occupation of Eastern Tennessee."

Johnson and Maynard then sent Buell a joint telegram: "We have just held interviews with the President and General McClellan, and find they concur fully with us in respect to the East Tennessee expedition. Our people are oppressed and pursued as beasts of the forest. The Government must come to their relief. We are looking to you with anxious solicitude to move in that direction." [19]

A few weeks later, on December 29, McClellan made another attempt to prod Buell into action. "Johnson, Maynard, &c., are again becoming frantic, and have President Lincoln's sympathy excited," he wired Buell. "Political considerations would make it advisable to get the arms and troops into Eastern Tennessee at a very early day; you are, however, the best judge." And a few days after that, on January 4, 1862, Lincoln himself telegraphed Buell: "Have arms gone forward for East Tennessee? Please tell me the progress and condition of the movement in that direction. Answer."

Buell answered promptly, and for a change he was quite frank. He said: "While my preparations have had this movement constantly in view I will confess to your excellency that I have been bound to it more by my sympathy for the people of East Tennessee and the anxiety with which you and the General-in-Chief have desired it than by my opinion of its wisdom as an unconditional measure." Buell's judgment had "from the first been decidedly against it" if it should interfere with a movement toward Nashville.

Lincoln showed Buell's long telegram to McClellan. Though the commander in chief and the general in chief were beginning to have their differences about strategy, the two men agreed completely on the urgency of the East Tennessee movement. McClellan telegraphed Buell that he was "extremely sorry" to learn that Buell attached so little importance to it. "My own general plans for the prosecution of the war make the speedy occupation of East Tennessee and its lines of railway matters of absolute necessity." Nashville was "of very secondary importance." And Lincoln replied to Buell:

> Your dispatch . . . disappoints and distresses me. . . . Of the two, I would rather have a point on the railroad south of Cumberland Gap than Nashville—first, because it cuts a great artery of the enemy's communications, which Nashville does not; and, secondly, because it is in the midst of a loyal people, who would rally around it, while Nashville is not. . . .
>
> But my distress is that our friends in East Tennessee are being hanged and driven to despair, and even now I fear are thinking of taking rebel arms for the sake of personal protection. In this we lose the most valuable stake we have in the South.

The "most valuable stake we have in the South"—the loyal men who, given a chance, would swell the ranks of the Union army![20]

After Ulysses S. Grant had taken Forts Henry and Donelson, thus opening the Tennessee and Cumberland Rivers, Buell proceeded up the Cumberland and occupied Nashville on February 25, 1862. This was the first Confederate state capital to fall. Though Lincoln would have preferred Knoxville to Nashville, he was now in an even better position to begin restoring Tennessee to the Union. His next step was to appoint a military governor to oversee the process.

The logical man for the job seemed to be Andrew Johnson, who from the outset had taken the lead in promoting Unionism in Tennessee. But some who knew him thought Johnson would antagonize too many Tennesseans and keep them from resuming their loyalty to the United States. William Nelson, for one, tried to forestall Johnson's appointment. After entering Nashville with Buell's army, General Nelson forwarded his advice to Lincoln by way of Lincoln's treasury secretary, Salmon P. Chase: "do not send Andy Johnson here in any official capacity. . . . He is too much embittered." Nelson's warning did not deter Lincoln from naming Johnson military governor, with the rank of brigadier general. (As for Nelson, he was shot and killed several months later by a subordinate, the Union general Jefferson C. Davis, who was never punished for the killing.)[21]

As military governor, Johnson would be responsible for supervising the recruitment of troops. "Authority to raise regiments of loyal Tennesseeans will be granted to all suitable persons," the new secretary of war, Edwin M. Stanton, had telegraphed to Nashville even before Johnson's arrival there. "Arms and ammunition for the Volunteers will be forwarded."[22]

Johnson readily joined with Northern governors in publicly urging Lincoln to call for additional troops in the summer of 1862. Lincoln, having complied, wrote to Johnson: "You are aware we have called for a big levy of new troops. If we can get a fair share of them in Tennessee I will value it more highly than a like number most anywhere else, because of the face of the thing, and because they will be at the very place that needs protection. Please do what you can and do it quickly." Lincoln asked Johnson for two more regiments, and Johnson assured him: "The number of troops suggested can and will be raised in Tennessee."

This quota did not satisfy Johnson very long. Fearing for the safety of Nashville, and learning that Buell needed cavalry, he telegraphed to Lincoln for permission to organize mounted regiments "for home purposes." Lincoln promptly replied through Stanton: "You are authorized to raise any amount of cavalry in your State that may be required for the service."[23]

Eager though Johnson was to see Tennesseeans enlist, he ran into difficulties with recruitment from the start. Instead of cooperating efficiently, he and his subordinates bickered among themselves. The Union army failed to get and hold a firm grip on as much of the state as he had hoped it would. Confederates intensified their efforts to prevent Tennesseeans from escaping into Kentucky. And then Lincoln's emancipation policy cooled the patriotic ardor of some Unionists, even in East Tennessee. Nevertheless, Union recruiting speeded up during Johnson's first year as military governor, and he was confident that it would accelerate still more during 1863.

After the capture of Nashville, the main forces under Grant and Buell had moved on southward, meeting the enemy at Shiloh in southwestern Tennessee and then advancing to Corinth in the northeastern corner of Mississippi. A Union naval expedition under Charles Davis took Memphis on June 6, and a Union army under George W. Morgan occupied Cumberland Gap on June 18, 1862. These gains were offset, however, by a Confederate invasion of Kentucky, which threatened the Union positions in Tennessee. Indeed, after holding the Gap for only three months, Morgan had to withdraw to Cumberland Ford, fourteen miles to the north. Johnson blamed Buell for leaving Nash-ville exposed and for failing to liberate East Tennessee. He tried unsuc-cessfully to persuade Lincoln to remove Buell.

To Johnson, Buell was a longstanding bête noire, but the Carters were Johnson's close associates—General Sam, Colonel Jim, and Preacher Bill—and Johnson turned against them also. The Carters had attracted the enmity of other Tennessee officers, who competed with the Carters and with one another for recruits. Among the officers were two whom Johnson particularly favored: his son Robert and the professional soldier Alvan C. Gillem.

While trying to put together the Third East Tennessee Regiment, in Kentucky, Leonidas C. Houk accused Colonel Jim Carter of trying to steal a company intended for Houk. "Some one did *swindle me* out of sixty odd men, by telling them that I would not be permitted to raise a Regt," Houk claimed. But Robert Johnson, organizing the Fourth Regiment, told his father that Houk was "a great *scoundrel*"—"he has done every thing against me that he possibly could, *lying* &c." Then Richard M. Edwards, the colonel of an incipient cavalry regi-ment, complained "that Robt had taken about 125 of his men." It appeared, for the time being, that there were not enough East Tennes-see refugees to go around.[24]

Robert Johnson succeeded in organizing an infantry regiment, then wanted to convert it into a cavalry unit. Morgan objected on the grounds that it would be impossible to equip and feed another such regiment in addition to the two that the governor had already autho-rized. Buell agreed with Morgan. Governor Johnson overcame the ob-jections of both generals, and his son's regiment was converted into the First East Tennessee Cavalry. The son's ambition and the father's nepotism were not yet exhausted. "I am informed that the four cavalry regiments from East Tennessee were to form a brigade, and be placed under the command of Col. Robert Johnson," the governor later

wrote to General William S. Rosecrans. "Can this be done and pro-
mote the public interest? If so, it would be gratifying to me as well as
others." But Johnson was not to be gratified this time.[25]

Johnson and the Carters were still on good terms at the time he was
appointed military governor. William B. Carter congratulated him
and winsomely said: "I was truly glad to meet with your son." But
Houk and other rivalrous officers were jealous of the Carters and kept
complaining to Johnson about them. "Col. J. P. T. Carter & Brother
are determined to stand preeminent," one officer charged, and another
alleged that the colonel was "obnoxious" to the men of his own regiment: "Many want transfers to go into other Regiments but he refuses
any as I am told." Even David Fry eventually wanted to "get out from
under the Carter boys." Fry had accompanied William B. Carter on
the latter's bridge-burning mission and had been captured and sentenced to be hanged, but had escaped.[26]

Rivals of the Carters held them largely responsible for the rebel persecution of Unionists in East Tennessee. One rival wrote to Johnson:
"Our friends blame a great deal of it on the Carters for having those
bridges burned. The very name of Carter seams to be hated by almost
all of them. They believe that the Carters don't care how much East
Tenn. suffers so that they *can make money*. The question is very
gravely asked, what became of all that money Carter took with him to
pay for the burning of those bridges?"

Of course, Johnson himself had been involved in the bridge-burning
scheme, and William Carter in carrying it out had stood to lose his
life, not to gain a lot of money. Yet Johnson was not above repeating
the ugly gossip to Lincoln: "This W B Carter procured some $20,000
from the War Dept. to aid in burning bridges in East Tenn. Many of
the men employed lost their lives and sacrificed large amts. of property. Their families have rec'd not one cent from this fund. This matter
should be looked into. I wish we were clear of the whole 'Carter Concern.'" William B. Carter was, at the moment, in Washington to lobby
for Samuel P. Carter's promotion to major general, and Johnson was
trying to dissuade Lincoln from it. Lincoln was not dissuaded. After
all, he was in a better position than Johnson to know the truth about
the War Department's financing of the William B. Carter mission.[27]

In Johnson's view, Alvan C. Gillem and not Samuel P. Carter deserved a generalship. Gillem, another East Tennessee native, had taken

part in the third Seminole War after graduating from West Point. More recently, he had been a quartermaster in the Shiloh and Corinth campaign. From Shiloh he had written to Johnson to ask for the command of a Tennessee regiment, and from Corinth he later wrote to accept the command that Johnson offered him, confiding to the governor: "before the liberation of Tennessee I was indifferent as to where I served, but now I desire to go to the aid of those Tennesseeans who have suffered. . . . among the oppressed are my father & brother."[28]

After the capture of Nashville, Gillem and other officers had access to new areas of the state from which they could draw recruits. "The glorious success of our arms at Forts Henry and Donelson has been most beneficial to the Union cause throughout South and West Tennessee and Alabama," a naval lieutenant reported after a gunboat voyage up the Tennessee. "Union men can now begin to express their loyal sentiments without fear of being mobbed, especially along the banks of the river." Before Grant moved upriver, Halleck instructed him: "Any loyal Tennesseeans who desire it may be enlisted and supplied with arms."

As Grant's and Buell's armies advanced southward from Nashville, large numbers of men joined them along the way. These Tennesseeans, the state adjutant general later reported, "did not pause to select a Regiment from their own State but eagerly enlisted in any Regiment they met. At the time of the Battle of Shiloh the banks of the Tennessee River in the neighborhood of Savannah and Pittsburgh Landing were crowded with loyal men who had come from a great distance to join the Army and they enlisted rapidly in such Regiments as they found nearest at hand. The ranks of Kentucky Regiments are well filled with refugees from East Tennessee and we may say the same of other Regiments from Northern States." Indeed, fifteen hundred or more Tennesseeans who had enlisted in Kentucky were already serving in out-of-state regiments.[29]

Gillem, in Nashville, proceeded to organize and command the First Middle Tennessee Volunteers, an infantry regiment that became the Governor's Guard. The First Middle Tennessee Cavalry was also in the process of formation in Nashville, the recruits making their way there "generally by night through a country infested by guerrillas." Four or five weeks passed and the officers and men received no pay. News of this discouraged enlistments in Nashville, and the same effects were felt in Kentucky, where the Third, Fourth, Fifth, and Sixth East Tennessee Regiments also went payless for several months. When Johnson complained, the U.S. paymaster general said he could not provide money until the regiments had enrolled a certain minimum number. It was a Catch-22 proposition.[30]

Despite the poor prospects for financial reward, East Tennesseeans continued to find their way into Kentucky to enlist. "Such suffering as they portray," one observer noted. "They have sacrafized thier property, left thier wifes & little ones and traveled hundreds of miles in the night (for they dare not travel in day light) to join the United States army. . . . These have come mostly from the counties bordering upon Kentucky; thousands in the interior and upon the border of North Carolina and Virginia would come & join the army but cannot, because they are hunted like the wolf in the forrest."[31]

Those from the more remote counties generally needed the help of a guide. At one time there were said to be nine hundred potential recruits "just waiting for some one . . . they can trust to pilot them through out of Dixie." They had to find someone they could afford as well as trust. One group of twenty-five "paid their own expenses and $50.00 to a pilate to pilate them through the mountains." A whole class of professional guides or "pilots" arose to meet the need and earn the money. If captured, they could be hanged, as was Spencer Deaton, of Knox County. The most famous of them was probably Daniel Ellis, who afterwards wrote a book about his experiences. The authors of another book provided "A Sketch of Daniel Ellis' Adventures as Union Pilot, With Many Thrilling Adventures and Hair-Breadth Escapes of This Brave and Daring Scout and Pilot Who Took More than 4000 Men into the Federal Army from East Tennessee, Southwest Virginia and Western North Carolina."[32]

The more the Confederates resorted to compulsion, the more the East Tennesseeans felt like volunteering for the Union. "A captain of Tennessee militia, who was notified to draft one-half of his command and report to [Confederate] headquarters at Monroe, Overton County, Tennessee, reported here with 44 of his men," the Union commander at Columbia, Kentucky, recorded on one occasion. "He expects 160 more *en route* for these headquarters." On another occasion an officer at Paducah, Kentucky, reported: "All [are] fleeing from Weakley County, Tennessee, to escape impressment." After taking command of the Confederate department of East Tennessee, in March 1862, E. Kirby Smith discovered: "Every effort made by the State authorities to call out the militia of East Tennessee has proved unavailing."

Even when East Tennesseeans did enlist in the Confederate army, they could not be depended upon, as Kirby Smith also discovered, to his dismay. Union raiders once "surprised and captured, without the fire of a gun," most of the men of two Confederate companies near Jacksborough. "From what I have learned of the character of the troops from East Tennessee in our service, of their strong Union proclivities, greatly increased by their near relationship to and from intimate association with many citizens who have fled the country and espoused the Federal cause," Kirby Smith informed the Richmond War Department, "I am satisfied the capture near Jacksborough was the result of treachery. Pickets detailed from them cannot be relied on, and even officers are not free from suspicion of more fidelity to the Federal than to our service." [33]

Kirby Smith wanted the East Tennesseeans in his army "sent South" and replaced with good Southern troops. He also wanted "incarceration South" for the recently elected county officials, who were "generally open advocates and supporters of the Federal Government," and whom he blamed for misleading the common people. He did issue orders for administering an oath of allegiance to the officials and for arresting those who refused to take it. Then, while imposing martial law, he proclaimed an offer of forgiveness: any man so "misguided as to leave his home and join the enemy" would not be "molested or punished" if he would "return within thirty days, . . . acknowledge his error, and take an oath to support the Constitution of the State and of the Confederate States." At the same time Kirby Smith announced he would "suspend the militia draft under the State laws." [34]

The flight of Unionists increased, further stimulated by the movement of the Union army under Morgan toward Cumberland Gap in June 1862 and by the passage of the first Confederate conscription act (April 16, 1862). From the Unionist point of view, impressment into the state militia (and then into Confederate service) was bad enough, though it had been a hit-or-miss affair. But a direct and systematic drafting into the Confederate army would be much worse.

Learning that "large numbers of Union men" were "intending to go through the passes of the Cumberland into Kentucky," Kirby Smith ordered cavalry to "attack and disperse these men," few of whom were armed. From Cumberland Ford, General Morgan reported the next day: "East Tennessee is in an uproar. Yesterday 1,000 fugitives tried to come over, but were attacked and 100 taken prisoners." Kirby Smith was making little progress toward stopping the flood. On April 20, 1862, he estimated: "At least 7,000 Unionists from East Tennessee have joined his [Samuel P. Carter's] command within the last three weeks."

Frustrated, Kirby Smith uttered a new threat. He had his provost marshal make the following announcement "To the Disaffected People of East Tennessee" (April 23, 1862):

> The undersigned, in executing martial law in this department, assures those interested, who have fled to the enemy's lines and who are actually in their army, that he will welcome their return to their homes and their families. They are offered amnesty and protection if they come to lay down their arms and act as loyal citizens within the thirty days given them by Maj. Gen. E. Kirby Smith to do so.
>
> At the end of that time those failing to return to their homes and accept the amnesty thus offered and provide for and protect their wives and children in East Tennessee will have them sent to their care in Kentucky or beyond the Confederate States lines at their own expense.
>
> All that leave after this date with a knowledge of the above acts [are hereby informed that] their families will be sent immediately after them. The women and children must be taken care of by husbands and fathers either in East Tennessee or in the Lincoln Government.[35]

The flight of Unionists decreased when, on May 13, 1862, Jefferson Davis telegraphed to Kirby Smith "directing or authorizing him to suspend the execution of the conscript act in East Tennessee." But the suspension lasted for only four months. Kirby Smith's successor in the Knoxville command, J. P. McCown, then noted: "Governor Harris' and General Bragg's conscription orders have thrown the whole country into a feverish state, and . . . thousands are stampeding to the mountains and to Morgan." McCown desperately sought advice from George W. Randolph, Davis's new secretary of war: "Large numbers are fleeing to the mountains and making their way to Cumberland Gap; if caught, what must be done with them?" [36]

Randolph recommended that Davis replace McCown with someone more decisive, and so Davis sent Samuel Jones to Knoxville with instructions that his "chief duty" would be "the execution of the conscript law in East Tennessee." After arriving, Jones found "the disloyalty and disaffection to the [Confederate] Government much more general and more bitter" than he had expected. He promptly sent out a detachment "to kill, capture, or disperse a party of some 200 or 300 armed men collected together in the mountains to join the enemy in Kentucky." Similar detachments were already pursuing other such bands. To facilitate arrests, Jones recommended that Davis again suspend the privilege of the writ of habeas corpus, the previous suspension having expired. Since he thought the troops being used to enforce the draft could be better employed at other duties, Jones also urged that Davis again suspend the conscription act in East Tennessee, at least for a short time, so as to give volunteering another chance. Davis declined to do so. [37]

Nevertheless, Jones was optimistic. He felt sure that the antislavery policies of the Lincoln government would soon counteract the Unionism of the East Tennesseans. On July 17, 1862, Congress had passed the second confiscation act, which provided that slaves of persons supporting the rebellion should be "forever free." On September 22, 1862—only about a week after the Confederates had begun to enforce the draft in East Tennessee—Lincoln issued his preliminary proclamation of emancipation. A few days later Jones had an interview with Thomas A. R. Nelson, who in 1861 had been one of the foremost East Tennessee Unionists, along with such men as William B. Carter and Andrew Johnson. Nelson now agreed to write an address to the people of East Tennessee for Jones to circulate.

In the address Nelson said he would have advocated secession in 1861 if he "had believed it was the object of the North to subjugate the South and to emancipate our slaves." Nothing yet done in the war equaled "the atrocity and barbarism of Mr. Lincoln's proclamation." "Many acts have been done in the South to which we were bitterly opposed . . . but the Union men of East Tennessee are not now and never were Abolitionists." Lincoln "has suspended the writ of *habeas corpus* . . . and thus destroyed a right essential to the liberty of the citizen"; he "has become a military dictator."

Jones congratulated Nelson: "I am satisfied that you and others can soon bring about such a state of feeling in this section of the country that the troops now in service in this particular section may with safety be withdrawn." Of course, the rank and file of East Tennessee Unionists had no slaves to lose, and they had no reason to fear Lincoln's suspension of habeas corpus—while they had much reason to fear Davis's suspension of the same writ. Still, the defection of Nelson and other prominent ex-Unionists doubtless led to discouragement of the Union cause among many of the rank and file.[38]

Certainly Andrew Johnson had cause to fear that Unionists would go over to the rebel camp. A "Peace Democrat" wrote him: "The confiscation act and the President's proclamation have also driven thousands of hitherto strong union men to side with the rebellion, where now are Hon. T. A. R. Nelson N. G. Taylor & others." Johnson was relieved when Lincoln issued his final proclamation on January 1, 1863; it omitted Tennessee from the states and parts of states that were considered still in rebellion and to which the proclamation therefore applied. "Your proclamation of the 1st excepting Tennessee has disappointed & disarmed many who were complaining & denouncing it as unjust & unwise," Johnson wrote to Lincoln. "I think the exception in favor of Tennessee will be worth much to us."[39]

Recruitment in 1862 had not gone quite so well as Johnson had hoped, and he was apologetic when he responded, near the end of the year, to a request from the War Department for a list of Tennessee units: "I regret to state that, owing to the peculiar condition of affairs in this State, and the almost entire withdrawal of Federal forces from that portion of the State which was supposed to be restored to Federal control, it has been impossible for us to organize anything like a military system, with the view of proceeding under the respective calls of the President for troops." Still, the following units had already been raised: six East Tennessee regiments of infantry and two of cavalry; one Middle Tennessee regiment of infantry and one of cavalry, as well as a battery of artillery; and one West Tennessee regiment of infantry and two of cavalry. "Authority has been granted various persons of influence in the several Divisions of the State to recruit Regiments, and, as soon as the Army of the Cumberland moves forward, extending our lines so as to embrace the whole State, Tennessee will, beyond all doubt, furnish her quota of troops."

In March 1863 Johnson went to Washington and talked with Secretary of War Stanton about the problems and prospects of recruiting Tennesseeans. Lincoln, now interested in the enlistment of blacks, sent Johnson a note with a hint: "I am told you have at least *thought* of raising a negro military force." But, for the present, Johnson was still thinking of white soldiers. Before returning to Tennessee he gave the military authorities this assurance: "I shall proceed at once to raise 25,000 troops, cavalry and infantry." [40]

"East Tennessee must be redeemed." Again and again Johnson repeated this demand to Lincoln. Other East Tennesseeans petitioned the President to the same effect. To one set of petitioners he responded, on August 9, 1863: "I do as much for East Tennessee as I would, or could, if my own home and family were in Knoxville." The delay, he explained, was due to the obvious "difficulties of getting a Union army into that region." But Lincoln gave the East Tennesseeans this assurance: "The Secretary of War, Gen. Halleck, Gen. Burnside, and Gen. Rosecrans are all engaged now in an effort to relieve your section." [41]

About a month later General Ambrose E. Burnside's Army of the Ohio occupied Knoxville, and General William S. Rosecrans's Army of the Cumberland entered Chattanooga. At last the Union forces were getting a grip on East Tennessee. It was a rather uncertain grip, however, and both Knoxville and Chattanooga had yet to fight off Confederate besiegers.

In its west and middle sections, too, Tennessee remained a battleground. After the battle of Stones River, at the beginning of 1863, the Confederate Army of Tennessee had withdrawn from the central part of the state, but the Confederates continued to raid central and western Tennessee from time to time. These regions did not become entirely secure until the rout and ruin of the Confederate Army of Tennessee in the battle of Nashville (December 15–16, 1864). Meanwhile, the area accessible for Union recruiting fluctuated with the fortunes of war.

Burnside had not been in Knoxville long before Lincoln indicated to him and others his deep concern about gathering additional recruits. Local Unionists had once more appealed to the President, this time imploring him "not to abandon them again to the merciless dominion of the rebels by a withdrawal of the U.S. forces." Lincoln wired back on October 17, 1863, that he would, at worst, only "withdraw them

[U.S. forces] temporarily for the purpose of not losing the position permanently. I am in great hope of not finding it necessary to withdraw them at all, *particularly if you raise new troops rapidly for us there.*" On the same day Lincoln telegraphed to Burnside: "I am greatly interested to know how many new troops of all sorts you have raised in Tennessee. Please inform me." [42]

Burnside had thought, at first, that he could easily raise "10,000 general-service troops and 5,000 home guards" in the area within his reach. While recruiting three-year men, he announced: "For the better defense of East Tennessee the loyal citizens are hereby invited and authorized to form themselves into companies, which will be known as the National Guard of East Tennessee." As soon as these companies were organized, they would receive arms, ammunition, and "necessary equipments" from the War Department. The National Guardsmen would be entitled to regular pay but only for the periods they actually served; when their active duty was over, they would be "ordered to their homes, retaining, however, their arms and equipments." Since the men could help provide for the security of their families, without long absences from them, Burnside hoped they would "come forward with promptness and do their part."

Neither army volunteers nor National Guardsmen enlisted quite so fast as Burnside had expected. One reason was the failure of arms and equipment to arrive on time, as he explained when he responded to Lincoln's query about the number of troops raised in Tennessee. "We have already over three thousand in the three year service & half armed," he reported on October 22, 1863. "About twenty five hundred home guards; many more recruits could have been had for the three years' service but for the want of clothing & camp equipage."

There was also another reason for the lag in enlistments: recruiting could be hazardous, because Confederate regulars or rangers continued to infest the countryside. On the same day that Burnside reported his numbers to Lincoln, he ordered Captain Goldman Bryson of the First Tennessee National Guard to "proceed with his command to North Carolina and vicinity, for the purpose of recruiting." In Cherokee County, in the westernmost corner of North Carolina, Bryson and his company ran into a rebel ambush. The rebels killed two of his men and captured seventeen men along with thirty horses; meanwhile Bryson and the rest of his men scattered. A band of Cherokee Indians under the lead of a Confederate lieutenant trailed Bryson for twenty-five miles, caught up with him, and shot him to death.[43]

While Burnside was anticipating manpower gains in Knoxville, Rosecrans was equally optimistic in Chattanooga. "The number of deserters from the rebel army is great," Rosecrans informed Stanton on September 11, 1863. "Men who were conscripted on account of their loyalty [to the U.S.], men who wish the *lex talionis,* are among them. Applications are numerous for permission to enter our service. An immediate decision, if possible, by the War Department authorizing the enlistment of these men is desirable." Stanton quickly gave Rosecrans the desired permission, adding: "I have been under the impression that this authority was given to you and Governor Johnson some time ago." [44] (Deserters from the Confederate army were already being enlisted in the Union army in Tennessee and other states.)

Nevertheless, one recruiter in Chattanooga had doubts about the wisdom of enlisting deserters and of organizing home guards. "The recruiting business for three years service is greatly retarded here in consequence of hopes entertained by many that you have or will authorize the raising of twelve months troops for state defence and also that you are authorizing the raising and arming of 'home guards' &c," Richard M. Edwards wrote to Johnson. Home guards, Edwards went on to say, had been useful enough in the old days "when our fathers contended with small bands of Indians." But in the present war, wherein large armies were engaging in offensive operations, home guards could "hardly be relied on to resist such forces." But Edwards brought up a "more serious objection": namely, that the companies being formed were "composed mainly of *deserters from Bragg's army,*" and such companies were unreliable. Two of them were already "robbing stealing and plundering both parties alike"—both Unionists and pro-Confederates.[45]

After Edwards raised the Fourth Tennessee Cavalry, Johnson appointed him as its colonel. But before Edwards could be mustered in he had to take an oath, and he wondered whether he could legitimately do so. A congressional act of 1862 required officeholders, civil or military, to swear that they had never supported the rebellion in any way. Then Lincoln, on December 3, 1863, offered pardon to practically all who would swear future loyalty to the Constitution and the Union. Nevertheless, in January 1864, Edwards received a copy of a "newly prescribed oath" requiring him to swear that he had "not sought nor accepted nor attempted to exercise the functions of any office whatever under any authority or pretended authority in hostility to the United States." The problem was that Edwards had served in the state legislature after the secession of Tennessee.

"About twenty other union men served in the same legislature with me who have maintained their position as loyal men to the present time," Edwards wrote to Stanton. "Some of them in fact like myself are organizing Regiments for our service, and I suppose the same question will be presented in their behalf." Edwards also noted that in East Tennessee the Unionists had "held nearly all the state offices," and nearly all were "forced by the Rebel authorities to take an oath 'to support the confederate constitution and the constitution of Tennessee.'"

> Having then held a state office, in a *state not out of the Union* (for if out the doctrine of secession must be true, which we can not agree to) and having been forced under military power to take an illegal unconstitutional void oath, am I as well as all the other state officers of Tennessee disqualified for holding a Federal office? Having raised a good Regiment many of whom voted for me for the aforesaid office, & now desire me to lead them, I only await a decision of the above question.

Seward turned Edwards's letter over to Lincoln. Obviously, the answer might have a serious effect on Union recruiting. "On principle I dislike an oath which requires a man to swear he *has* not done wrong," Lincoln jotted down on the letter. "I think it is enough if the man does no wrong *hereafter*." That disposed of the Edwards case, though it was hardly a complete answer to his question.[46]

Despite Edwards's objection to both twelve-month troops and home guards, Johnson continued to authorize the raising of twelve-month and even three-month, or hundred-day, companies as well as three-year units. Five companies of hundred-day men signed up for one regiment in East Tennessee, their hundred days to begin when the regiment was complete. By the time the remaining five companies were raised, five months had passed, and the earlier enlistees were unwilling to stay for another three months. "We hope you will instruct the mustering officer to muster out all the men in this Regt. who have served a hundred days," Johnson told Stanton. "Many of them will enlist in three year organizations if released from their present enlistment." [47]

In Chattanooga the commanding officer imposed a special kind of draft when, in December 1864, John Bell Hood's Confederate army invaded the state (to run ultimately into the disastrous defeat at Nashville). The Chattanooga commander was Thomas F. Meagher, born in Ireland, a leader of New York City's Irish Americans. In preparation for a possible attack, Meagher ordered that "all civilians within the lines of the post be enrolled and organized into a military force," to be "known as the Civic Guard of Chattanooga." Each civilian, when enrolled, would receive a certificate, and anyone found without it would be "arrested on the spot." If the civilian had no good excuse, he would "immediately be sent by the post provost-marshal to work for thirty days on the streets or fortifications." [48]

In West Tennessee, recruitment was proceeding less rapidly than in the East. In Memphis, Stephen A. Hurlbut commanded the XVI Army Corps for a time. Born and brought up in South Carolina, Hurlbut was an old Illinois friend of Lincoln, who had made him a brigadier general at the start of the war.

In September 1863 Hurlbut directed division commanders in Kentucky and Tennessee to see to the organization of home guards, who were to serve for twelve months. He prepared an authorization form for his subordinates to use. Someone in each county was to be "hereby authorized to recruit and organize a company of mounted men to be denominated Union Guards, the object of which shall be to operate offensively and defensively in the suppression of the rebellion and all freebooting and marauding combinations which have been or may hereafter be found in this State." Hurlbut informed Andrew Johnson: "I believe the people of West Tennessee can be trusted to put down the Guerillas—against regular & organized force I must of course protect them." [49]

In April 1864, during a Confederate cavalry raid into West Tennessee, Nathan Bedford Forrest reported to Jefferson Davis that "many men heretofore Union in sentiment" were "openly expressing themselves for the South." But Forrest did not find many who were willing to join his army. "There are yet a large number of men in West Tennessee who have avoided the service, and there is little prospect of adding

to our strength by volunteering," he elaborated. "Conscription, however, would, I think, give us from 5,000 to 8,000 men, perhaps more."

But conscription, whether Union or Confederate, was no more popular in West Tennessee than elsewhere. When, in February 1865,
Johnson heard that "a draft of one man in seven" had been "ordered
in that district," he urged that the draft be postponed at least until
after the elections that were soon to be held for ratifying a new free-
state constitution. The draft nevertheless went ahead on schedule.
General N. J. T. Dana, then in charge at Memphis, reassured Johnson:
"The quota for West Tennessee had previously been so nearly filled by
voluntary enlistment of colored men that only a very small number
were drafted, and of these it is not at all probable that a man will leave
the State, and I do not think the election will be influenced by the draft
a single vote." [50]

In Middle Tennessee, as in other parts of the state, recruitment
would have proceeded faster if the War Department could have been
more prompt with money and materials. "The organization of the
Tennessee Regiments now at Nashville is progressing well, but there
are neither arms nor horses for them here," General Gillem reported
to Johnson in March 1864. "Much discontent has been caused by the
neglect or failure . . . to pay bounty."

Johnson kept badgering the War Department for arms, ammunition, and other supplies, but he had to contend with a lot of army red
tape. At one time arms for him were present in Nashville but, as he
complained to Stanton, were being "withheld without instructions
from you to issue." Consequently, Stanton authorized him to "make
requisitions upon the Ordnance officers and quartermaster at Nashville." Soon conflicts arose between Johnson's orders on the local ordnance depot and those of Ulysses S. Grant and other officers. So Stanton revoked the authorization and compelled Johnson to make
requisitions, as before, on the Ordnance Bureau in Washington. When
Johnson made another trip to Washington to expedite one of his re-
quests, he was promised: "Horse equipments will be sent at once—
carbines as soon as they can be procured." [51]

On June 24, 1864, the Nashville *Dispatch* boasted that Johnson had
raised 25,000 men—the number that, a year earlier, he had promised
Lincoln he would raise. Johnson had recently been nominated for the

vice presidency, as Lincoln's running mate on the Union ticket, and the *Dispatch* was campaigning for him. But the Nashville *Press* denounced him for endorsing Lincoln's Emancipation Proclamation and contended that the Tennesseeans in the U.S. army had not joined it to fight for abolition, so they were no longer obligated to serve in it.[52]

The emancipation issue was wedging Tennessee Unionists apart. The Carters, among others, combined with Thomas A. R. Nelson to oppose the Lincoln-Johnson ticket. James P. T. Carter condemned the use of black troops and argued that Tennessee laws, including those to punish antislavery utterances, were still in effect. Johnson and his political friends Maynard and Brownlow suspected that the Carters sympathized with the rebels because of relatives who were fighting on the rebel side.[53]

No longer were the Carters willing to cooperate with Johnson in recruiting for the Union army, as they had done so eagerly and so effectively earlier in the war. Still, recruiting in Tennessee does not seem to have fallen off much during Johnson's final year as military governor. During that time, seven new regiments of mounted infantry were organized in addition to miscellaneous other units.[54]

When the state adjutant general put together a troop summary on January 10, 1865, he could not do full justice to the Tennessee contribution for reasons that he explained:

Owing to the limited information on file pertaining to the military organizations in this State it is impossible to furnish as elaborate or concise a report as could have been done had they been recruited and organized under more favorable circumstances, which was impossible owing to the peculiar and unfavorable position the loyal portion of the inhabitants of this State occupied at the breaking out of the rebellion. Many of them were obliged to flee from the tyrannical laws of the Confederate States, into the Federal lines where they joined our army at the first opportunity, others remained at home and organized themselves into Home Guard companies and even into Regiments to act in defence of their homes and families. Some of these organizations were kept in this irregular manner until our forces under Maj Genl Burnside entered East Tennessee in the month of [September] 1863. As soon as this relief came to them they came forward promptly by Regiments and Companies in squads and singly to show their devotion to the Federal Government, and to perfect if possible the organizations of troops that they had so nobly collected together.

There being at first no state adjutant general's office, "much confusion arose in the designation of Regiments," so that for a while there were "for instance six 1st Tennessee Regiments viz. 1st East Tenn Cavalry, 1st East Tenn Infantry, 1st Mid Tenn Cavalry, 1st Mid Tenn Infantry, 1st West Tenn Cavalry, 1st West Tenn Infantry." In June 1863 all the regiments were renumbered serially, and as of January 1, 1865, the adjutant general could list the First through Fourteenth Cavalry, the First through Eleventh Infantry, and the First through Seventh Mounted Infantry (in addition to five separately numbered "colored" regiments), for a total of thirty-two white regiments. Several regiments were still in the process of recruitment, and some of those already organized had much fewer than the normal complement of about a thousand officers and men.

The state adjutant general's count of "the enlisted men and officers mustered into the U.S. service," as of January 1, 1865, totaled 28,161. Of these, 5,201 were blacks, leaving a balance of 22,960 whites. But the adjutant general pointed out not only that his tally of men in Tennessee units was incomplete but also that many Tennesseans had fled to "the Federal lines for protection" and had enlisted in regiments from other states. "It is thought that an estimate of the number of Tennesseans in the army not in Tennessee Regiments placed at 7000 would not be an overestimate. These men cannot be officially credited to the State but attention is called to the fact for the purpose of showing that we have furnished men for the army for which Tennessee has received no credit." [55]

The pro-Union state militia must also be taken into account. On September 13, 1864, Johnson issued a proclamation ordering the enrollment of the militia. Enrolled in consequence were 15,400 whites (and 3,834 blacks) who declared for the Union. These men were not necessarily organized and armed; they merely constituted a potential force upon which Johnson and Lincoln could draw. In the course of the war, some of the local militia companies or home guards were mustered into the U.S. service, and others were not.

The U.S. provost marshal general, in his April 1865 report, credited

Tennessee with a white "aggregate furnished" of 31,092. A later compilation of "Federal Rosters" listed the names of nearly 40,000 men who belonged to Tennessee outfits and were mustered into the U.S. service. Not included in either of these figures are those Tennesseeans who enlisted in out-of-state regiments and were credited to other states. Nor are those included who served in state and local units that never became part of the U.S. army.[56]

3   Carolina and Arkansas Recruits

North Carolina

*I*N THE SUMMER of 1861 U.S. troops under
General Benjamin F. Butler landed on Hatteras Island and compelled
the Confederate forces there to surrender. Soon the Confederates
abandoned their other positions on the Outer Banks, the string of narrow islands that shelter the coast of North Carolina. President Lincoln, already recruiting from Virginia and Tennessee, now had an opportunity to recruit from one more Southern state.

Lincoln did not see any such opportunity when his old friend Ward
Hill Lamon, busily recruiting Virginians, forwarded a letter from
Charles Henry Foster. A New England native, recently a North Carolina resident, Foster offered to raise a regiment of loyal North Carolinians if the Federal government would accept it and would furnish arms
and equipment for it. On August 31, 1861, three days after Butler's
troops had landed on the Outer Banks, Lincoln turned Foster's letter
over to Secretary of War Simon Cameron after noting on it: "Respectfully submitted to the War Department, with the remark that if arms
were in the hands of a Union Regiment in N.C. they probably would
not remain in their hands long." [1]

Colonel Rush C. Hawkins of the Ninth New York Volunteers,
whom General Butler left in command at Hatteras Inlet, soon discovered possibilities for recruitment on the Outer Banks. A delegation of
thirty residents called on him and gave him two pieces of paper. In one
they asked for the protection due loyal citizens, averring: "We did not
help by our votes to get North Carolina out of the Union." In the other
paper the signatories swore allegiance to the United States, promised
not to give aid or comfort to its enemies, and agreed to provide infor-

mation about the movements of the rebels. "On my part," Colonel
Hawkins reported, "I have agreed verbally to give them all the necessary protection against the vigilance committees which infest all parts
of the State, and are organized for the purpose of suppressing Union
sentiments and pressing men into the service of the Confederate Army,
and to afford them such other protection as may appear necessary.
Two hundred and fifty men have taken the oath, and they are still
coming in."

In his plans for cultivating the support of Unionists, Hawkins received a setback when some of the occupation troops, men not of his
own regiment but of the Twentieth New York, went on a vandalistic
rampage. They not only plundered the abandoned camps of the Confederates but also broke into houses and stores belonging to private
citizens. Hawkins restored to the inhabitants as much of their stolen
property as he could, and he recommended that the Federal government provide $5,000 as compensation for the rest. He also issued a
proclamation to correct the "erroneous impression" that his forces
had come with the object of "pillage and plunder."

Before long, Hawkins had another suggestion for his superiors.
"My belief is that troops could be raised here for the purpose of suppressing rebellion in North Carolina upon the assurance that they
would not be called on to go out of the State." This suggestion came
to Lincoln's attention, and the President talked it over with his general
in chief, Winfield Scott. Lincoln then reconsidered the question of
arming North Carolina Unionists. He wrote to Scott on September 16,
1861:

> Since conversing with you I have concluded to request you to frame
> an order for recruiting North Carolinians at Fort Hatteras. I sug-
> gest it be so framed as for us to accept a smaller force—even a
> company—if we cannot get a regiment or more. What is necessary
> to say about officers, you will judge. Governor [Secretary of State]
> Seward says he has a nephew (Clarence A. Seward, I believe) who
> would be willing to go and play colonel and assist in raising the
> force. Still, it is to be considered whether the North Carolinians will
> not prefer officers of their own. I should expect they would.

Orders went to Hawkins the next day "to accept the services of such
loyal North Carolinians, not to exceed one regiment, as in his neigh-

borhood may volunteer." Hawkins, "on the recommendation of the volunteers," was to nominate the officers, who would be commissioned by the President. The upshot was the enlistment of fifty or sixty local men and their assignment to garrison duty.[2]

It seemed possible, for a time, not only to recruit troops in North Carolina but also to set up a loyal state government there—one comparable to the Wheeling government of "reorganized" Virginia. The promoter of the North Carolina project was Charles Henry Foster, the man who had failed to arouse Lincoln's enthusiasm when he earlier proposed to raise a regiment of loyal North Carolinians. The Lincoln administration encouraged this newer project. Foster and an associate, the Reverend Marble Nash Taylor, talked with "certain citizens of North Carolina" residing in New York City, who concurred "unanimously and heartily" in the plan. Secretary of State Seward obtained a pass for Foster to go to Hatteras. There Foster ran for Congress and received 400 votes, but Congress refused to seat him, since the district (including its larger mainland portion) contained 9,000 voters. Nothing ultimately came of Foster's scheme for a "provisional" state government.[3]

Once they had secured the Outer Banks, the Union forces were in a position to threaten the mainland. Hawkins sent three Hatteras Islanders to "the opposite shore" to assay the Union feeling there. According to Hawkins, the three returned with information that Unionists were holding secret meetings and hoping for peace under the old government; "they have resolved to allow our forces to land without molestation if we will come in a force strong enough to protect them from the vigilance committees." But Confederates caught and imprisoned eight other islanders who carried copies of Hawkins's proclamation and the oath of allegiance and who "attempted communication with the people in Hyde County."

Confederates were apprehensive. North Carolina Governor Henry T. Clark was "urgent in his demand to have troops sent into Hyde County to counteract evil influences said to have extended from Hatteras to the main-land." There was also "an unhappy state of feeling among a portion of the citizens" in Washington County, according to a judge in nearby Williamston, and the feeling was not confined to that county but had "ramifications along the sounds in many settlements." So many pro-Confederate citizens of the coast were away in the army that the judge wondered whether there would be "a reliable majority of the people in case of invasion." [4]

Confederates had reason for alarm: Unionism was indeed deeply rooted and widespread in the coastal counties. In Washington County during the summer of 1861 farmers and laborers secretly organized a mutual-aid society and an irregular militia. They swore they would never support the Confederacy either by paying taxes or by giving military service. Taking heart from the Federal occupation of Hatteras, they prepared to assist the Yankees as soon as the Yankees approached the mainland. From all around Albemarle Sound and Pamlico Sound fearful planters were moving to the interior with their slaves. "The poorer classes remain," a U.S. naval officer at Hatteras heard, "waiting for protection to avow their Union sentiments."

General Ambrose E. Burnside, with a large amphibious expedition, succeeded in taking Roanoke Island in February and New Bern in March 1862. On reaching the mainland, the Union officers found ample confirmation of the rumored loyalism. "The hearts of the people of North Carolina are not with the rebels; the woods and swamps are full of refugees fleeing from the terror of conscription," Commodore S. C. Rowan reported from New Bern. "The people say they won't fight us, and if they must fight it will be on our side."

Burnside soon decided to enlist such men as were available. "I have authorized the organization of the First North Carolina Union Volunteers," he wrote from his New Bern headquarters to Secretary of War Edwin M. Stanton on May 5, 1862. "The movement was initiated by the Union men in and about Washington [N.C.], and I have encouraged it to the extent of feeding, clothing, and arming." [5]

Union recruiters could apparently do still better in Elizabeth City and the surrounding area. A naval officer going ashore here was visited by "100 people who only wish[ed] a leader in order to take arms in their own defense," and they "requested that a recruiting officer be sent here." Learning of this, Lieutenant Charles W. Flusser of the USS Commodore Perry thought "if the general [Burnside] would send two companies here he would meet with much greater success than at Washington." "Men from 20 odd miles around here have come to see the gunboats, and all are anxious to enlist." Lieutenant Flusser feared that if these men were not accepted, they would "soon be pressed into the Confederate Army."

Early in June 1862 Flusser took possession of Plymouth, the Washington County seat, located near the mouth of the Roanoke River. He urged upon Colonel Hawkins the possibilities for recruitment in this vicinity. Hawkins spoke with Burnside, who gave him a free hand. On June 12 Commodore Rowan reported from the USS *Philadelphia*, standing off Plymouth:

> A meeting of the country people took place on board this vessel this morning and adjourned to the custom-house, where Colonel Hawkins and myself made a few remarks, the tenor of which was to the effect that the Government was prepared to aid them in throwing off the tyranny that now oppressed them, and to put arms in their hands to defend and assert their rights, if they would organize into companies and come under military discipline. Twenty-two signed their names and the meeting was adjourned to the 16th, when many more would come in, enough, perhaps, to form a company. The commanding general, at my suggestion, has authorized Colonel Hawkins to place a company in Plymouth as a nucleus around which the Union men can rally under the protection of the gunboats.

On the day before the scheduled June 16th meeting, Hawkins detailed Company F of the Ninth New York for duty in Plymouth.[6]

Protection by the gunboats was not assured until President Lincoln intervened to assure at least a measure of it. Commodore Goldsborough had begun to withdraw the vessels from positions close to the shore, Burnside protested to Stanton: "In every place that has been visited by either the Army or Navy some Union feeling has been displayed, and in some of the places the American flag has been hoisted upon the public buildings by citizens of their own volition, and it would be manifest injustice to leave the people without a protecting force to the oppression of the rebel Government." Again: "When the boats were taken away it created much alarm among the Union people who had made demonstrations in our favor in the towns occupied by these boats." Stanton replied to Burnside: "Your dispatch in relation to the gunboats has been laid before the President. He has directed the Hunchback and Perry to remain where they are, and that Goldsborough's order for their removal be countermanded."[7]

Unionists certainly needed protection against Confederates seeking to impress or conscript them. As early as September 23, 1861, the Confederate secretary of war, Judah P. Benjamin, had advised Governor Clark to call out the militia "by volunteers or by draft," though the Confederate Congress did not pass its conscription act until April 16, 1862.

The conscription act did not work well in Bertie and adjoining counties, as a Bertie resident explained to the new governor, Zebulon B. Vance, on September 18, 1862: "Some [men] have been taken out [for the Confederate army] by the Conscript law—& the attempted execution of the law has driven many, of not very reliable character, to the enemy at Plymouth—& many more, of little better character, are in readiness to repair to Plymouth or to the gunboats, if its further execution is attempted." The "thinking men" of Bertie County had met and agreed to ask Governor Vance to intervene with President Davis and persuade him to exempt the county from further conscription—since, to repeat, "any attempt at executing the law, instead of getting soldiers for our Army, would send recruits to the enemy."

Vance eventually complied by urging Davis to suspend the draft in the counties bordering on Albemarle Sound. Instead of doing so, Davis suspended the privilege of the writ of habeas corpus, so as to make it possible to arrest and hold without trial those who resisted or evaded the conscription officers.[8]

The Confederate government was doing more for Union recruitment than was Edward Stanly, the Beaufort County native (who had been residing in California) whom Lincoln had appointed military governor soon after the Union landing on the North Carolina coast. As a military governor, Edward Stanly proved to be no Andrew Johnson. He received authority to "enlist independent volunteer companies of loyal citizens to serve within the State or their respective counties and districts." Dutifully, he went out from New Bern to visit Roanoke Island and communities around Albemarle Sound in the hope of stimulating Unionism and enlistments. But he made little progress with this endeavor, since he sympathized with and concentrated his attention upon the slaveholding planters, practically all of whom were unalterably pro-Confederate.

Stanly was and remained a rabid proslaver. He embarrassed Lincoln by provoking the House of Representatives to inquire of the President whether Stanly had "interfered to prevent the education of children, white or black." Lincoln referred the matter to Stanton, who demanded a "full and immediate answer" from Stanly. Stanly replied that he had, indeed, discouraged a man from operating a school for black children. "I thought the negro school, if approved by me, would do harm to the Union cause," Stanly explained.

Convinced that any antislavery stance would turn people away, Stanly thoroughly disapproved of Lincoln's emancipation policy. But most of the local Unionists, having no slaves of their own, did not seem to mind about emancipation so long as the blacks, once freed, would be removed from North Carolina. Men in Carteret, Craven, and Hyde counties, many of whom were serving in the First North Carolina Union Regiment, formed "Free Labor Associations" to support Lincoln's program. "They are generally down on the negro as well as his master, and desire his deportation out of the country," a *New York Tribune* correspondent reported, "but they heartily wish the slaves were free as the first necessary step in getting rid of them." Loyalists had no use for Stanly, and they wanted Lincoln to get rid of him, too. On January 15, 1863, after less than eight months as military governor, Stanly resigned. Lincoln appointed no successor.

The Emancipation Proclamation did not appear to "fill the hearts of Union men with despair," as Stanly had said it would in his letter of resignation. Union recruitment made as rapid progress after the proclamation as before. Charles Henry Foster, whom Lincoln had appointed a recruiting officer with the rank of captain, and who aspired to run for Congress again, was popular with the Free Labor Association.[9]

By January 1863 the First North Carolina Union Volunteers numbered 534 officers and men, about half as many as a full regiment, and Charles Henry Foster was organizing the Second North Carolina Union Volunteers. One company of the First Regiment was stationed at Beaufort, and a Unionist civilian there was much impressed by the men's appearance. They looked "first-rate with their sky-blue pants and dark blue hats and coats on. I believe that they make a better appearance than the Yankee soldiers do."[10]

Not all the local Union recruits were quite so impressive, and the recruiting service itself deteriorated with the passage of time. An investigator reported in April 1864 that there were recruiting stations in New Bern, Washington, Plymouth, Beaufort, and Morehead City.

These were trying to raise men for several "colored" units and also for the First and Second North Carolina Union Volunteers plus the First North Carolina Cavalry, which had just been authorized.

> Each of these organizations has sent a number of officers and men to conduct the recruiting operations in this district. Many of them are here without proper authority, and there seems to be a great lack of organization and unity of action.
>
> Some of the officers engaged have done well, and proved themselves very energetic and efficient, while others have evinced no very remarkable traits except utter incapacity and general uselessness, both as regards recruiting and care of troops. As a general thing, too large detachments are sent upon this duty. The result is that they become mere idlers, with no other object in view than to draw pay and consume rations. Some of these officers, zealous without knowledge, perhaps, seem to labor to enlist all the men they can possibly persuade, without the slightest regard to their capacity, either mental or physical.[11]

It was, perhaps, no wonder that the cavalry regiment never materialized or that the two infantry regiments never quite attained full strength.

There was, however, a much more important reason than the inefficiency of recruiters to explain why the Union enlisted no more white men in eastern North Carolina than it did. The men needed the protection of the U.S. army or navy to feel safe in volunteering, and such protection never extended beyond a fairly narrow coastal strip. Only five months after arriving, General Burnside departed with half of the occupation force to assist General George B. McClellan in the latter's Peninsular Campaign. For the rest of the war, the remaining Union troops, including the North Carolina recruits, had to content themselves with occasional raids into the interior when they were not defending themselves against Confederate counterattacks.

Once the U.S. forces had landed on the North Carolina mainland, the hope revived for an early reconstruction of the state. Lieutenant Flusser of the USS *Commodore Perry* got the impression that "the loyal people [were] two to one against the disloyal" and that, if they were given arms, "the State would soon return to her allegiance."[12] On taking over as military governor, Stanly expected that before long he would be exercising jurisdiction over the entire state. Flusser, Stanly, and others no doubt overestimated the pervasiveness of Unionism in North Carolina. Still, it was even stronger in parts of the Piedmont and in the mountains than on the coastal plain. If Lincoln could have spared enough troops to occupy key points all the way from east to west, he might not have achieved reunion at an earlier date, but he certainly could have recruited a much larger number of North Carolinians than he did.

During the first year of the war, Governor Clark received frequent reports of serious disaffection in several of the Piedmont counties. In Randolph County there were said to be numerous "abolitionists and Lincolnites," men who would boldly "hold up for the Republican Party and the North," and who were organizing and arming themselves to defy the Confederate authorities. In Guilford they were doing the same, and also in Alamance, where "some of the militia [had] in the field refused to muster under the Flag of the Confederate States and [had] defended themselves from arrest with arms in their hands." In Davidson there was "known to exist a combination of persons [who were] opposed to the Southern Confederacy, and who openly advocate[d] the Union . . . and [were] in favor of the coercion policy of Lincoln." These persons were "in the habit of mustering under the old U S Flag," and one of them "openly declare[d] it to be the design of the band to fight in support of the Lincoln government whenever an opportunity [should] present."

When Governor Clark undertook to draft militiamen to resist the Union landings on the coast, men in Guilford, Randolph, Davidson, and Moore counties demonstrated against the draft and in favor of peace. The governor sent three hundred state troops and also a regiment of Confederate soldiers to put down the demonstrations. Moore County draftees asked the slave-owning farmer and farm implement manufacturer Bryan Tyson to lead them in resisting the Confederacy. "All that was lacking was for the stars and stripes to have been planted there, with a force sufficient to defend them," Tyson later wrote. "They [the draftees] would have enlisted under the banner almost unanimously."

By resorting to force, the governor succeeded in quelling the disturbances, at least for the time being. But if the Unionists temporarily desisted from open defiance, they kept busy with underground activities. They formed a secret society, which came to be known as the

Heroes of America or the Red Strings. The members promoted the Union cause by engaging in espionage and sabotage and by assisting draft dodgers, deserters, escaped prisoners of war, and people who wanted to reach the Federal lines in eastern North Carolina or in Kentucky, Ohio, Virginia, or Tennessee.

Lincoln's emancipation policy does not seem to have diminished the zeal of the Piedmont loyalists. One of them afterwards wrote that he thought it his duty to "help defend our flag and demolish Slavery," which was "an evil thing," and thus "let the country be free and united." As the U.S. presidential campaign of 1864 was getting under way, a conscription officer reported that Montgomery County contained two hundred draft evaders whom he could not arrest because they had the sympathy and support of most of the local citizens. "[T]wo third[s] of the county are Lincoln men, they would vote today for Abe Lincoln," he said.

Between 1861 and 1865 the Confederates carried on six military campaigns against the Unionists of Randolph County. Only a month before abandoning Richmond, General Robert E. Lee sent about five hundred of his veterans to Randolph with orders "to take no prisoners among those deserters [that is, to shoot all those] who resist with arms the civil and military authorities." All together, at least sixty-eight were killed and twenty-one wounded on both sides in the various campaigns. Houses and barns of Unionists were burned, their crops and livestock destroyed. This was guerrilla warfare. As a twenty-one-year-old deserter from the Confederate army remarked of the dead Unionists, "thes[e] men were fighting for the union cause."

Indeed, all those who resisted the Confederacy, who caused a diversion of its military and other resources, were fighting for the Union just as surely as the men from the Piedmont who managed to reach the Federal lines and join the U.S. army. Uncounted numbers of them did so. There is evidence that at least one hundred Union soldiers came from the counties of Randolph, Davidson, Chatham, Moore, Montgomery, and Guilford. The total was probably much higher than that.[13]

In the North Carolina mountains Unionism was probably even more pervasive than in the Piedmont. But there were fewer people in the mountains, and it took some time for Union recruiters to gain access to the loyalists there. Fairly early in the war, Confederates expressed concern about an "organization of tories from North Carolina" that was operating in East Tennessee. Some of the "tories" made their way into Tennessee or Kentucky to join Tennessee or Kentucky regiments. Not till Ambrose E. Burnside had occupied Knoxville in September 1863, however, did western North Carolinians begin to enlist in Union regiments of their own. Before long, the Second North Carolina Mounted Infantry was organized (there was no First North Carolina Mounted Infantry).

Serving in that regiment was George W. Kirk, a native of Greene County, Tennessee, a carpenter before the war, and a former captain of East Tennessee cavalry. On February 13, 1864, General John M. Schofield (who had replaced Burnside in command at Knoxville) authorized Kirk to "raise a regiment of troops in the eastern front of Tennessee and western part of North Carolina." Kirk could mount his regiment, or part of it, but only "upon private or captured horses"; the War Department would not supply them. The outfit would be known as the Third Regiment of North Carolina Mounted Infantry.[14]

To obtain arms and men, Kirk and his associates would have to make forays from Tennessee into North Carolina. In April 1864, while Kirk distracted the local defenders by threatening another point, his subordinate Montreval Ray and a "band of tories" raided the headquarters of the Confederate home guard at Burnsville, Yancey County. "The county is gone up," the commander of the home guard reported to Governor Vance. "Swarms of men liable to conscription are gone to the tories or to the Yankees—some men that you would have no idea of—while many others are fleeing east of the Blue Ridge for refuge."[15]

In June 1864 Kirk himself led a raid on Morganton, North Carolina, far beyond the Great Smoky Mountains and the Tennessee line. He was, as the Confederate state commander of conscripts put it, "commanding a detachment of the Third Regiment North Carolina Mounted Infantry Volunteers, the same notorious tory and traitor, vagabond and scoundrel, who organized those four companies of thieves and tories at Burnsville, N.C., last April." The raiders surprised and captured Camp Vance, a rendezvous of conscripts near Morganton, and set fire to all the buildings except the hospital.

The raiding party numbered . . . between 150 and 200 men, being composed of a very few soldiers, some 25 Indians, and the remainder of deserters and tories from Tennessee and Western North Carolina. All of them were armed magnificently, the most of them with Spencer repeating rifles. They released some recusant conscripts and deserters from the guard-house here and armed them immediately. They are retreating and gathering horses and negro men, whom they arm instantly.

The commander of conscripts thus gave the impression—which Confederates generally held—that Kirk and his men were guerrillas and bushwhackers. But the commander had not been on the scene at the time of the raid. The army surgeon at Camp Vance, an eyewitness, observed: "Colonel Kirk claimed to be a regular U.S. officer, carried a U.S. flag, and his men were all in Federal uniforms." [16]

General Schofield, who had ordered Kirk's raid, sent General William T. Sherman an account of it. Kirk, he said, had not accomplished his main object, which was the destruction of the railroad bridge over the Yadkin River. But Kirk had "destroyed a large quantity of rebel property" and had captured 277 prisoners, "of which number he succeeded in bringing into Knoxville 132, together with 32 negroes and 48 horses and mules, besides obtaining 40 recruits for his regiment, and perfecting arrangements for others."

Sherman, in the field near Atlanta, was glad to hear of Kirk's exploit but thought that Kirk's recruiting was more important than his raiding. "You may encourage him all you can, more in organizing the element in North Carolina hostile to Jeff. Davis rather than in undertaking those hazardous expeditions," Sherman advised Schofield. "If he could form a series of companies in North Carolina that could protect each other, and give us the information needed, he would fully earn his compensation and our thanks." [17]

One of Kirk's recruiters was Gideon S. Smoot, a native North Carolinian, a miller in civilian life, formerly a sergeant in the Tenth Tennessee Cavalry, U.S.A., and now a first lieutenant in the Third North Carolina Mounted Infantry. Smoot aspired to raise and command another regiment, which would have been the Fourth North Carolina Mounted Infantry. He was recommended as a man who had "kept the old flag, the stars & stripes, up in Wilkesboro the longest of any town" in North Carolina. "He has brought a great many recruits out and as there are many more in that country and a great many deserters coming through, he could recruit fast." But Smoot never managed to raise his own regiment, though potential recruits were beginning to appear in fairly large numbers.[18]

By the spring of 1865 defeatism lay heavily on the Confederates in western North Carolina, as elsewhere in the South. Desertions from the Confederate ranks multiplied. The Confederate commander at Asheville heard of secret meetings being held in nearly all the counties west of the Blue Ridge with the purpose of choosing delegates to send to a secret convention, which would "organize a new State of the eastern portion of Tennessee and Western North Carolina." These meetings, the officer informed General Robert E. Lee, were "preliminary to the desertions which have occurred in this command." As the Union army of Tennesseeans and North Carolinians moved eastward through the mountains, it was, as one officer said, "considerably augmented by recruits enlisted in the North Carolina and colored regiments."[19]

At the end of the war the number of recruits credited to North Carolina, eastern and western, in the provost marshal general's report, was 3,156. This figure did not include the uncounted numbers who had enlisted in regiments of Tennessee, Kentucky, and other states. From twenty-one counties of western North Carolina alone, more than 4,000 men managed to make their way to such regiments and join them, according to a Unionist congressman from one of those counties.[20]

Arkansas

Governor Henry M. Rector of Arkansas had cause to worry. It was November 1861, seven months after he had told Lincoln bluntly that Arkansas would never give him a single soldier. "A conspiracy has been discovered in the northern part of this State against the Confederate Government," Rector now alerted Jefferson Davis from the governor's office in the capitol at Little Rock. "The intention seems to be to join Lincoln's army if it gets into Arkansas."

More than 150 of the accused pro-Lincoln conspirators were arrested. Most of them avoided prison by agreeing to join the Confederate army. Rector disapproved of this, but there was not much he could do about it. The only advice he could get from the Davis administration did not help: "You must use your best judgment in acting on the information before you." According to the information Rector had before him, there were still large numbers of secret Unionists in the state.[21]

Lincoln's army got into the state before the end of the first winter of the war. After gaining control of most of Missouri, Union forces crossed into the northwestern corner of Arkansas, where they defeated the Confederates at Pea Ridge on March 7–8, 1862. The main Confederate army then withdrew from the area.

Commanding the Union forces was General Samuel R. Curtis, a New Yorker by birth, an Iowan by residence. After the victory at Pea Ridge, Curtis started on an expedition across Arkansas to the east. "On reaching Little Rock you will assume the direction of affairs in Arkansas as military governor," General Henry W. Halleck notified him. But, on this expedition, Curtis did not manage to reach Little Rock, which was to remain in Confederate hands for more than a year.

At Batesville, on the edge of the Ozark hills northeast of Little Rock, Curtis stopped to take advantage of the recruitment opportunities that the vicinity seemed to offer. "I find the Union sentiment in the country strong and in town considerable," he reported on May 5, 1862. "The people of Arkansas are much more ready to abandon a desperate and despicable cause than some I have had to contend with [in Missouri]. They seem rather cheered by the arrival of their ancient and time-honored flag."

Curtis requested and received permission to raise ten regiments of infantry in Arkansas, but he never came close to attaining that ambitious goal. "I have earnestly and immediately complied with every order authorizing the recruiting of regiments, with poor results, because I have been so far from depots," he explained after several weeks of effort. "About 200 are in my camp and four other companies are nearly formed."[22]

One of the recruits blamed Curtis for the Union's failure to enlist a larger number of Arkansans. According to this critic, Curtis should have either stayed in Batesville or advanced upon Little Rock instead of swinging around, as he did, to Helena, below Memphis on the Mississippi River. At Batesville he would have had "an accessible point of refuge" in high and healthful country. At Helena, in the miasmatic lowland, the men became sickly and miserable; many deserted.

To make matters worse, Curtis imposed upon the men a colonel from outside the state; they would have preferred a fellow Arkansan. The colonel opened a recruiting office on Main Street in Helena but did not bother with medical examinations. "Among those recruits almost every grade of physical condition were [*sic*] represented, from the aged and infirm to the puny and effeminate boy."

Despite the low standards and a short term of enlistment—only six months—not enough men signed up to fill what was intended to be the First Arkansas Union Infantry Regiment. The resulting battalion was mustered in on July 21, 1862, and, after garrison duty in St. Louis, was mustered out on December 31, 1862.[23]

Meanwhile, with Lincoln's encouragement, Union recruiters were doing much better in the hill country near the northwestern corner of Arkansas. From Cassville, Missouri, just over the state line, the colonel of the Thirty-seventh Illinois Volunteers, Julius White, had written on May 25, 1862, to the governor of Illinois, Richard Yates:

> I have the honor to state that large numbers of loyal citizens in Northwestern Arkansas express a desire to enter the military service of the United States. I believe a regiment can be raised in two or three counties near this post (Cassville, Mo., where my regiment is now stationed), composed exclusively of Arkansans, with no expense to the Government for subsistence of recruits prior to the mustering in of the regiment entire. I respectfully ask Your Excellency to present the matter to the consideration of the President or Secretary of War. If authorized to say that a regiment or more from Arkansas would be accepted, I believe I could make a cheering report from this people, who have hitherto since the war commenced been prevented from any exhibition of their undoubted loyalty until the battle of Pea Ridge.

Governor Yates duly referred to the President this letter from Colonel White. Lincoln endorsed the envelope (unwittingly giving the colonel a boost in rank): "The President respectfully refers the inclosed to the Secretary of War, with the expression of his confidence in the energy and faithfulness of General White."[24]

The secretary of war responded by authorizing three persons to recruit in Arkansas. M. La Rue Harrison, a civilian New Yorker residing in Missouri, was to raise a cavalry regiment that would be "mustered into service, clothed, mounted, and armed at Springfield, Mo." The prospective recruits, to be organized in Missouri, were refugees from Arkansas—comparable to the refugees from Tennessee who were recruited and organized in Kentucky. Colonel W. James Morgan, on duty in Washington, D.C., was to "proceed to the State of Arkansas" and raise a regiment of cavalry there. And General Egbert B. Brown, commanding Missouri state militia in Springfield, was to organize a brigade of volunteer infantry. All these troops were to enlist for three years or the duration of the war.[25]

At his headquarters in Springfield, General Brown was optimistic. "The [Confederate] conscription is making Union people fast," he heard; "4,000 or 5,000 men can be armed against the South in Western Arkansas." Many of the conscripts being taken to Fort Smith, he also heard, were such die-hard Unionists that the Confederates were "unwilling to trust them with arms." One day the "secret agent of a Union organization" visited Brown "with a view to arranging some place by which a large number of Arkansas citizens could escape." "He reports that a regiment was made up, and through the indiscretion of some of its officers, the plot was discovered and the whole captured—a large number having arms; about 200 put in prison."

But Brown did not depend only on patriotism to fill the ranks. As fleeing Arkansans continued to seek shelter at the U.S. army posts in southwestern Missouri, he "ordered that no subsistence be given to able-bodied refugees" who failed to enlist. He demanded that to be fed they must "join one of our regiments ordered into service"—one of the Missouri or the Arkansas regiments. Nor did he simply wait for refugees to arrive; he also sent an expedition into Arkansas to fetch recruits. As a result of his efforts, men were enlisted faster than they could be equipped. "The First Arkansas and Eighth Missouri will be completed before the arms can get here if forwarded immediately," he reported on August 10, 1862.[26]

While the Union forces were still a long way from the Arkansas capital, Lincoln appointed a new military governor of the state (to serve from July 1862 to March 1863). His appointee, whom he also made a brigadier general, was John S. Phelps, a Democratic politician and former Connecticut congressman who had recently been a resident of Missouri. Lincoln's general in chief informed Phelps: "The President authorizes and empowers you to commission all officers of Arkansas Volunteers." As a military governor, Phelps of Arkansas differed from Johnson of Tennessee and Stanly of North Carolina in being a stranger to the state he was to govern.

Setting up his headquarters in Helena, Phelps started to recruit a cavalry regiment, for which he promptly commissioned the officers. But in this Mississippi River town he succeeded little better than Curtis had done in persuading men to enlist. He "made an entire failure" in procuring arms and mounts for the recruits, as one of them complained. Eventually the regiment, the Second Arkansas Cavalry, was filled up and mustered in a long way from Helena—at Pilot Knob, Missouri. As for Phelps, he went back upriver to St. Louis, where for the rest of his gubernatorial term he maintained his office in a hotel, the Planter's House.[27]

During the first year of Union recruiting in Arkansas, the results were, on the whole, disappointing to U.S. officers and local Unionists. In late 1862, stationed at Fayetteville or nearby were a cavalry regiment with 887 Arkansans and part of an infantry regiment with 370. At Helena three companies of the Second Arkansas Cavalry had been formed, comprising fewer than three hundred men. Other Arkansans, in indeterminate numbers, were serving in Missouri units, and still others in companies of Union home guards. Whatever the total, it was far less than the ten regiments that Curtis had originally asked permission to raise.[28]

The outlook for 1863 was uncertain. From Fayetteville, on January 2, General Schofield wrote to Governor Phelps in St. Louis and requested authorization to organize and equip farmers as militia so that they could protect their homes from guerrillas. "Very few volunteers for the general service can be obtained," Schofield said, "but I believe all the loyal men will gladly do duty as local militia."

Such militia might help with the enlistment of three-year volunteers, it seemed to Colonel Harrison, who was commanding the Fayetteville post. James M. Johnson, a native Arkansan, was trying to recruit infantrymen there. "Fifteen Home Guard companies ask to be organized as militia for home defense," Harrison reported on January 27. "Dr. Johnson can raise his infantry regiment from these organizations." He could "take command of these men and use them as auxiliaries" until his regiment was full. "These men will require no pay, and only a little sugar, salt, and coffee, and will be a bulwark here in raising volunteer regiments."[29]

Apparently, Lincoln's emancipation policy was not the cause of the slowdown in Union recruitment—certainly not in the mountainous northwestern part of the state, though Confederate recruiters tried to exploit the issue there. In a March 1863 proclamation "To the People of North and West Arkansas," Confederate General William L. Cabell announced: "I hope . . . to rid that section of the State of the presence of an insolent and unscrupulous abolition invader." But abolition did not seem to bother the typical Arkansas mountaineer. "The old frontiersman, sitting musingly in his chimney corner, on the slope of a mountain spur, could not see wherein the election of Abraham Lincoln had injured him," an Arkansas Unionist wrote in an 1863 book. "The fear of negro equality had never disturbed him," nor did it disturb him after Lincoln's proclamation of emancipation.[30]

Another Arkansas Unionist, also writing a book in 1863, attributed the slowness of recruitment to U.S. mismanagement and mistakes. Not only had General Curtis erred in sidling around to Helena instead of moving directly on Little Rock. Too many outsiders, including Governor Phelps, had been imposed upon the state, and too many Arkansans had been taken into Missouri and other foreign regiments, where they were "absorbed, as it were, in non-existence" and had "no share in the glory and fame."

> If all the men, who are in the Union army from Arkansas, and all those who would have joined it if saved from the rebel conscript, could have been collected together, organized, properly armed and equipped, and officered from their own State by men of their own choice, and then turned loose upon their rebel neighbors, with authority to deal with them in their own way, Arkansas would have been long since, to say the least, as clear of rebels as Missouri.[31]

Once the Union forces in northwestern Arkansas were able to reach the Arkansas River—and then to advance down it to Little Rock—recruitment could be expected to improve. "The infantry regiment of Colonel Johnson will be filled up whenever we can go forward to the river, and one other regiment," one officer predicted. General Curtis also heard that "in all Southern Arkansas" there was a "strong Union element." His correspondent added: "I also learn that the Union men of Clark and Sebastian Counties, [in southern and western] Arkansas, have from the rebels armed themselves, and I am assured by them that as soon as we get near Little Rock they will co-operate with us." [32]

As General Frederick Steele moved downriver with his army in August and September 1863—to take Little Rock while Burnside was taking Knoxville—the cooperation of local Unionists was fully as great as had been predicted. They certainly gave notable assistance to Colonel William F. Cloud, commanding the Second Kansas Cavalry, when he approached the enemy at Dardanelle, above Little Rock. On the march "we were joined by six companies of Union men, about 300 all told, with the Stars and Stripes flying, and cheers for the Union," Cloud related. "These men assembled at one day's notice and accompanied me in the attack upon the town, and justly share the victory."

Cloud also received aid from a more surprising source. "In the attack upon Dardanelle," he continued, "I was assisted by three officers and about 100 men, who had fought me at Backbone, under Cabell, and it was a novel sight to see men with the regular gray uniform and Confederate States belt-plate fighting side by side with the blue of the army, and this novelty was intensified by knowing that they were fighting their old command."

Afterward, Cloud set these Confederate deserters to hunting Confederate guerrillas. He hoped to "make good soldiers out of many of them"—soldiers for his own Kansas regiment. He anticipated still other recruits. "I am convinced that thousands of men stand ready to take up arms as soon as they can be furnished, and this is the case also with Northern Texas."

Another Union officer, General C. B. Holland, was "surprised to find such a thoroughly Union sentiment prevailing" in Carroll, Marion, and Searcy counties in the north central part of the state. "A feeling of security, inspired by the presence of Union troops in the country, caused many to come in and acknowledge their faith in and devotion to the old flag." Troops should be stationed at various points, Holland thought, until the Unionists could "organize themselves into home-guard companies" so as to "protect themselves and families from the outrages of guerrillas, outlaws, and jayhawkers." [33]

Once he was in control of Little Rock and most of northern Arkansas, General Steele decided to take advantage of the Unionism that was being so openly expressed. Arkansans could organize home guards to protect themselves, they could help fill up depleted regiments from the North, and they could also form new Union regiments of their own. Steele gave tentative orders for the organization of a third and a fourth regiment of cavalry. A. H. Ryan, the colonel-to-be of the Third Arkansas, went to Washington to get the War Department's approval for the raising of his regiment.

While Ryan was away, aspiring recruiters were busy. In Arkansas, as in other states, there was much competition among them, for if a recruiter raised a company he could expect to be its captain, and if he raised more than one company, he could aspire to still higher rank. For the time being, the terms of enlistment were unclear. Enlistees would supposedly receive $25 of their $100 bounty plus a month's advance pay as soon as they were mustered in. Some were promised these emoluments for only one year's service instead of the usual three. Several men went to Little Rock to join the Fourth Regiment—as one of them ruefully testified later—and were dissuaded by the prospective captain of Company H of the Third, who "said we were fools for going into the fourth for three years when we could go into his company for one year."

A number of the new recruits were to suffer grievously on account of the competition and the confusion. Having enlisted for what they thought was to be a one-year hitch, they were surprised to find that the muster-in rolls and payrolls they were asked to sign specified a three-year term. They were assured that this was an error and would be corrected; they were advised to go ahead and sign—they would receive no pay unless they did so. Some signed and others did not.

The length of service remained uncertain until December 15, 1863, when Colonel Ryan got back from Washington with the news that the War Department would allow no enlistments for less than three years. What happened then, Private W. J. Burris of Company A, Third Arkansas Cavalry, subsequently related:

> Some time in December, 1863, the captain came into camp [near Lewisburg] one afternoon and appeared to be very much excited. He stated to his company that he had just understood that they had been mustered in for three years instead of twelve months, but said

he was satisfied that it could not be so, and advised us not to sign any pay or bounty rolls, for fear of committing ourselves for a longer service than twelve months . . . the captain told the men that we were no longer bound, as the order under which we had been recruited had been revoked by the War Department. I then turned over my arms and accouterments . . . and went home. . . .

I was immediately arrested and put in the guard-house, and compelled to labor in the fortifications at Lewisburg, under guard, forty-five days, when I was sent to Little Rock under guard and placed in the penitentiary, where I remained till the 11th June, 1864.

In the Little Rock prison Private Burris found several other alleged deserters, like him, from the Third Arkansas Cavalry.

Burris and the others appealed to the provost marshal general of the Department of Arkansas, who referred their letter to the regiment's lieutenant colonel, Irving W. Fuller. Fuller maintained that all the men had enlisted for three years and that the prisoners should be released only if they agreed to serve for that time. They refused.

Finally, on June 1, 1864, the adjutant general of the District of Little Rock ordered the convening of "a board to inquire into and report upon certain alleged difficulties existing in the Third Arkansas cavalry volunteers." After nearly a month of hearings, at which the men disputed the word of Lieutenant Colonel Fuller, the board came to the following conclusion: "all the men . . . who were recruited previous to the 15th day of December, 1863, and have not signed enlistment papers for three years' service, cannot be held to service, and should be immediately discharged." So Burris and his fellow inmates were freed from both the prison and the army.

That, however, was not the end of the difficulties in the Third Arkansas Cavalry. Sixteen members of Company H, after enlisting for what they understood to be a twelve-month stint, had declined to sign the three-year papers but had nevertheless stayed in the army, serving without pay. When their one year was up, they refused to do further duty. Twenty-nine-year-old Corporal Simon Harkey, for one, thought he had done his bit. Besides, Harkey argued, "I have an old mother, a sister in Yell County, and a family of my own, all depending on me for a living, and are living in a part of the country where there are plenty of 'bushwhackers,' and I wanted to get them out."

Again, Lieutenant Colonel Fuller insisted that the men had committed themselves for three years, and he charged them with mutiny. The case came before the district judge advocate in February 1865. Fuller tried desperately to defend himself. "I had no idea of trying to deceive the men into the service, for we could have had the regiment filled for three years, as cavalry, if we had known that we would be accepted," he said in a sworn statement. "There were whole companies presented themselves, and asked to be taken in, which we could not receive, as we had all the men we wanted to fill the regiment."

But the judge advocate decided that Fuller and others had misled the accused soldiers. "These men should be discharged from further service," read the verdict. Furthermore, "they should be paid. It is not necessary, in disposing of the claims of these men, to refer to the conduct of the mustering officer or the regimental officers. Whatever view may be taken of the criminality or neglect of duty manifested by these officers . . ."[34]

Despite the difficulties, General Steele had succeeded in adding two cavalry regiments to his army. He had also authorized Elisha Baxter to raise a regiment of mounted infantry. Baxter, a native of North Carolina (who would later become a Reconstruction governor of Arkansas and be a party to the "Brooks-Baxter War"), soon recruited nearly four hundred men. But his regiment never filled up, because the War Department refused to confirm the authority that Steele had granted him.[35]

After U.S. troops occupied the Arkansas capital, Unionists living north of the Arkansas River began to think of bringing their state back into the Union. President Lincoln, with his "10 percent plan," offered to let voters commence the reorganization of a seceded state when as many as 10 percent of them had taken an oath of future loyalty to the United States. In March 1864 he named Isaac Murphy provisional governor to start the state-making process, and the voters elected Murphy governor in April.

Murphy, born and brought up in Pennsylvania, had moved as a young man to northwestern Arkansas, where he made a living as a schoolteacher, legislator, lawyer, and judge. At the state's 1861 convention he was the only delegate who voted against secession to the bitter end. Though nearing sixty at the start of the war, he served in the Union army until the occupation of Little Rock. During his absence from his home in Huntsville, Confederates raided the town and "committed depredations on all the Union families in that vicinity, more especially that of Judge Murphy, the ladies of whose family they stripped of everything but what was on their bodies, leaving them in a destitute condition." [36]

On taking office, Governor Murphy warned President Lincoln: "Should the army leave the line of the Arkansas unprotected, terror would prevail [in] the State." The main army, under General Steele, was already leaving that line. Steele had orders to move against Confederate forces in Louisiana and thus assist General Nathaniel P. Banks in the Red River campaign. After having been repulsed again and again, Steele was back in Little Rock by early May, but the Confederates continued to harass much of Arkansas throughout the summer of 1864.

All along, Governor Murphy had been trying to raise troops to meet the emergency. "Will the Government accept of two regiments of artillery (one black) and a regiment of cavalry, armed for pursuit of guerrillas?" he asked Lincoln early on. "The swamps and mountains are full of armed rebels waiting for the movement of the army, to pounce upon unprotected points and cut off communications." Murphy wanted to attract recruits with the enhanced bounty of $300, and he was frustrated by a want of funds when Stanton told him that amount would no longer be payable.

He was also disappointed when his request for permission to raise cavalry was denied. Word came from the War Department that (because of a shortage of horses) no more cavalry or mounted infantry would be authorized in Arkansas. It would be all right to raise as many three-year infantry regiments as possible, but only one at a time: "In other words, as soon as one regiment is recruited, organized, and mustered into service, a second one may be commenced by you, not sooner." [37]

Murphy did not think the Lincoln administration's response was adequate to the Arkansas crisis, and neither did the state legislators who had been elected with him. The General Assembly adopted two sets of resolutions, which the governor forwarded to the President.

In the first set of resolutions, the legislators implored the President to "furnish additional soldiers at the earliest possible day"; they recommended "mounted rangers" as "most suitable"; and they suggested "the propriety of employing the Arkansas troops" for the state's defense (not for pursuing Confederates in Louisiana), "believing that their intimate acquaintance with the different sections of the State" would "give them an advantage in usefulness superior to other troops."

The second set of resolutions asked for "ten thousand stand of arms and ammunition to arm a loyal State militia," for which the governor would call for ninety-day volunteers, these to be "distributed as near as possible" to the places where they had been recruited. And "no person shall be commissioned as an officer in said organization who has held an office, civil or military, by authority of the Confederate States government, or by authority of any State while acting with the so-called Confederate States of America." (This restriction was similar to the one in the oath required of enlistees in Tennessee's Union regiments. In the case of the loyal Tennessee colonel who had served in the state legislature after secession, Lincoln had thought the restriction should be disregarded.)[38]

Murphy complained bitterly to Lincoln about the administration's neglect of Arkansas after the occupation of Little Rock. (Murphy's opposite number, the governor of Confederate Arkansas, complained just as bitterly to Jefferson Davis, as will be seen.)

Not much came of the proposal that Murphy call for ninety-day militia, though he did raise a few of them. Already Federal officers in the state were taking steps to raise local defense forces by means of a kind of draft. First, the commander of the District of the Frontier, at Fort Smith, on the edge of Indian Territory, issued the following orders:

I. All male persons capable of bearing arms in this district are required to proceed to the nearest military post and enroll themselves for military duty.

II. The enrolled persons will be divided into two classes. The first class to be composed of persons mounted for active field service, to be called rangers. They furnish their own horses. The second class to be composed of the balance of the enrolled persons, for home protection, to be called the reserve.

Later the commander of the District of Little Rock ordered that "all able-bodied males between the ages of eighteen and forty-five" should be "immediately enrolled in the service, in the militia." But the U.S. provost marshal general disapproved the plan for conscription, and "no drafted men from Arkansas entered the service."[39]

By summer's end in 1864 the worst of the crisis was over for Governor Murphy and the Arkansas Unionists. Now it was time for the pro-Confederate governor and his followers to worry. Upon the Federals' approach to Little Rock, Harris Flanagin had moved his government to the tiny village of Washington in the southwestern corner of the state. Governor Flanagin took a rather gloomy view of Confederate prospects in Arkansas, and he blamed the Confederate government for the state's predicament. Jefferson Davis and his generals, the governor thought, had not tried hard enough to hold the state. They had taken twenty-three of its infantry and three of its cavalry regiments away to serve east of the Mississippi, leaving only nine infantry regiments at home.

This neglect, according to Flanagin, accounted for the willingness of so many Arkansans to sign up with the Federals. "The citizens of Missouri and Arkansas became satisfied that they were abandoned to their enemies," he complained to Davis, "and thousands of men who might have been obtained for our army from Missouri either remained neutral or joined the Federal army." When "our forces fell back from the Arkansas River" in the summer of 1863, "at least one-half the State was regarded by the citizens as being abandoned." Since the taking of Little Rock, Flanagin contended, the Federal army had recruited eight thousand Arkansans, black and white, and the Federals could get many more in the southwestern part of the state: "If this department were in their possession they could recruit 30,000. This is under rather than over the fact."[40]

So, by the testimony of the pro-Confederate governor himself, there was a tremendous reservoir of Unionism even in the southwestern part of the state. Yet in the northwest, the most loyal area of Arkansas, Unionists remained insecure to the very end of the war. On their behalf the assemblyman from Marion County appealed to Governor Murphy in February 1865:

Several counties in Northwestern Arkansas have been almost depopulated in consequence of the withdrawal of U.S. troops from that section of the State. Those persons are now in Missouri, and have left their property to be destroyed by the numerous bands of guerrillas that infest that country, one of the most fertile regions of Arkansas. In Southwest Missouri, [in] the counties adjoining Arkansas, are 200 or more families, the male portion of which would have long since gone into the U.S. service, but destitution (the result of moving) has necessarily compelled them to remain at home and provide for their families. We desire to raise four companies in the counties mentioned (enlisting those Arkansans in Missouri), to protect and defend our property, that we may cultivate it and assist in supporting our armies.

General Sanborn, commanding at Springfield, agreed to arm, clothe, and subsist the militia companies.

Refugees and other Arkansas Unionists were suffering from extreme want. It was urgent that they be enabled to attend to their spring planting and to the care of their crops. Colonel Harrison of the First Arkansas Union Cavalry took charge of a unique project to arm and organize farmers in the northwest and establish them in fortified settlements. By April 1865 he could boast of sixteen such "colonies," 1,200 organized and "mostly armed" men, and 15,000 acres to be brought safely under cultivation.[41]

By this time, the U.S. army included the following white Arkansas units: two batteries of artillery, four regiments and one extra company of cavalry, and four regiments, one battalion, and one company of infantry. The Arkansas adjutant general credited the state with a total of 8,789 white troops. He pointed out that this figure was less than the real total of enlisted Arkansans: "To quite a considerable extent, citizens of Arkansas were enlisted during the war in Missouri, Kansas, Iowa, Indiana, and Illinois regiments, but this number . . . I am unable to give," he explained. His overall estimate was a conservative one: "The State of Arkansas furnished more than ten thousand [white] men to the loyal army." And he was not counting the Arkansans who had served on the Union side in state and local militia of one kind or another.[42]

When Confederate Governor Flanagin said that the Federal army could have recruited more than 30,000 additional men (including blacks) if it had gained control of southwestern Arkansas, he quite likely exaggerated the number to make his point with Jefferson Davis. Still, there can be no doubt that the U.S. army would have been a great deal more successful at enlisting volunteers in Arkansas if it could have got an earlier, broader, and firmer grip on the state and if it had been able to arm and equip all the available troops.

4   Enlistees from Other States

Louisiana

$\mathcal{N}$EW ORLEANS was the next state capital in the Confederacy after Nashville to fall under Union control. As that control was gradually expanded, much of Louisiana became a Federal recruiting ground.

Thousands of Louisianans were more willing to fight for the Union than for the Confederacy. The Cajuns of the southwestern parishes and the Germans, Irish, and Yankees of New Orleans (the most polyglot of Southern cities) were particularly reluctant to aid the rebellion. But there was also a great deal of what Confederates called "disaffection and disloyalty" among native whites in some of the northwestern parishes.

When the Louisiana governor called out the militia on September 21, 1861, the reluctant ones had to be dragooned into the state service. And when some of them were ordered downriver to Fort Jackson, they went aboard the transports only at the prodding of bayonets. Both Fort Jackson and Fort St. Philip, on opposite sides of the Mississippi and guarding the approach to New Orleans from the south, were garrisoned largely by such impressed, unwilling men.

Late in April 1862 a Union fleet under the command of the Tennessee-born Rear Admiral David G. Farragut passed the forts. Men of the Fort Jackson garrison mutinied, firing on their own officers, spiking the guns, and surrendering to the Federal besiegers. Then transports, with the prisoners, proceeded upriver and landed General and Mrs. Benjamin F. Butler and an occupation force at New Orleans. Butler, a Democratic politician from Massachusetts, took command of the occupied city on May 1, 1862.[1]

In one of his first official actions, Butler saw to the hanging of William B. Mumford, a professional gambler who had pulled down a recently raised U.S. flag and ripped it to pieces. Butler later ordered that any female insulting his troops should be regarded as a "woman of the town plying her avocation." For these and other affronts to Southern sensibilities, Confederates dubbed him "Beast" Butler, and Jefferson Davis declared him an outlaw who was to be hanged without trial if captured.

Before the end of the year, President Lincoln would remove the controversial commander and replace him with the blander Nathaniel P. Banks, another Massachusetts politician, though not a Democrat. Lincoln appointed a military governor, George F. Shepley, and under Lincoln's 10 percent plan the voters eventually elected a free-state governor, Michael Hahn. But neither Shepley nor Hahn would have much, if anything, to do with recruiting in Louisiana. Recruiting would be undertaken by Butler and Banks—especially Butler, with his remarkably energetic and enterprising spirit.

From the beginning of his New Orleans command, Butler feared a Confederate counterattack that he might not be able to repulse with the force available to him. He needed more troops and he needed them right away. Luckily he found willing volunteers already at hand. "Large numbers of Union men—Americans, Germans, and French— have desired to enlist in our service," he telegraphed to Secretary of War Edwin M. Stanton after a couple of weeks in New Orleans. "I have directed the regiments to fill themselves up with these recruits. I can enlist a regiment or more here, if the Department think it advisable, of true and loyal men." Stanton authorized him to "raise 5,000 loyal white men," to organize them in regiments and nominate the officers, and to "organize a portion of home guards" if he deemed it expedient. "That class of troops have been found very embarrassing," Stanton added.

Within three months Butler had "enlisted a thousand men in the old regiments" that he had brought with him from the North. He also had "1,200 being organized as the First Regiment of Louisiana Volunteers, National Guards, and two companies of cavalry." He expected to get two more regiments, but this would take time and he was in a hurry. Still believing an attack imminent, he asked General-in-Chief Henry W. Halleck for additional troops, only to learn that "it was impossible to expect re-inforcements in time to meet the expected movement." So he began to enlist parolees and deserters from the enemy ranks, including prisoners taken at the surrender of Forts Jackson and St. Philip. "I have called upon a portion of a brigade of soldiers who were in the Confederate service, and are now ready and desirous of doing loyal service to the Union here," Butler notified Halleck.[2]

There was one other possible source of military manpower to which Butler might turn in the emergency. Why not enlist Louisiana blacks? One of Butler's subordinates, General John W. Phelps, an abolitionist Vermonter, told Butler he already had at Carrollton, Louisiana, "upwards of 300 Africans organized into five companies" and eager to serve. "The President has not yet indicated his purpose to employ the Africans in arms," Butler replied. "The arms, clothing, and camp equipage which I have here for Louisiana volunteers are by the letter of the Secretary of War expressly limited to white soldiers."

Nevertheless, after failing to get the reinforcements he demanded, Butler decided in late August to accept Phelps's recommendation and go ahead on his own. "I shall call on Africa to intervene," he reported to Stanton, "and I do not think I shall call in vain." He began to organize and arm blacks—freemen, not slaves—before Lincoln had issued even his preliminary proclamation of emancipation (September 22, 1862), and Lincoln did not officially approve of arming blacks until after his final proclamation of emancipation (January 1, 1863).[3]

In September 1862 Butler could boast to Stanton from New Orleans:

> I have succeeded wonderfully in my enlistments of volunteers here—a full regiment, three companies of cavalry, 600 to form a new regiment, and more than 1,200 men enlisted in the old regiments to fill up the ranks. I shall also have within ten days a regiment, 1,000 strong, of Native Guards (colored), the darkest of whom will be about the complexion of the late Mr. Webster [Daniel Webster, the swarthy "Black Dan"].
>
> I shall have the honor to have increased my division by at least 3,000 men (one-fifth of the whole) after a nine-months' campaign in the unhealthy South.[4]

After general conscription went into effect in the Northern states in 1863, Butler's successor Banks decided to try it in part of Louisiana. He ordered an enrollment "for general military service" of men in the First and Second Congressional districts (New Orleans). He exempted from general service "those well-disposed persons who, in the event of capture by the enemy, would not be entitled to the full immunity of soldiers of the United States." He was referring to deserters from the Confederate army. Such recruits would be designated the "New Orleans Volunteers," and their service would be limited to "the protection and defense of New Orleans." (Despite Banks's assumption, there is no reason to believe that these deserter-recruits would have been immune from treatment as turncoats if captured.) From the two sources—deserters and others—Banks hoped to obtain a total of four thousand to five thousand men. He never came close to enlisting so large a number, even with the stimulus of a threatened draft.[5]

In the French-speaking Cajun country of southwestern Louisiana, men seemed more willing to volunteer, at least for local defense. General E. O. C. Ord reported in October 1863 that "at Vermillionville many white citizens came in and, taking the oath of allegiance, desired to arm, to protect the country from further inroads on the part of the rebel forces." He thought he "could have procured nearly 1,000 good men in that section with the aid of his scouts and of some Union citizens of influence."

These influential citizens bore such Cajun names as Honoré Béreaud, Joseph Boudreau, and Zephraim Doucet. Another local leader, also bearing a Cajun name, O. Currier, had already raised men west of Opelousas and had "successfully resisted the enemy when attempting to enforce the draft." (Undoubtedly, the early recruits whom Butler referred to as French were not foreigners but Cajuns.)[6]

After the formation of the free-state government, Governor Hahn preoccupied himself with matters other than military defense. Lincoln's friend Stephen A. Hurlbut, temporarily replacing Banks, felt compelled to step in and take over recruiting, which he considered the governor's responsibility. "The militia is unorganized," Hurlbut wrote to Hahn on December 1, 1864, "and at last, after four months waiting for the action of the State, it is being done by military authority."[7]

Almost to the very end, Union recruiters continued to compete with Confederate recruiters in Louisiana. As late as February 1865 Lieutenant Pomponeau (another Cajun name) of the First Louisiana Cavalry, U.S.A., was sent out from Thibodaux, not far southwest of New Orleans, to make a reconnaissance "for the purpose of surprising and capturing any rebel recruiting parties" that he might find. According to his orders, "Lieutenant Pomponeau will be authorized to bring in with him any recruits who may desire to join the U.S. service."[8]

By April 1865 the following white Louisiana units had been organized for the U.S. army: three batteries of light artillery, three regiments of infantry, and five of cavalry. The aggregate of white Union troops officially credited to the state was 5,224.[9] This figure did not include the Louisianans who had joined out-of-state regiments, of whom Butler had counted more than 1,200 soon after the occupation of New Orleans. Nor did the figure include the large but uncounted numbers who served the Union in some military capacity or other but had never been mustered into the U.S. army.

Texas

Texas was embraced in the Department of the Gulf, which Butler and then Banks commanded from their headquarters at New Orleans. Both men wanted to enlist as many Texans as possible, and so did Lincoln, but they confronted the problem of getting a foothold in the state. Quite early it began to appear that if they could set up rallying points on Texas soil, they would find no lack of willing recruits.

At the very start of the war, in April 1861, anti-Confederate feeling flared in Zapata County, which bordered the Rio Grande more than a hundred miles above its mouth. About forty Mexican-Texans, or *tejanos,* took their guns and went to the county seat to prevent officials from swearing allegiance to the Confederacy. Pro-Confederate troops fired on them and drove them away, causing heavy losses. But the *tejanos* remained defiant. "[T]hey openly declared their intention of supporting no government except that of the United States," a Confederate officer reported months later. Another officer, the Fort Brown commander, stated in November 1861: "They are backed by a strong party . . . who avow the intention to take service with the North, should Mr. Lincoln send an invading force to the Rio Grande."[10]

Unionism was strong not only among Mexican-Americans but also among German- and Anglo-Americans, and it was not confined to southern Texas but appeared here and there throughout the state. In the central counties anti-secessionists formed a Union Loyal League in June 1861. In the north they joined a secret peace society in late 1862 to resist the draft and to spy for the Union. A mob lynched about twenty-five Unionists, and local authorities hanged forty-five more after arrest and trial. Still other killings occurred from time to time in northern and central Texas.[11]

Union sentiment was most widespread in the western counties, where hundreds of Unionists attempted to flee the state. "Many Germans and some Americans are leaving here to avoid a participation in our struggle," the local Confederate commander reported from San Antonio in March 1862. "I have directed the troops to permit none to go to Mexico, unless they have a pass from me." The commander thought a "considerable element" of the "opposition, or Union men," would have to be "crushed out, even if it [had] to be done without due course of law." That same month, martial law was declared throughout the state, and a military court began to try suspected Unionists.

In consequence, three companies of loyalist militia decided to disband. One company—consisting of sixty-three Germans, five Anglos, and one Mexican—set out for Mexico under the leadership of Fritz Tegner. Ninety-five Confederates, under Lieutenant C. D. McRae of the Texas Mounted Rifles, caught up with the fleeing Unionists at their Nueces River camp and killed thirty-two and wounded many others in a surprise attack. Afterwards McRae commended his men for their "deeds of daring chivalry."[12]

The plight of the Texas loyalists and the possibility of recruiting them had already come to Lincoln's attention. His secretary of state, William H. Seward, was learning about the matter from the U.S. consuls at Matamoros and Monterey. The consul at Matamoros wrote in May 1862: "The crowds of refugees from Texas do not diminish in the least, although it is very difficult, owing to the strict watch kept upon their movements, for them to get out. Many are arrested; some are hung; others are taken and pressed into service." The Monterey consul added, "Let me urge that a force be sent into this frontier; it may not be very large, if they have plenty of arms. I am assured that there could be 3,000 enlisted from Texas as soon as it was known."

This message was reinforced by a report from Captain Charles Hunter of the USS *Montgomery,* which was blockading the mouth of the Rio Grande. Captain Hunter had "brought off through the surf" seventy escaping Unionists. "The poor refugees still come to us," he wrote on June 16, 1862, in a private letter that the recipient turned over to Seward. "There is a large number of Union men in the State who only want arms and protection to organize themselves and drive the secessionists out."

In forwarding to Stanton the communications from the consuls and the captain, Seward noted that the "condition of the loyal inhabitants of Texas" was "represented to be so miserable" that "most of them of a suitable age to bear arms might be most readily and effectually relieved if they would accept service in our Army." He therefore suggested that "an arrangement be made with the Secretary of the Navy for receiving any such persons on board the blockading vessel or vessels in that quarter as recruits." He also proposed to expedite the recruiting through "a military occupation of Texas in the neighborhood of Brownsville." [13]

Among the refugees whom the U.S. navy carried to New Orleans, two were to prove the most important of all the Texas Unionists— Edmund Jackson Davis and Andrew Jackson Hamilton, both of whom were native Southerners and well-to-do, successful men.

Edmund J. Davis was born to wealthy parents in St. Augustine, Florida. After entering West Point as a cadet and volunteering for the Mexican War, he moved to Corpus Christi, Texas, where he prospered as a lawyer. He was in his fifth year as a state district judge when the Civil War began.

Andrew Jackson ("Colossal Jack") Hamilton came from Madison County in the hill country of northern Alabama. As a young man, he settled in Austin, Texas, to practice law. He became attorney general of the state, a member of the legislature, and a congressman—one of the few from the South who stayed in Congress when their states seceded.[14]

In August 1862 Davis visited the White House with a delegation of Unionist Texans to make a personal appeal to the President. "Please see these Texas gentlemen, and talk with them," Lincoln asked Stanton in a note he sent along with the gentlemen. "They think if we could send 2500 or 3000 arms, in a vessel, to the vicinity of the Rio Grande, that they can find the men there who will re-inaugerate [sic] the National Authority on the Rio Grande first, and probably on the Nuesces [sic] also." But Lincoln agreed with Stanton that the undertaking was impracticable at the moment.[15]

In September 1862 Hamilton was in New Orleans, preparing to make a trip to the North. He received a letter of introduction to Secretary of the Treasury Salmon P. Chase from George S. Denison, a native Vermonter who had resided in Texas and who held a Treasury Department job as collector of revenue in New Orleans. Denison also wrote directly to Chase on Hamilton's behalf. "Col. Hamilton can raise a Brigade of Union troops in Texas more quickly than any other man in the State, and I believe he only wants an authority to raise such a Brigade when an expedition goes there," Denison assured Chase. "Mr. H. is to Western Texas what Brownlow, Maynard and Johnson are to East Tennessee." He was "the man to make Western Texas a Free State"—an independent state like West Virginia.[16]

Hamilton, once in the North, went on a speech-making tour, appearing at such places as Faneuil Hall in Boston and Cooper Union in New York to arouse public support for his cause. At Cooper Union on October 4, 1862, he said: "In Mexico there are now 500 men who left as I left. They are in the mountain fastnesses, hunted like wolves. Are they to have help? Give them a chance, and they will bleed for their country, die for it, redeem it; and there are men enough there today to redeem it, if they were organized and had arms in their hands."[17]

While in New York City, Hamilton met John A. Stevens, Jr., secretary of the local chamber of commerce and chairman of the War Committee of the Citizens of New York. Stevens had planned to lead several committee members to Washington to plead the Texas case, and Hamilton accompanied them. Stevens took Hamilton to dinner at Chase's house, where Stanton also was a guest. "After dinner, Col. Hamilton spoke fully of Texas," Chase recorded in his diary, "—described his escape and hiding in the woods—said that many hundred loyal Texans were now concealed in Texas as refugees—declared the War was a war of the oligarchy upon the people—that Slavery was the basis of the oligarchy, but that the perpetuation of slavery was not more their object, then the despotic power of the class over the mass."

Chase arranged an interview with Lincoln for Hamilton, which took place on October 9, 1862. The next day Stevens and his associates presented their petition to Lincoln. In it they argued that if the Texas Unionists "could be positively assured of the assistance of the Federal Government, large numbers would immediately flock to the . . . old flag."

Lincoln and Stanton doubted whether the Federal government, considering its other manpower needs, could afford to give much assist-

ance to the Texas project. Lincoln did not want the Texas expedition
to interfere with the opening of the Mississippi River, an objective
with a higher priority. He and Stanton were partly persuaded by the
argument that they would not have to provide a great many men—
that, given a little help, the loyal Texans would rise up and liberate
themselves. Lincoln must have thought this outcome fairly imminent,
for he concluded it was time to prepare for the governance of liberated
Texas. Shortly thereafter he appointed Hamilton as brigadier general
and military governor "with the authority to raise troops." [18]

Loyal Texans were soon enlisting in New Orleans. From there,
Denison optimistically wrote to Chase on October 27, 1862:

> Seventy-three refugees from Texas have just arrived here from Ma-
> tamoros, about one-third of whom are Germans, the remainder
> Americans. At my request Gen. Butler is organizing them into a
> company for Gov't military service. Judge Davis, from Texas, is
> now here, and will receive authority to enlist and organize a full
> Texas Regiment. There will be no difficulty about this, as besides
> the company here, three or four companies can be raised in Galves-
> ton. There are hundreds of refugees in the vicinity of Matamoros,
> anxious to join the army, for whom Gen. Butler will send a steamer.

Davis, with a colonel's commission from Lincoln, proceeded to train
the inchoate First Regiment of Texas Volunteer Cavalry, U.S.A. [19]

A small Union naval force having landed at Galveston, and the place
being under blockade, Butler was confident that he could establish a
beachhead there. He asked the consul at Matamoros to "notify all
loyal Texans" willing to enlist that they should gather there for transport to Galveston. In another message to the consul, he elaborated:

> I propose to send down the First Regiment Texas Volunteers with
> some other troops to Galveston. I will arrange with Colonel Davis,
> of that command, and with Rear-Admiral Farragut that refugees
> who may desire may be sent to Galveston from Texas and Mexico;
> some of them will enlist, doubtless, in the service of the United
> States. The preference in granting passage, as a rule, will be given
> to those who are physically able.
>
> Of course, it will be improper to enlist even Americans as soldiers
> on Mexican soil, but there can be no impropriety in sending Amer-
> icans to do their duty to their country.

But before Butler could carry out this plan, he had to turn his command over to Nathaniel P. Banks.[20]

When Banks sailed from the North with an expedition of several regiments and dozens of transports, Lincoln did not announce the destination. Accompanying the expedition were Hamilton, Stevens, and other advocates of Texas liberation, who assumed that their special enterprise was now under way. Hamilton, as military governor, expected soon to set up headquarters in his home state. "When it became known that our destination was New Orleans and not Texas, which was not until our arrival here," Banks recalled a little later in New Orleans, "those connected with him [Hamilton] became very violent, and denounced unsparingly the Government and all connected with the expedition for what was called bad faith in its management." Hamilton, taking up residence in the City Hotel, looked forward impatiently to his installation on the soil of Texas.

Banks, according to his recollection, heard from Butler about the plan for Galveston—"that he [Butler] had contemplated ordering a small force there to assist in recruiting Texas refugees." Urged on by the fretful Hamilton and his entourage, Banks did not wait long to begin putting the Butler plan into operation. Three companies of the Forty-second Massachusetts Volunteers were immediately available, and Banks sent them on ahead with their colonel, Isaac S. Burrell. "The situation of the people of Galveston makes it expedient to send a small force there for the purpose of their protection," Banks instructed Burrell, "and also to afford such facilities as may be possible for recruiting soldiers for the military service of the United States."[21]

Having landed his three companies at Galveston on Christmas Eve 1862, Colonel Burrell ascertained that there were "still living upon the island about 3,000 persons," largely women and children and mostly loyal. The enemy had the island covered by batteries on the mainland and one gun in the middle of the connecting drawbridge. There appeared to be about 2,000 of the enemy in the immediate vicinity. Burrell had only 260 men. Still, he could presumably count on protection from the blockading vessels, which stood directly offshore.

And reinforcements were soon on the way. Transports were bringing the rest of the companies of the Forty-second Massachusetts. Aboard one of the ships was William L. Burt, General Hamilton's aide-de-camp, who was ready to make arrangements for the military governor's subsequent arrival. Burt's ship approached Galveston on New Year's Eve—in time for him to view the Confederates' assault early the next morning. The rebels under General John B. Magruder not only overran the island, killing or capturing Burrell and his men, but also seized the *Harriet Lane* and destroyed other vessels of the blockading fleet.

Another transport, the *Cambria,* anchored outside the island on the following day, January 2, 1863. On board were numerous civilian refugees, some horses, and the two companies of the First Texas Cavalry that had been organized so far. The *Cambria,* along with the other transports, managed to get safely back to New Orleans. But the Confederates held Galveston for the rest of the war.[22]

After the Galveston catastrophe, Governor Hamilton thought of looking to Matamoros again to enlist refugees. "From the United States consul at that place," he informed Banks, "I learn that there are quite a number there, and I shall order Lieutenant-Colonel Stancel, of the First Texas Cavalry, and Dr. William J. Moore, of the Second Texas Cavalry (who speaks the Spanish language), to go as soon as transportation may be furnished them to Matamoros, to bring off such refugees, most of whom are ready to join the service." Banks referred the proposal to his quartermaster, who squelched it by explaining that no transport could go up the Rio Grande as far as Matamoros yet, since the Confederates still controlled the river.

A couple of months later, in March 1863, the Federal steamer *Honduras* anchored off the Mexican coast, and Colonel Davis proceeded overland to Matamoros. There he picked up his family and at least a hundred recruits. Confederate General H. P. Bee, commanding at Fort Brown on the other side of the river, was incensed at what he considered the "palpable violation of the neutrality of Mexico by the authorities at Matamoros in permitting soldiers to be enlisted openly in their streets for the service of the United States." Bee complained further of the many deserters from his own command who were "openly enlisted, fed, and clothed by the American consul at Matamoros." He denounced Davis as "a Texas renegade, who was the proved originator of all the troubles on this frontier."[23]

The most spectacular desertion from Bee's command was yet to occur. Bee, in his own words, "had a company of Mexican citizens, under command of Capt. Adrian I. Vidal, stationed at the mouth of the Rio Grande," who had "done good service." Vidal, twenty years old, was the son of a rich Anglo businessman and a Mexican woman. On October 26, 1863, Bee sent two couriers with orders for Vidal to bring his company to Fort Brown. Word came back to Bee that his two messengers had been shot and that he himself "was to be attacked during the night by men from below, consisting of Vidal's company and renegades and deserters from Matamoros." But instead of attacking Brownsville, the mutineers proceeded on upriver, plundering ranches as they went.

At this very time, a much greater threat to Brownsville and Fort Brown was about to materialize. Also on October 26 an expedition of three warships and 3,500 men left New Orleans to "raise the flag in Texas." The men landed near the mouth of the Rio Grande, marched the thirty miles to Brownsville, and easily took the place.[24]

Recruits now flocked to Brownsville, among them Captain Vidal and his fellow deserters from the Confederate army. "Vidal's command has been mustered in, armed, and equipped to the number of 89 men, for one year," General N. J. T. Dana reported on December 2, 1863. Two hundred other men had been mustered in for the First and Second Texas Cavalry, and two hundred more were waiting to be brought to Brownsville. Also thirty-three blacks joined the Corps d'Afrique. A few Germans came all the way from Monterey, where they had gone for refuge, sent by Philip Braubach, a German who had settled near San Antonio and had become a recruiter of his fellow Unionists from Germany. Braubach was personally shepherding other refugees to Brownsville. "When he comes," Dana said, "they expect to be mustered in 'for the campaign in Texas.' "

Having secured a foothold at Brownsville, General Banks hoped to launch from there a campaign to recover the entire state. More immediately, he expected large additions to his military manpower. On Christmas Day 1863 he emphasized this objective in orders he gave to General F. J. Herron, who was taking charge of the U.S. forces on the Rio Grande. Preparations had been made for recruiting "from the citizens of Texas and also from the citizens of Mexico," Banks wrote. "It is of the utmost importance that our army be increased as far as possible by recruits in that country."

Banks cautioned that Herron should "avoid all complications or difficulties with any foreign power." The foreign power to be most concerned about was France, which was attempting to get control of Mexico. An army of Mexican patriots under Benito Juárez resisted the invading French and the cooperating Mexican Imperialists, as the country entered upon its own civil war. The warring Mexicans competed with the warring Americans for recruits and had the advantage of being able to pay well and pay in gold.

Colonel Davis, commanding the cavalry brigade at Brownsville, questioned both the feasibility and the desirability of recruiting Mexicans or, for that matter, Mexican-Americans. On February 10, 1864, Davis summarized the progress and prospects of his own cavalry forces thus:

> The enlisted men of [that is, with regard to] nationality are about divided as follows: 433 Mexicans and 500 Americans (including in this designation Germans, Irish, &c.), the whole (including the part brought from New Orleans) having been recruited here [that is, on the lower Rio Grande], and those not of Mexican birth being refugees from the interior of Texas.

> The Mexican recruits have not been as numerous as expected. For this several reasons may be alleged: First, the bounty promised them has not been paid, nor have they received any of their monthly pay, and this cannot be explained to their satisfaction; accordingly there is among them an impression that they have been badly treated. Second, the difficulties on the other side of the river, commencing at the time of our arrival here, have driven into the ranks of the contending parties most of the available men. Third, there has not sufficient clothing been given to those enlisted. In some cases men have been in the service more than two months without a pair of shoes.

> All this has operated to check recruiting of that class. I must say, however, that I do not believe the Mexicans in large numbers can be induced to enter our service and remain without paying them with regularity in specie, which is obviously not advisable, even were it possible to do so.

Davis thought it inadvisable to recruit Mexicans because, under the circumstances, they had too great a tendency to desert. There was, among many others, the example of Vidal and his Partisan Rangers. After a few months in Davis's command Vidal and most of his men decamped for Mexico, where they fought for the *juaristas* until the *imperialistas* captured Vidal and executed him as a traitor.[25]

Hamilton had set up his headquarters as military governor in Brownsville but had done little to assist in recruiting. A greater concentration on Anglo recruits could presumably be expected from John Hancock, a Texas Unionist who arrived in Brownsville in May 1864. Hancock, an Alabamian by birth, was a law partner of Hamilton.

In Hancock's behalf, General Herron appealed directly to Lincoln. "The loyal Texans now within our lines ask of you the appointment of Judge John Hancock as a brigadier-general of volunteers, with authority to take charge of recruiting in this State and at once form a brigade," Herron wrote. "I think he has more influence among the Unionists than any other one man . . . he could fill up a brigade within a few months." The War Department gave its permission with the proviso that Hancock raise the brigade within sixty days. This he failed to do. He spent most of the rest of the war trying to recruit in New Orleans.[26]

While demanding enlistments from both sides of the Rio Grande, Banks kept hoping to advance into the interior and to tap the rich manpower there. He was encouraged by General James H. Carleton, who commanded the U.S. forces in New Mexico. "From information derived from Union refugees from Western Texas," Carleton assured Banks, "there will be thousands of loyal hearts who will gather around the colors as you advance, and so that you have arms and materiel for them you can hardly fail to have an army of Texans."

Certainly, northern Texas was ripe for Union recruiting by the beginning of 1864. From his headquarters at Bonham, not far from Indian Territory (Oklahoma), General Henry E. McCulloch sent gloomy messages to his fellow Confederates. Soldiers kept leaving his command and going over to the Yankees, even though the nearest Yankees were some distance away. "A Dr. Penwell left here two days ago for Fort Smith with a party of men to join the Federals, and there is a constant stream of them going." General Samuel Bell Maxey, who led Indian troops from Indian Territory, was having no better luck, according to McCulloch. "General Maxey's command are deserting by the score, and they will fall in with the brush men and resist or go to the Federals."[27]

When Banks undertook his Red River campaign (March–May

1864), one of his objectives was to reach the reported multitudes of loyalists in the interior of Texas and to add them to his army. Unfortunately, his expedition never made it up the Red River through Louisiana even as far as the Texas state line. So Banks had no chance of finding out how real the multitudes were in Texas.

The numbers of loyal Texans appear to have been real enough. It has been estimated that no more than a third of the people of Texas actively supported the Confederacy. Possibly, if they had had an opportunity to do so, at least as many Texans would have joined the Union army as joined the Confederate army. Certainly the U.S. recruiters would have done much better than they actually did if they had been able to penetrate the state more deeply and on more fronts. The gap between the potential and the actual yield of Union troops was probably greater in this state than in any other.

At the end of the war the U.S. provost marshal general credited Texas with only 1,965 white troops (including Hispanics). A tally of names from the service records produces a slightly larger total of 2,164. The troops attributed to Texas had been organized in two regiments of cavalry, one company of partisan rangers, and one company of scouts. Not included in the totals were those men, such as the uncounted numbers making their way to Arkansas, who enlisted in units from states other than Texas.[28]

Mississippi, Alabama, and Georgia

While one Union army was occupying New Orleans, another was moving from Tennessee southward into Mississippi. By the summer of 1862 the U.S. forces held not only the town of Corinth, Mississippi, but also strategic points in Alabama north of the Tennessee River. The U.S. forces strengthened their hold on the area when they undertook the East Tennessee campaign in 1863 and the Atlanta campaign in 1864. Thus they gradually enlarged their recruiting ground in the hill country of northern Mississippi, Alabama, and Georgia.

There were a good many Unionists in this region, especially in northern Alabama, where a majority of the people in several counties had opposed secession in 1861. Even in west central Alabama the Confederates soon began to worry about rumors of Unionism. An officer in Greene County, southwest of Tuscaloosa, warned the Confederate war secretary, Judah P. Benjamin, in January 1862: "I have been credibly informed that another company of Union men are secretly organizing, and have elected their officers, in [an] adjoining county to the one where the 300 are encamped I wrote you about." A citizen of Columbus, across the state line in Mississippi, had other alarming information for the Confederate War Department in April 1862:

> The northern counties of Alabama, you know, are full of Tories. There has been a convention secretly held in the corner of Winston, Fayette, and Marion Counties, Alabama, in which the people resolved to remain neutral; which simply means that they will join the enemy when they occupy the country. Since Mississippi seceded people from these counties have been in this State carrying the United States flag. There are suspected men even in this [Lowndes] county.[29]

These fears were not entirely idle, as became apparent when the U.S. forces finally arrived. No sooner had they established a base at Huntsville, Alabama, in July 1862, than Alabamians began to come in to enlist. Some said many more were trying to get in but were prevented by rebel cavalry and guerrillas. Colonel Abel D. Streight offered to go with his Fifty-first Indiana Volunteer Infantry and bring the other Unionists in. He and his men had to march through a rough and hostile country for a distance of twenty-five miles south of the Tennessee River. Still, he succeeded in adding about four hundred Alabamians to his own Indiana regiment.[30]

General Don Carlos Buell, commanding at Huntsville, soon ordered that "Alabama men desiring to enlist" be sent to or left in Huntsville and organized in companies of their own. (Buell asked for and obtained authorization from Stanton after having already issued the order.) By August 8, 1862, he needed rifles and accouterments for 180 men in the Alabama Volunteers. These two companies became the nucleus of the First Alabama Cavalry, U.S.A.[31]

As the Union forces advanced eastward in Tennessee and Alabama, recruits kept appearing, some to join the First Alabama and others to enlist in Northern regiments or in independent Alabama units. "A good many mountaineers are enlisting," one Union officer reported in August 1863 from Larkinsville, Alabama, far up the Tennessee River. About twenty of them joined the Fourth Indiana, and seventy-six others (some of them from Tennessee) formed a company of loyalist partisans. As soon as General Rosecrans arrived in Chattanooga, he began to accept loyal Alabamians for the service. "Since the occupation of this country and East Tennessee," he said on September 11, 1863, "men are fast organizing and applying to be mustered—some for one year, some for three." 32

General Grenville M. Dodge, headquartered at Pulaski, Tennessee (north of Decatur, Alabama), aspired to raise a second and even a third Alabama cavalry regiment. "I recruited one regiment at Corinth, Miss.—the First Alabama Cavalry, nearly 1,000 strong—and that fact being well known in North Alabama nearly all the refugees from there seek my lines," Dodge claimed in January 1864. He wanted the First Alabama, under the command of his friend George E. Spencer (who became a carpetbag U.S. senator from Alabama after the war), to be stationed at Decatur so as to "form a nucleus that would soon give us another mounted regiment."

Later, at Athens, Alabama, just north of Decatur, Dodge found there was a Confederate "cavalry picket line" running for miles along the south side of the Tennessee River "to catch the deserters and refugees seeking our lines. The mountains are full of them, and they hold the mountain district in spite of all efforts of the rebels to catch them. I know of several companies of at least 100 men, each led by our scouts and members of the First Alabama Cavalry." Confederate Joseph E. Johnston with the Army of Tennessee was at Dalton, Georgia (soon he would begin retreating toward Atlanta under pressure from William T. Sherman). According to Dodge, "The desertions from Johnston's army are very large, and a great many come to us." But most of them went to the First Alabama Cavalry, U.S.A.; there would never be a second or a third.33

Alabama loyalists continued to join Northern regiments and independent companies as well as the First Alabama. In January 1864 Colonel Morgan L. Smith moved far up the Tennessee Valley with the Eighth Missouri, the Forty-seventh Ohio, and the One Hundred and Sixteenth Illinois to break up a picket line that was intercepting deserters from Johnston's army. "This movement created great consternation," Smith reported.

It also enabled men to come out of the fastnesses of Sand Mountain who had been secreted a great part of the time for two years, several of whom have raised companies for the First Alabama Cavalry, and some have enlisted in [Missouri, Ohio, and Illinois] infantry regiments. One man, McCurdy, mustered his company with a pencil on brown paper, christened it, assumed command, ordered an advance into Sand Mountain, and actually made captures of rebel home guards in the same hiding-places they had themselves just vacated. These loyal Alabamians are invaluable, and exceed in number and are equal in zeal to anything we discovered in East Tennessee.

Many of the Home Guards, including 1 officer, have resumed their allegiance by taking the amnesty oath [prescribed by Lincoln in his December 1863 proclamation], and the always-loyal people of this part of Alabama have learned from the general good conduct of the men [in the Northern regiments] who their real friends are.[34]

All that some of the Alabama Unionists asked for was the means by which to do their own fighting. One of them went to Nashville to appeal to Governor Johnson, who sent him on to Washington with an introduction to President Lincoln. On November 16, 1864, Lincoln in turn sent the man on to Secretary Stanton with this note: "Hon. Sec. of War please see Mr. Gear [Jean Joseph Giers], on the question of furnishing some small arm am[m]unition to loyal people in Northern Alabama."[35]

By the end of the war the U.S. provost marshal general could credit Alabama with 2,576 white troops. The state's contribution to the Union cause was, in fact, considerably larger than that, since many Alabamians had served in out-of-state regiments and were counted with them, and many had belonged to home guards or independent units that were never mustered into the U.S. service and hence were not counted at all.

At least 65 members of the First Alabama Cavalry were Mississippians by birth (but were, of course, credited to Alabama, not Mississippi). As early as the beginning of 1863 a company of Mississippi Rangers existed. About a year later the First Mississippi Mounted Rifles was organized, but this regiment was never completely filled. A couple of companies of Mississippi militia were mustered into the Federal service. The total credited to the state was 545.

At least 271 members of the First Alabama Cavalry were native Georgians. By April 1865 the First Georgia Battalion had come into existence—too late to be counted in the provost marshal general's report. At least 98 men in the First Alabama Cavalry were native South Carolinians, and some South Carolinians doubtless served in other regiments, but South Carolina (alone among the Confederate states) provided no organization of white troops for the Union.[36]

Florida

It was almost as hard to get access to Florida as to Texas. From the outset of the war U.S. forces controlled offshore positions such as Fort Pickens, on an island opposite Pensacola, and other forts on the Florida Keys. The U.S. navy early set up a blockade of Florida ports. But most of the state was sparsely settled and much of it completely uninhabited. Along large stretches of the coast lay almost impassable marshes and swamps. The Confederates maintained picket lines that added to the difficulty of reaching possible recruits.

In the spring of 1862 the Confederates withdrew from their positions around Pensacola Bay, and the Federals permanently reoccupied Forts McRae and Barrancas, which they had abandoned after Florida's secession. Meanwhile Union troops took Jacksonville four times and evacuated it three times. During the final occupation of Jacksonville they started in the direction of Tallahassee but were stopped and badly defeated in Florida's one big battle at Olustee (February 20, 1864.) Tallahassee, along with Austin, Texas, was one of only two state capitals that remained immune to Union capture throughout the war.

As early as September 1861 the U.S. authorities had received evidence of Florida Unionism when nine Confederate deserters and two civilians arrived at Fort Pickens. "They represent there being many Union men in this country," the post commander then reported to the War Department, "but the expression of Union sentiments to be dangerous." A year later Governor John Milton wrote to Jefferson Davis:

> You are apprised that in Florida a very large minority were opposed to secession, and in many parts of the State combinations existed to adhere to and maintain the United States Government, and even now in some portions of the State there are men who would eagerly seize any opportunity that promised success to the United

States. . . . The enforcement of the conscript act has had a most unhappy effect . . . enrolling officers have reported to me that a greater number of men, able to perform military service, have evaded them than the number of men capable of being useful which they have enrolled.

While the Union forces occupied Jacksonville, a "considerable number of the inhabitants . . . avowed themselves publicly in favor of our cause," as one of the occupying officers noted.[37]

Not until the fall of 1863, however, did the Federals make a serious effort to recruit the dissident Floridians. The Hungarian-born veteran of the Austrian army Alexander Sandor Asboth then took command of the District of West Florida. He received orders, dated October 29, 1863, to undertake to raise a regiment of cavalry.

As he began to organize the First Florida Cavalry, U.S.A., Asboth convinced himself that "not only one but several regiments could be raised in Western Florida, by offering to all those who are anxious to enlist into the Union Army proper assistance to come within our lines." For bringing in recruits, down the rivers and through the bays, he had the use of two vessels, a schooner owned and operated by a local Unionist and a small steamer from the blockading fleet. On one trip across Choctawhatchee Bay the schooner brought in 25 able-bodied men, all it could carry. "They enlisted at once, and, in addition to these, 33 more, who have found their way through the rebel pickets, at the risk of their lives; of those [the total of 58 troops], 18 have enlisted in Company M, Fourteenth New York Cavalry, and 40 in the Florida regiment." Asboth was confident that the steamer would "return in a few days with at least 200 recruits."

If Asboth were to realize his full recruiting potential, however, he thought he would need additional help. He must have reinforcements, two steamers that would be completely at his disposal, and money for paying bounties. The steamers and the reinforcements would open new recruiting territory for him. They would enable him to "enter the Escambia and Perdido Rivers, scout to the interior of the State, and, capturing the isolated rebel posts, with their horses, collect also the refugees and deserters secreted in the woods and islands." An officer at Fort Barrancas was holding $2,000, "sent to him to be disbursed in payment of bounties to recruits at Key West." Asboth urged that this money be used at Pensacola instead. "Considering the general destitution of the people here, it would be an act of humanity, as well as good policy, to grant advance payment of bounty."

Though he failed to get all the support he asked for, Asboth succeeded in organizing before the end of 1863 a few companies of the First Florida Cavalry, which consisted largely of deserters from the Confederate army. By that time there was also a company of Florida Rangers, which was stationed at Charlotte Harbor, in the District of Key West and Tortugas.[38]

For some Union commanders in Florida, the objective was to recruit blacks rather than whites. As General Rufus Saxton informed Stanton from Jacksonville in March 1863, "the object of the expedition was to occupy Jacksonville and make it the base of operations for the arming of negroes and securing in this way possession of the entire State of Florida." Yet in the state as a whole the Union recruiters obtained a somewhat larger number of whites than blacks.[39]

When the Confederates won the battle of Olustee, on February 20, 1864, they did not win the minds and hearts of all the people in the area. Soon after the battle they sent troops to "operate against the deserters and disaffected citizens of Taylor and Lafayette Counties," located to the southwest of Olustee and the southeast of Tallahassee. The commander of the troops depended on two friendly swampers to show the way. According to him, "It would have been impossible for me to have penetrated these swamps even with a compass without their aid."

The commander could not find the deserters, but he came upon their unoccupied huts, and he obtained a muster roll of thirty-five members of the Independent Union Rangers, who had sworn "true allegiance to the United States of America." "At William Strickland's house (who is the leader of the gang)," the commander noted, "was captured the muster-roll referred to, 2,000 rounds of fixed ammunition for the Springfield musket, several barrels of flour from the U.S. Subsistence Department, and several other articles which evidenced the regularity of their communication with the enemy's gun-boats." The Confederate officer "ordered the destruction of every house on the east and west banks of the Econfina and Feuholloway Rivers belonging to these people." He advised: "The only practical way of hunting them will be with dogs and mounted men under the command of an experienced woodsman who is familiar with the country."[40]

Union forces remained in control of Jacksonville and its vicinity. "If it is the intention of the Government to occupy the State of Florida," the officer in charge at Jacksonville wrote on April 3, 1864, "I would urge upon the general commanding the granting me authority to raise a Florida regiment of white men, to serve only in this State." Two months later the general commanding the Department of the South issued the following orders:

> That the general superintendent of the recruiting service for the Department of the South be, and is hereby, instructed and authorized to enlist and organize into companies and regiments all white male persons that can be recruited within the State of Florida.
>
> The men so enlisted shall be organized as Florida volunteers, but will be governed by the same rules and regulations and receive the same premium, bounty, pay, and pension as all volunteers now being enlisted into the service of the United States. They will not be required to do duty outside of their own State except in cases of extreme necessity.
>
> Every white male person between the ages of eighteen and fifty, capable of bearing arms, now within this department or such as may hereafter come into it, who are not in the U.S. service, shall be immediately enrolled and organized into companies and battalions and drilled as infantry at least two hours one day of each week. Said militia shall be called into active service in case of an attack upon the post where they reside, or be required to do garrison duty should it be necessary, and while actually employed shall receive from the commissary one full ration per day.
>
> All refugees from within the rebel lines, or deserters from the rebel armies, and all aliens subject to foreign powers in amity with the United States Government, are exempt from the operation of this order.[41]

At the end of the war, six companies of the First Florida Cavalry and five companies of the Second Florida Cavalry were on duty. The provost marshal general credited the state with 1,290 white troops. This figure does not include those Floridians who were drafted into the pro-Union militia for defense or garrison duty, nor does the figure include those (such as the eighteen enlistees in the Fourteenth New York Cavalry) who joined Northern regiments.[42]

5   Galvanized Yankees

ORIGINALLY, the term "Galvanized Yankees" referred to Union soldiers who, after capture, joined the Confederate army. The term came to be applied also to rebel prisoners who joined the Union army (though these men might more logically have been called "Galvanized Confederates"). The North was slow and the South still slower to make use of Galvanized Yankees. President Lincoln finally took it upon himself to facilitate their recruitment for the U.S. forces.

At first, prisoners did not accumulate in large numbers on either side. Officers usually exchanged captives or released them on parole, that is, on a pledge that they not take up arms again until exchanged. In July 1862 the two sides agreed to a cartel by which a system of large-scale exchanges was set up, but in December of the same year Jefferson Davis took a step that led to the breakdown of the cartel. Davis proclaimed that the Confederacy would not treat all its captives as legitimate prisoners of war. The Confederacy would consider Benjamin F. Butler and all commissioned officers serving under him "robbers and criminals deserving death," and it would refuse to parole any other commissioned officer until Butler had "met with due punishment." Furthermore, the Confederacy would kill or reenslave black soldiers and would execute their (white) officers. For nearly two years, there were no systematic and large-scale exchanges under the cartel, though batches of prisoners continued to be exchanged from time to time, often on an informal basis. Consequently, the prison population grew.[1]

Until Lincoln opened the way to wholesale recruitment of prisoners, U.S. policy fluctuated but remained quite restrictive. As early as February 1862 Colonel James A. Mulligan, in command of the prison at

Camp Douglas, near Chicago, asked permission to recruit men he had paroled. General Henry W. Halleck referred the question to General-in-Chief George B. McClellan. Receiving no reply, Halleck authorized Mulligan to go ahead. Mulligan proceeded to enlist 228 ex-Confederates in the Twenty-third and Sixty-fifth Illinois Volunteers. Then came word that the War Department was prohibiting the enlistment of prisoners. It was too late. The two Illinois regiments were already in the field—with their new recruits.[2]

Before long, Secretary of War Edwin M. Stanton seemed about to reverse the department's policy when, on July 10, 1862, he informed the U.S. marshal at New York City: "You are authorized to visit and hold communication with the persons now held as prisoners of war at New York for the purpose of ascertaining whether any and how many of them are willing to enter into the military service of the United States." Certainly, quite a few prisoners were willing to do so at other prisons, as, for example, at Camp Morton in Indianapolis. "A number of the rebel prisoners in camp here desire to volunteer into our Army instead of being exchanged," Indiana Governor Oliver P. Morton assured Halleck. "I am in favor of accepting them, believing they can be trusted and it will have a good effect."[3]

Months later, however, the War Department was still objecting to proposals for prisoner recruitment, persuasive and even touching though some of the proposals were. In February 1863 the commandant at Camp Butler, near Springfield, Illinois, reported that nearly half of his prisoners, who had recently been captured at Arkansas Post, were eager to join the Union army.

The prisoners of war now confined at Camp Butler are principally from regiments raised in and about Texas. A large number are of Irish, German, and Polish nationality. They state that they were conscripted and forced into the rebel army against their will; that the battle of Arkansas Post was the first in which they were engaged. Some are known to have gone from Illinois to the South for employment, and some have near relatives and friends in Illinois. They are willing to take the oath of allegiance and fight for the Union, and but for the misfortune of locality would ere this be found in the ranks of loyal regiments.

On behalf of the Germans at Camp Butler and also those at Camp Douglas, the colonel of the Sixteenth (German) Illinois Cavalry, Christian Thielemann, who was seeking recruits, made another appeal to the War Department. Illinois Governor Richard Yates and Congressman Isaac N. Arnold (a friend and later a biographer of Lincoln) seconded the appeal. The response to both Thielemann's and the Camp Butler commandant's proposals: "The Secretary of War forbids the enlistment into our ranks of prisoners of war." [4]

Yet the secretary of war was apparently moved by the argument that among the prisoners were men who had always been loyal at heart and had never willingly fought for the enemy. So he began to make exceptions to the rule "not to permit Confederate prisoners to join our Army" in cases where the prisoners were "sincerely desirous of renouncing all connection with the rebels." An unspecified number of prisoners were allowed to enlist at Camp Douglas. At Somerset, Kentucky, General Samuel P. Carter, commanding loyal Tennessee troops, received the welcome news: "East Tennesseeans will not be compelled to be exchanged if they wish to remain with us." At Camp Morton in Indianapolis 50 Tennesseeans joined an Indiana regiment and 55 joined a Tennessee regiment. At Fort Delaware, 82 prisoners enlisted in the First Connecticut Cavalry and 461 (later 120 more) were added to the Third Maryland Cavalry. Finally, on June 20, 1863, Stanton made the new policy definite: "The Secretary of War . . . directs that, when it can be reliably shown that the applicant was impressed into the rebel service and that he now wishes in good faith to join our army, he may be permitted to do so on his taking the oath of allegiance." It would be "left for the examining officer to satisfy himself of the reliability of the prisoner's statements."

When each officer in charge of prisoners had to decide which of the prisoners to enlist, the result was a considerable increase in recruited prisoners. But so many of them afterwards deserted that Stanton decided to tighten up the recruiting procedure. On August 5 and 7, 1863, he sent the following instructions to the commanders of all the military departments (geographical areas):

It must be shown . . . that the applicant was forced into the rebel service against his will and has taken advantage of the first opportunity to endeavor to free himself from it; or it [the privilege of enlisting] may be granted as a favor to his family or friends, they being all loyal people and vouching for his sincerity in desiring to become a loyal citizen; or it may be granted on account of the youth of the applicant, it being shown that he was led away by vicious companions, his Union friends guaranteeing his future good conduct. Cases must be presented substantially after this manner, with all the papers, through this office [Commissary General of Prisoners], for the approval of the Secretary of War, on whose order alone the discharge [from prison] can be granted.

All this paper work, plus the requirement of Stanton's personal approval, would obviously put a limit on the number of prisoners that could be recruited.[5]

General William S. Rosecrans, commanding the Department of the Cumberland, gave the lieutenant colonel of a Tennessee regiment "permission to go to Indianapolis and recruit from Vicksburg prisoners, first obtaining approval of [Tennessee] Governor Johnson." The officer should take care to "have them so distributed as to be under control of Union forces and sentiment." More than a hundred Irish Catholics at the Indianapolis prison were allowed to join an Indiana regiment. But at Indianapolis and elsewhere there remained a great many other prisoners who were "willing and eager to enlist in the U.S. service."[6]

The numbers of willing men were especially large at Point Lookout, the prison at the tip of Maryland between the Potomac River and Chesapeake Bay. About eight thousand men were confined there (in tents) when, in November 1863, Benjamin F. Butler became commander of the Department of Virginia and North Carolina and also commissioner for the exchange of prisoners. (Here was a nice, ironic touch—this man, whom the Confederates would kill instead of exchanging, was now supervising the release of imprisoned Confederates!) Butler sent the following telegram to Stanton on December 27, 1863: "Is there any objection to my enlisting as many prisoners as may desire to do so—after they know they can be exchanged—either in the regular or volunteer force of the United States or that of any State?"[7]

Before answering Butler, Stanton consulted Lincoln. Having recently offered amnesty to rebels taking an oath of future loyalty, Lincoln hoped to give as many rebels as possible an opportunity to take the oath. He decided to allow those prisoners choosing amnesty at Point Lookout to have several options, one of which would be to enlist in the U.S. service. On January 2, 1864, he sent his private secretary John Hay to carry a letter to Butler and present the plan to him. Stanton telegraphed Butler on the same day to tell him Hay was going to Point Lookout. "You will please meet him there, if convenient, and come to Washington for the purpose of explanation and further instruction."

According to Lincoln's new program, which applied only to Point Lookout, a prisoner would not be required to prove that he had originally been a Unionist, or that he had been taken into the Confederate service against his will, or that he had left that service at the first opportunity. He would be asked only four questions:

First. Do you desire to be sent South as a prisoner of war for exchange?

Second. Do you desire to take the oath of allegiance and parole, and enlist in the Army or Navy of the United States, and if so in which?

Third. Do you desire to take the oath and parole and be sent North to work on public works, under the penalty of death if found in the South before the end of the war?

Fourth. Do you desire to take the oath of allegiance and go to your home within the lines of the U.S. Army, under like penalty if found South beyond those lines before the end of the war?

Each prisoner was to be read these questions "alone and apart from any other rebel prisoner." Once a man had made his decision, he was to sign his name under the question to which he was giving an affirmative answer.

"Every prisoner at Point Lookout has recorded his name under one of the four questions," Butler reported on March 11, 1864. "I have nearly a regiment recruited. I can get more when I get more prisoners." He soon had enough men to fill the First Volunteer U.S. Infantry. They had enlisted for three years or during the war "upon the same terms as other soldiers in the U.S. Army." This meant that they could be assigned to duty anywhere. If they should be sent back to the South,

as earlier prisoner recruits had been, they would run the risk of capture, and if captured and recognized as ex-Confederate soldiers, they
would be treated as deserters.[8]

Not only deserters but all Southerners caught serving in the Union
army ought to be punished as traitors, in the opinion of some Confederates. (Lincoln and his advisers had taken a similar view at first: they
threatened to try captured rebels for treason rather than hold them as
prisoners of war, but they never carried out the threat.)

In September 1861 the governor of North Carolina, Henry T. Clark,
inquired of the attorney general of the Confederacy, Judah P. Benjamin, about the "legal course to be taken against these prisoners" who
had been arrested for having "taken the oath of allegiance to Lincoln's
government." Though the prisoners had not joined the Union army as
yet, perhaps they were encouraging others to do so. The governor
cited a law that the secession convention had passed: "Treason against
the State of North Carolina shall consist only in levying war against
her or in adhering to her enemies, giving them aid and comfort." Yet
when North Carolinians who had joined the Union army and participated in levying war against the Confederates in that state were captured, none was tried for treason on that count alone.

But some loyalist captives were treated differently from ordinary
prisoners. Three of them, taken in March 1863, languished in Castle
Thunder, a former tobacco warehouse in Richmond where alleged
spies and traitors were commonly put. These three "had been confined in an awful dungeon, from the effects of which two of the men
had died," according to their commanding officer. "Thus my men are
treated as felons of the deepest dye instead of as prisoners of war because they are North Carolina Union Volunteers."[9]

Governor John Gill Shorter of Alabama raised the treason issue
again after the Confederates had captured Abel D. Streight and his
raiders in May 1863. Streight, with seventeen hundred men, had set
out from Nashville to destroy railroads and other property in northern Alabama and Georgia. Included in his force were about four hundred Alabamians he had enlisted in his own Fifty-first Indiana Infantry and also two companies of the First Alabama Cavalry, U.S.A.
Governor Shorter seemed unaware that there were Alabamians in the
Indiana regiment, but he was incensed about the Alabama compa-

nies—who he erroneously believed had been arming slaves and inciting them to insurrection. He was convinced that, even apart from this supposed crime, there was good cause to hang the Alabamians. He explained his strong convictions in a long and impassioned letter to James A. Seddon, the Confederate secretary of war:

> If the uniform of our enemy is to continue to protect their officers and men . . . is it also to protect our recreant and traitorous citizens who still claiming themselves as Alabamians afford to our enemies the means of striking at the heart of the State and when captured claim the flag of our enemy as their protection? Ample opportunity was given to these traitors to cast their lot with the enemy and remove this reproach and stigma from the State. With a forbearance before unknown one of the earliest acts of the Confederacy was to invite those who preferred the rule of our enemies to leave our borders in peace and establish themselves in the Government of their choice. But these traitors preferred to remain that their crime might strike deeper and their blow fall heavier, and having chosen their status as citizens of a State of the Confederacy they should not be allowed to escape the penalty of treason which they have invited. They stand as citizens levying war [against the state] as well as giving aid and comfort to our enemies.

Governor Shorter of Alabama requested that "these marauders be delivered up to the authorities of this State for trial."

Governor Morton of Indiana read in an "account from the rebel newspapers" that "the men were paroled except the four companies of renegade Alabamians"—which he took to be the four companies in the Fifty-first Indiana Regiment. He demanded of Stanton that twice as many rebel prisoners be "held as hostages for the safety of these loyal Alabamians." Governor Yates of Illinois also protested to Stanton: "A number of citizens of Alabama, now residents of this State, have addressed me by letter asking me to interest myself in securing for citizens of Alabama, relatives and friends of theirs captured with Colonel Streight's command, the rights and immunities of prisoners of war." The Illinois governor demanded "instant retaliation."

On behalf of the War Department, E. A. Hitchcock, at that time commissioner for the exchange of prisoners, replied to the governors of Indiana and Illinois that retaliation would only provoke further outrages and that hostage-taking would be fruitless, since the Confederacy held more prisoners than the Union did. "The question involved is plainly that which brought on the war, to wit, the right of a State over its own people in denial of their obligations as citizens of the United States," Hitchcock explained. "It can only be settled on the battle-field."

Responding to Governor Shorter of Alabama, Confederate Secretary of War Seddon said the governor's letter about the Alabamians captured with Streight had been referred to Jefferson Davis, and "considerations of public policy in his judgment" made it "more advisable that the cases should be brought under the cognizance of the tribunals of the Confederacy and remain subject to the final determination of the Executive." But the Confederacy could do nothing about the present case, for all the Alabamians in Streight's command either had "made their escape before the capture" or had been released "through the speedy action of the officials intrusted with the duty of exchanging prisoners." [10]

Neither the Confederacy nor any of its member states ever adopted a policy of trying Southern Federals, as such, for treason. But the treatment of deserters or alleged deserters from the Confederate army—and especially those who joined the U.S. army—was another matter.

In dealing with deserters, the Confederacy was quite inconsistent. Early in the war it imposed a variety of punishments: a week or two on bread and water in a stockade, bucking and gagging, fifty lashes, and occasionally shooting or hanging. In April 1863 the Confederate Congress eliminated whipping and specified death or imprisonment at hard labor. Lee and Davis (like Lincoln) sometimes pardoned a convicted deserter or commuted his death sentence. As desertion increased, the government now and then resorted to offers of amnesty to persuade the absent to return. [11]

The more lax policies were intended for the soldier hiding out in the woods or spending time at home with his family and did not necessarily apply to men who had left the Confederate army and had gone over to the other side. Such men, if identified as deserters after their capture, ran a greater risk of imprisonment or execution.

(A Southern accent was not a reliable mark of identification. Tens of thousands of Union soldiers had Southern accents of one kind or another—soldiers from Maryland, Kentucky, and Missouri, and even from southern Ohio, Indiana, and Illinois. Also, Confederate soldiers who were born in the North or abroad, or who came from some of the mountainous areas of the South, lacked the familiar Southern patterns of speech.)

Two men from the Eighth Vermont Infantry and one from the Second Massachusetts Cavalry were recognized as deserters when rebels brought them to Vicksburg, Mississippi, after the surrender of a Federal outpost. At the time of the Farragut-Butler expedition against New Orleans (April 1862), these men had been among the Fort Jackson garrison troops who mutinied and helped bring about the capitulation of the fort. The prisoners now fell into the hands of their former outfit, the First Louisiana Heavy Artillery. They were made an example to their previous regimental comrades and to many other Confederate troops. "Cloudy day," Lieutenant William T. Mumford of the First Louisiana Heavy Artillery noted in his diary on March 6, 1863. "Private Thos. Graham, Co B La. Arty., Denis Kean, 1st La. Arty., and Sergt. W. H. Brown, 1st La. Arty. executed today in presence of Smith's, Maury's, and Stephenson's Divisions. They were . . . tried by court martial and sentenced to be shot." [12]

From time to time other such executions occurred, without attracting much attention in the North, but then there occurred a most horrendous mass execution that provoked a great deal of consternation among some Northerners. It took place in North Carolina in February and March 1864 shortly after Confederate forces had attacked New Bern and taken a number of prisoners. The man responsible for the executions was George E. Pickett, who was to Southerners the hero of "Pickett's Charge" at Gettysburg, though his role in that exploit was later questioned. He had graduated last in his class at West Point. It was said of him that he was "dapper and alert" and "wore his dark hair in long, perfumed ringlets that fell to his shoulders." [13]

John J. Peck, a New Yorker with a much better West Point record, was commanding the Union's District of North Carolina, with his headquarters at New Bern when the Confederates attacked. Afterward General Peck read in the *Richmond Examiner* that a black soldier, who had been seen to shoot a Confederate colonel, "was watched, followed, taken and hanged." Peck sent Pickett a letter of protest, enclosing a copy of Lincoln's order of July 30, 1863, which included the following words: "for every soldier of the United States

killed in violation of the laws of war a rebel soldier shall be executed."
In reply, Pickett said the newspaper story was false, but "had I caught
any negro who had killed officer, soldier, or citizen of the Confederate
States I should have caused him to be immediately executed." Pickett
added: "I have in my hands . . . some 450 officers and men of the U.S.
Army, and for every man you may hang I will hang 10 of the U.S.
Army."

Before receiving this reply, Peck had sent Pickett another letter and
with it a list of fifty-three (white) soldiers who presumably had fallen
into Pickett's hands during the recent action at New Bern. "They are
loyal and true North Carolinians and duly enlisted in the Second
North Carolina Infantry," Peck wrote. "I ask for them the same treatment in all respects as you will mete out to other prisoners of war."
Soon Peck read in the *Fayetteville Observer:* "We learn by an officer
just from the spot that two of these [prisoners] have already been executed and others are undergoing trial." He then notified Pickett: "If
the members of the North Carolina regiment who have been captured
are not treated as prisoners of war the strictest retaliation will be enforced." He did not yet know that twenty other members of that regiment had already died on the gallows at Kinston, North Carolina.

Peck learned of this in a sarcastic letter from Pickett, who expressed
his gratitude for

> the list of 53 with which you have so kindly furnished me, and
> which will enable me to bring to justice many who have up to this
> time escaped their just deserts. I herewith return to you the names
> of those who have been tried and convicted by court-martial for
> desertion from the Confederate service and taken with arms in
> hand, "duly enlisted in the Second North Carolina Infantry, U.S.
> Army." They have been duly executed according to the law and the
> custom of war.
>
> Your letter and list will, of course, prevent any mercy being
> shown any of the remaining members, should proper and just proof
> be brought of their having deserted the Confederate colors, many
> of these men pleading in extenuation that they have been forced
> into the ranks of the Federal Government.
>
> Extending to you my thanks for your opportune list . . .

And, as if to return the favor, Pickett enclosed his list of the names of
the twenty-two who had been executed.

Pickett's action, together with his threat of ten-for-one retaliation, evinced "a most extraordinary thirst for life and blood on the part of the Confederate authorities," Peck retorted. "Such violent and revengeful acts, resorted to as a show of strength, are the best evidence of the weak and crumbling condition of the Confederacy." Peck sent copies of his correspondence with Pickett to his own superior, Butler, who forwarded them to the general in chief, Ulysses S. Grant, with the following argument:

> Many of these men were conscripted by the rebels. All of them were citizens of the United States, who owed their allegiance to our Government; if misguided, they forfeited their allegiance, repented, and returned to it again. They have only done their duty, and, in my judgment, are to be protected in so doing. I do not recognize any right in the rebels to execute a United States soldier because either by force or fraud, or by voluntary enlistment even, he has been brought into their ranks and has escaped therefrom. I suppose all the rights they can claim as belligerents is to execute one of the deserters from their army while he holds simply the character of a deserter during the time he has renounced his allegiance, and before he has again claimed that protection [from the Union army] and it has been accorded to him. Therefore by no law of nations and by no belligerent rights have the rebels any power over him other than to treat him as a prisoner of war if captured.

Butler's argument—that a deserter is a deserter only so long as he is on his own between the two belligerents—failed to convince Grant.[14]

Grant held a quite different view, as he had recently indicated in correspondence with Joseph E. Johnston regarding "soldiers belonging to the 3d West Tennessee Cavalry, U.S. Service," who were "confined at Atlanta Ga. charged with belonging to the C.S. Army." Grant conceded: "Of course I would claim no right to retaliate for the punishment of deserters who had actually been mustered into the Confederate Army, and afterwards deserted and joined ours." He would exclude from punishment those men who joined the Union service to escape from Confederate conscription, but only if they did so before being sworn into the Confederate army.

Besides, Grant was a personal friend of Pickett's, an army associate of the prewar years. When a son was born to Pickett and his wife, in July 1864, Grant along with two other Union officers signed the following letter to Pickett: "We are sending congratulations to you, to the young mother and the young recruit."

After the war, Grant would intercede to save Pickett from possible prosecution as a war criminal. Pickett failed to get a pardon when he applied to President Johnson on June 1, 1865, and he risked punishment when an army board of inquiry met at New Bern on October 15, 1865, and again at Raleigh on January 17, 1866.

The testimony at the army board's hearings indicated that some of the executed men had belonged to local home guards, had never agreed to serve in the Confederate army, and therefore could not have been rightly adjudged deserters. "These troops were raised for local defence," ex-Governor Vance himself testified. He thought "the Confederate Government did not keep faith with these local troops," whose "transfer to the regular service" was a "violation of their enlistment agreement."

After hearing Vance and other ex-Confederate witnesses, the investigators came to the following conclusion with regard to General Pickett, General Robert F. Hoke, the members of the court martial, and others responsible for the executions: "these men have violated the rules of war and every principle of humanity, and are guilty of crime too heinous to be excused by the Government of the United States; and therefore there should be a Military Commission immediately appointed for the trial of these men and to inflict upon the perpetrators of such crimes their just punishment." Secretary Stanton and Judge Advocate General Joseph Holt agreed with the findings and hoped to see at least Pickett and Hoke punished for "the barbarous slaying upon the gallows of certain Union soldiers at Kinston, N.C."

Pickett, of course, took a quite different view. "It has come to my knowledge that certain evil disposed persons are attempting to re-open the troubles of the past," he wrote to Grant on March 12, 1866, "and embroil me for the action taken by me whilst the Commanding Officer of the Confederate Forces in N.C." Not much was left of Pickett's bloodthirstiness or bravado as he now begged for assurance that his parole at the war's end would protect him from "the assaults of those persons desirous of still keeping up the War."

Grant agreed. He believed that the terms he had given Lee at Appomattox—and the terms Sherman had given Johnston at Bennett's farmhouse—would exempt Confederate officers and men "from future trial or punishment by Military or Government authority, for past offences, so far as these offences consisted in making war against the Government of the United States." And Grant seemed to think that Pickett's offense involved no more than waging war against the U.S. government.

Grant sent Pickett's letter on to President Johnson with a "recommendation that clemency be extended in this case or assurances given that no trial will take place for the offences charged against G. E. Pickett."

> I know it is claimed that the men tried and convicted for the crime of desertion were Union men from N.C. who had found refuge within our lines and in our service. The punishment was a harsh one but it was in time of war when the enemy no doubt felt it necessary to retain, by some power, the services of every man within their reach. Gn. Pickett I know personally to be an honorable man but in this case his judgement prompted him to do what can not well be sustained though I do not see how good, either to the friends of the deceased or by fixing an example for the future, can be secured by his trial now. It would only open up the question whether or not the Government did not disregard its contract entered into to secure the surrender of an armed enemy.

Johnson, as commander in chief, did nothing to bring Pickett to trial. After a month, on April 16, 1866, the House of Representatives impatiently called upon the secretary of war for information about what steps had been taken "to bring to justice and punishment the murderers" of the loyal North Carolina soldiers who had been killed "under the pretext of their being deserters from the Confederate service." Stanton responded with the relevant documents, including the proceedings of the army boards of inquiry. By this time, the Republicans in Congress were beginning to override Johnson's vetoes of their reconstruction bills but were powerless to dictate his actions as commander in chief.

Pickett was never tried for war crimes, but he was included in the "amnesty for the offence of treason" that Johnson proclaimed on Christmas Day, 1868.[15]

In July 1864 the First U.S. Volunteers, who had been recruited at the Point Lookout prison, went on an expedition from Norfolk, Virginia, to Elizabeth City, North Carolina, "for the purpose of capturing

horses, cotton, and other contraband property" in the eastern counties of the state. For these deserters, 40 percent of whom were North
Carolinians, this was a particularly dangerous mission. If any of the
men had been captured, they might well have suffered the same fate as
had the twenty-two victims of General Pickett in February of that
year. As things turned out, the expedition returned safely to Norfolk,
with large quantities of loot.

General Grant was troubled by the possibility that the loyal soldiers
of the First U.S. Volunteers could be punished as deserters if they were
captured by Confederate forces in North Carolina. He promptly ordered the First U.S. Volunteers to leave for the Department of the
Northwest, where General John Pope, from his headquarters in Milwaukee, commanded the forces that were defending the frontier
against the Indians. "The 1st Regt. U S Vols. numbers 1000 for duty
and is a first class Regiment," Grant explained, "but it is not right to
expose them where to be taken Prisoners they must suffer as deserters." He directed that Pope "send an equal amount of troops to Genl
Sherman," who was bearing down upon Atlanta.[16]

It was not an entirely new idea to send ex-rebels out to fight the
Indians. Detachments of "rebel deserters" were already serving, along
with companies of the Second Minnesota and the Thirtieth Wisconsin
Cavalry, on the Northwestern frontier. But Grant now made it a fixed
policy to enlist no more prisoners in regiments that might take them
south to fight their former comrades.

Lincoln had yet to learn of Grant's new policy. Running for reelec-
tion, in a contest he feared he would lose, he was concerned about the
electoral vote of Pennsylvania, the second most populous of all the
states. He had issued another call for troops, and Pennsylvanians, like
other Northerners, were weary of the war and leery of the draft. The
draft could be avoided—and voters could be mollified—if rebel prisoners could be used to fill up quotas.

This possibility occurred to a couple of Pennsylvania Republicans,
one of them Colonel Henry S. Huidekoper, and they urged it upon
Lincoln, who authorized it in the following order of September 1,
1864:

It is represented to me that there are at Rock Island, Ills., as rebel
prisoners of war, many persons of Northern and foreign birth, who

are unwilling to be exchanged and sent South, but who wish to take the oath of allegiance and enter the military service of the Union. Col. Huidekoper on behalf of the people of some parts of Pennsylvania wishes to pay the bounties the government would have to pay to proper persons of this class, have them enter the service of the United States, and be credited to the localities furnishing the bounty money. He will therefore proceed to Rock Island, ascertain the names of such persons (not including any who have attractions Southward) and telegraph them to the Provost Marshal General.

Lincoln later revised this program so that the whole process of mustering in could be done at Rock Island (without the names having to be first approved by the provost marshal general) and also so "that the restriction in the President's order limiting the recruits to persons of foreign and Northern birth be removed."

Stanton objected to the scheme when he learned of it, and Lincoln went to Stanton's office to persuade him to carry it out. Provost-Marshal-General James B. Fry, whom Stanton summoned, argued that prisoners "could not be used against the Confederates" and that "to give them bounty and credit them to a county which owed some of its own men for service" would "waste money and deprive the army . . . of that number of men." But Lincoln insisted on the War Department's going ahead, since he had already committed himself to the Pennsylvanians. As he explained, apologetically, to Grant,

I was induced, upon pressing application, to authorize agents of one of the Districts of Pennsylvania to recruit in one of the prison depots in Illinois; and the thing went so far before it came to the knowledge of the Secretary of War that in my judgment it could not be abandoned without greater evil than would follow its going through. I did not know, at the time, that you had protested against that class of thing being done; and I now say that while this particular job must be completed, no other of the sort will be authorized without an understanding with you, if at all.

The Pennsylvania politicians were elated. "Nothing has helped our cause here as your order," one of them wrote Lincoln from Meadville, "and the manner [in] which you have so justly sustained it when assailed has quickened their efforts and renewed their energies." The people would not forget: "Their gratitude will be mannifested at the Polls." [17]

As for the Rock Island recruits, Grant telegraphed to Stanton: "I would advise that they be placed all in one regiment, and be put on duty either with Pope, or sent to New Mexico." At the same time, Stanton approved a request from Butler that he be allowed to recruit another regiment at Point Lookout for service on the frontier.

The First U.S. Volunteers were already on the way to Minnesota, and in return for them Pope was reluctantly giving up both the Eighth Minnesota and the Thirtieth Wisconsin, which were on the way to Georgia. Pope was relieved when he first saw some men of the First U.S. Volunteers en route in Milwaukee. He informed H. H. Sibley, the commander at St. Paul: "The regiment is well organized and officered, and to my great satisfaction (as also somewhat to my surprise) it is in a most excellent state of discipline."

But Sibley was quickly disillusioned with the new arrivals, who certainly were not the equals of the Minnesota and Wisconsin troops he had given up. Many were "desperate characters," capable of any crime and ready to desert at the first opportunity, Sibley wrote to a member of Pope's staff on October 6, 1864. They could be controlled in large garrisons, but the frontier service required the force to be divided into small parties, in which the "rebel deserters" could not be trusted. "I respectfully request that no more of this class be sent here." Pope forwarded Sibley's letter to Halleck, who wired Grant: "The conduct of the regiment of rebel deserters enlisted by Genl Butler & sent to the northwest has been such that no more of that class should be received." [18]

So, for the time being, the War Department did nothing with the men who, under Lincoln's order, had been recruited at Rock Island. They remained in a kind of limbo. They accumulated to a total of more than two thousand and were crowded into barracks where they were kept separate from the rest of the prisoners by a high board fence. On November 18, 1864, the commandant of the prison appealed to the provost marshal general:

Since they are no longer prisoners of war they are entitled to the rights of U.S. soldiers. Consequently this pen is close and tiresome, and the men are becoming dispirited and long for that freedom of action which they gained by their enlistment. Again, their clothing is of the poorest description and cannot be bettered. As they are no longer prisoners of war clothing cannot be issued to them from the prisoners' portion, and as they are not organized [as troops] clothing cannot be issued by the quartermaster. Consequently these cold days and nights find them shivering around the barracks stoves, which are kept red-hot in order that they do not freeze. These men are to be pitied.

Finally, after months more of waiting and shivering, the Rock Island recruits were saved by news of Indian troubles on the Great Plains. Troops were needed to guard the overland mail route from Leavenworth to Laramie. "I will be glad to have the two regiments of rebel deserters from Rock Island to post on the Overland route," Pope informed the War Department, "if experienced and suitable officers can be appointed." Stanton authorized Pope to take the regiments and appoint the officers.[19]

Meanwhile Grant undertook to remove Southern deserters from state units and put them with the U.S. Volunteers. "Every day I receive letters from rebel deserters who, in the absence of employment, have enlisted and now find themselves confronting their old regiments or acquaintances," Grant telegraphed to Halleck from City Point, Virginia, on December 7, 1864. "I wish you would ask the sec. of War to give me discretionary authority to transfer such as I think deserving of it." Stanton readily gave him the authority but let him know that there were more than two thousand recruits at Rock Island who, at that time, were still "of no use."

Stanton, as well as Grant, continued to oppose the enlistment of prisoners in state regiments. The major of the Second North Carolina Mounted Infantry hoped in January 1865 to recruit men captured at Cumberland Gap in September 1863 and since confined at Camp Chase (Columbus, Ohio), Camp Douglas (Chicago), and Johnson's Island (Lake Erie). "The larger number of those men were and now are Union men and have written from time to time to me to come and get them out of prison," the major said. Stanton ruled, however, that it was not expedient to approve the major's request. If those men were to get out of prison by signing up for the Union, they would have to serve in the West, not in the South.[20]

The two regiments from Point Lookout plus the two from Rock Island made four regiments of U.S. Volunteers in service by early 1865. A fifth was soon to follow. General Grenville M. Dodge, who had earlier organized the First Alabama Cavalry, U.S.A., had taken command of the Department of the Missouri and needed additional troops on the frontier. On March 5, 1865, Dodge informed Pope

> that there are some 250 men in confinement at Alton, Ill., known as the "galvanized Yankees," *i.e.*, men who were taken prisoners by the enemy during the last year, and who, to avoid starvation and death, enlisted in . . . the Confederate Army, and who in the recent raid [by Benjamin Grierson in Mississippi] deserted on the approach of our forces to us. These men have already applied to be sent back to their regiments, but it is not considered safe to send them where they will be in danger of capture by the enemy. There are also 1,000 prisoners of war and conscripts who refuse to be exchanged—claim to be deserters, unwilling conscripts, &c. These men have applied to enlist in our Army. I respectfully submit if we had not better organize a regiment of these men and put them on the plains.

Stanton authorized Pope to recruit for the Fifth U.S. Volunteers at Alton, and when it appeared that he could raise only five companies there, Stanton directed him to "complete the regiment by enlistments from prisoners at Chicago and Rock Island." By the time this was done, the war was over.[21]

While the Union was discontinuing the use of rebel prisoners against the South in the summer of 1864, the Confederacy was beginning to employ captured Federals against the North. The Davis government had approved such a policy earlier, in March 1863, when General J. C. Pemberton at Jackson, Mississippi, inquired about it. "Use your discretion with regard to men taken as prisoners of war," Confederate Secretary of War Seddon replied. "Enlist if any are willing." Instead of taking many more prisoners, however, Pemberton surrendered his army at Vicksburg a few months later.

By the fall of 1864 there was an abundance of potential recruits in Confederate prisons. "Many Yankee prisoners here profess to be highly indignant with their Government for not exchanging them,"

General Sam Jones observed at Charleston, South Carolina, in September 1864, "and they express an earnest desire to take the oath of allegiance, and many of them to join our army if we will permit them." Seddon responded: "A battalion or two might be formed of the foreigners—the Yankees are not to be trusted so far, or at all." Seddon also sanctioned the "enlistment of Irish and other foreign prisoners" when the commandant at Macon, Georgia, told him that a thousand or more Roman Catholic Irishmen there desired to enlist. Later Seddon approved the acceptance of "about 260 prisoners, foreigners," who had volunteered at Florence, South Carolina.[22]

The numbers grew. According to Confederate reports, there were soon 807 enlistees at Florence, 1,100 at Richmond, and 349 at Camp Lawton, Georgia, an outlet for overcrowded Andersonville prison, where there were at least a few hundred more. According to Union reports, there were "between 1,300 and 2,000 U.S. soldiers" who had sworn allegiance to the Confederacy on James Island and at Summerville, South Carolina. "Reports from Savannah represent that many of our prisoners now in that city have also taken service in the rebel army," J. G. Foster, commanding the Union Department of the South at Hilton Head, South Carolina, wrote to General Halleck on November 12, 1864. Halleck forwarded the letter to Grant with this note on it: "Advices from other sources indicate that many of our foreign troops and substitutes, prisoners of war, are joining the rebel service."[23]

Robert E. Lee himself took an interest in prisoner recruitment. He heard from the prison commandant at Salisbury, North Carolina, that "2,000 or 3,000 foreigners" being held there could be enlisted, and that "by proper management this force could be increased to 7,000 or 8,000." Lee inquired of Seddon: "How would it answer to organize these men into the Regular Army, with officers appointed by the President, and the whole under one good officer?" Replying on November 17, 1864, Seddon described the existing Confederate policy:

> For some time past my attention has been attracted to that mode of recruiting, and I have given to officers supposed to be competent, in several instances, permits to raise battalions, directing them to prefer Irish and French, and to enlist no citizens of the United States. The latter, especially native born, I hold in great distrust. . . .

I have, too, authorized several officers, whose commands had been greatly depleted, to recruit for them from this source. Among others, General [Zebulon] York, while wounded here, has obtained this permission and proposes to visit the prisons, taking with him one or more Catholic chaplains, whose influence, he thinks, may be profitably exercised upon those of the same religious persuasion. . . .

You have, I believe, a Virginia battalion, originally composed of Irish, now greatly reduced by the casualties of service, which might, probably, in that way be re-established in numbers and efficiency.

Seddon thought it preferable to organize the men in units no larger than battalions and to enlist them for the provisional army rather than the regular army.[24]

None of the Confederate generals was more enthusiastic about recruiting prisoners than William J. Hardee, but he was soon disillusioned with regard to their usefulness. After Sherman had taken Atlanta and had begun his march to the sea, Hardee was responsible for resisting the march and finally for defending Savannah. After Savannah had fallen, he reported to his government:

Colonel [J. H.] Brooks' battalion, composed of Federal prisoners of war enlisted from prison into Confederate service, was found at Savannah to be utterly untrustworthy. The men deserted in large numbers, and finally mutinied, and were narrowly prevented from going over in a body to the enemy. The ringleaders were shot and the remainder sent back to prison. These men were selected with great care, and were principally foreigners, and this is, therefore, a fair test of such troops. I recommend that all authority to organize similar commands be revoked.[25]

The Confederates had another bad experience with Galvanized Yankees on December 28, 1864, a few days after the fall of Savannah. Union General Benjamin Grierson, on a raid in Mississippi, attacked at Egypt Station on the Mobile and Ohio Railroad and captured nearly a thousand men, of whom a fourth or more proved to be former U.S. soldiers. On the riverboat taking them to the prison at Alton, Illinois, some of the former U.S. soldiers talked with Colonel John W. Noble of the Third Iowa Cavalry. Noble reported that their accounts agreed "in the following particulars":

That they were prisoners of war at Andersonville, Ga., when they enlisted in the Confederate service; that at the time they were in great want of food, fuel, and clothing, which, with exposure to weather, rendered disease and death imminent to them all, that many dead were carried from among the prisoners daily; . . . that they were enlisted . . . with the design and determination on their part to rejoin our ranks at the first opportunity, and that they did avail themselves of the only opportunity that had presented itself; that they were never fully trusted by the Confederates, being deprived of many privileges extended to other troops, kept under strict camp guard and unarmed; that they were given muskets on the day before the affair in which they were captured, and ammunition; but on the night before, that foreigners were first solicited, but many others finally taken, and that they now wish to be sent to their old regiments to fight for the Union.

General Grierson did not treat these deserters in quite the same manner in which General Pickett had treated the twenty-two North Carolinians. Most of the present captives, Grierson reported, "were induced to join the [Confederate] ranks from a desire to escape a loathesome confinement. I commend them to the leniency of the Government." General Dodge wanted them for service on the frontier, and General Pope recommended such service as a way to "get rid of the whole question of 'galvanized Yankees.'" None of the men was hanged or shot; most of them were enlisted in the Fifth U.S. Volunteers.[26]

By early 1865 the Confederacy was so desperate for troops that, despite the undependability of its prisoner recruits, even the foreign-born, as shown at Savannah and at Egypt Station, Confederate leaders began to look for more of them. Seddon advised that such recruits "should not be placed in new organizations, nor collected in large numbers in those now existing, but should be distributed as much as possible among companies, regiments, and brigades of undoubted fidelity." It had been a mistake, he thought, to concentrate them in a single battalion, as at Savannah. "In one case in which a new battalion was formed from such material a conspiracy was discovered; and although it was promptly crushed, yet it was found expedient to disband the battalion," he wrote with Savannah in mind. "Nevertheless, the experiment is now in course of trial by other officers, who believe that by recruiting among Catholic Irish and other foreigners and obtaining the influence of the Catholic priesthood they may secure faithful soldiers."

The disabled General York—who earlier had secured permission to make the rounds of the prisons with Catholic chaplains—again set out on the same mission. From Salisbury he reported to Lee that he had between six hundred and seven hundred recruits in camp there, and if he "could have the exclusive privilege of recruiting in all the prisons for some weeks," he "could shortly muster a brigade composed of such material as would reflect no discredit upon our army."

Even Hardee—who after the Savannah debacle had urged an end to the prisoner recruitment—once more resorted to it. On February 14, 1865, he ordered Lieutenant Colonel J. G. Tucker, "commanding First Foreign Battalion," to "recruit his command from the prisoners of war." Tucker was to "take only men of Irish and French nationality," who were to be "used for engineering service," not for combat.[27]

The war was over before the later recruits had much of a chance to show whether they would be any more reliable in action than the earlier recruits had been.

6   What Manner of Men

*T*AKEN AS A GROUP, the loyalists differed *with* the rebels much more than they differed *from* them. True, the loyalists were somewhat atypical in their geographical distribution: they did not come in proportionate numbers from all parts of the South. The great majority, perhaps 75 percent of them, lived in the mountainous or hilly country of Appalachia or the Ozarks—in northwestern Virginia, in East Tennessee and the neighboring areas of northern Alabama and western North Carolina, and in northwestern Arkansas. But a considerable minority inhabited the lowlands of West Tennessee and eastern North Carolina and those of Texas, Louisiana, and even Florida. Loyalists represented, in some measure, every state of the Confederacy.

In those highlands where there was the most Unionism, there was the least cotton, rice, or tobacco growing and the least slaveholding. Very few Union volunteers, whether from the highlands or from the lowlands, owned slaves or had close relatives who owned them. But in this respect the loyalists differed from the rebels only to a limited degree. Comparatively few of the ordinary Confederate soldiers belonged to slaveowning families, though nearly all the commissioned officers did. In the Confederacy as a whole, only one family in three held as many as a single slave.

Confederates may have thought of themselves as constituting a noble chivalry, but they did not impress the Tennessee Unionist William G. Brownlow that way. In "Parson Brownlow's Book," published in the midst of the war, he had this to say about them:

And whilst many of the substantial men of the country entered the army,—for the most part as officers, contractors, wagon-masters, and furnishers of supplies in various forms,—a much greater number entered the service who were pusillanimous and worthless, lazy and sensual, having no visible means of support. Many of these were known to me in East Tennessee and other portions of the South; and I can safely say that when they entered the service, and were fitted out with suits of coarse jeans and supplied with army-rations, they were bettered dressed and fed than they ever had been before. . . .

It was a common thing to hear men of this class, dressed in uniform, and under the influence of mean whiskey, swearing upon the streets that they intended to have their rights, or kill the last Lincolnite north of Mason & Dixon's line! Ask one of them what rights he had lost and was so vehemently contending for, and the reply would be, the right to carry his negroes into the Territories. At the same time, the man never owned a negro in his life, and never was related, by consanguinity or affinity, to any one who did own a negro![1]

This is, of course, a bitter and biased view of rebel soldiers, but no more bitter or biased than the attitude of most Southerners toward loyalist troops.

Confederates generally thought they were far superior to Unionists. One eastern North Carolinian referred to himself and his fellow secessionists as the "thinking men of this county" and the "substantial men of the county"—in contrast with the Lincolnites, who were "of not very reliable character." A Confederate colonel said of a group of East Tennessee "traitors" he had captured: "They are the most ignorant, poor, ragged devils I ever saw." Another colonel called the East Tennesseeans "savages." Still another officer thought his enemies in western Virginia were "imbued with an ignorant and bigoted Union sentiment."[2]

Contempt for loyalists and hatred and fear of them went to extremes among the planters near the North Carolina coast. A "secesh lady" expressed their feelings in her diary:

this company of Union men which they boast so of raising in Chowan & Gates [counties] is composed of the offscouring of the people & foreigners, people who can neither read or write & who never had a decent suit of clothes until they [the Yankees] gave it to them, poor ignorant wretches who cannot resist a fine uniform and the choice of the horses in the country & liberty to help themselves without check to their rich neighbors belongings. We should judge them leniently, but justice to ourselves demands that we shoot them down like wolves on sight.

To planters, the men of the First and Second North Carolina Union Volunteers were "Buffaloes," a term that was synonymous with "murderers" and "thieves." [3]

In eastern North Carolina and in some other parts of the South, U.S. officers themselves often assumed that the Confederates were the rich and prominent, the Unionists the poor and insignificant. Actually, the division of Carolina society was somewhat more complex than that, as is suggested by the 1860 census figures for Washington County. (The county furnished approximately the same number of Union and Confederate troops.) On the one hand, Union soldiers from that county owned an average of only $269 in personal property, Confederate soldiers an average of $3,759. None of the Unionist heads of household reported more than $1,000 in real estate; a couple of dozen pro-Confederate families did. On the other hand, all but one of the Unionists were landowners, while nineteen of the pro-Confederates were completely landless.

As recent scholarship has shown, the Confederates of Washington County consisted of the following: "Large planters and . . . dependents—their sons, the merchants with whom they dealt, the lawyers and clergymen they patronized, and the poor white men who worked as day laborers and . . . cut shingles on land owned by planters . . . an alliance of the very rich and the very poor." The Unionists were "men of middling means, yeoman farmers and their sons, many of whom owned land . . . [and] personal property, but seldom any slaves." The distinction was not simply between the rich and the poor, for "many poor men (mainly day laborers who worked for planters) fought for the Confederacy, and a few rich men (mainly merchants who traded with yeoman farmers) supported the Union." [4]

Throughout the South, many members of what was locally the middle or even the upper class served as commissioned officers of loyalist troops. A lieutenant of the First North Carolina Union Volunteers was a son of the mayor of Washington; the mayor himself was imprisoned in Richmond on account of his Unionism. The colonel of the

Second Virginia Union Infantry, a native Virginian, was a graduate of the University of Pennsylvania medical school; he had long practiced as a physician. The lieutenant colonel of the same Virginia regiment was the proprietor of a farm, which he rented out, and of a general store and tavern, which he operated in peacetime. The organizer and colonel of the First Texas Union Cavalry, born of wealthy parents in Florida, had become a successful Texas lawyer and a district judge. So it went with most of the loyalist regiments that were officered by local men.[5]

In northwestern Virginia "the most intelligent and influential citizens" favored the Union cause, as their leader Francis H. Peirpoint truthfully declared. In East Tennessee a Confederate pointed out that the men of "influence and some distinction in their counties" encouraged the loyalist resistance to the Confederacy. "The influence of their wealth, position, and connections has been exerted in favor of the Lincoln Government, and they are the parties most to blame for the troubles in East Tennessee," according to this Confederate. Also in the mountainous areas of the South the prominent and well-to-do were generally Unionists.[6]

Elsewhere the local establishment was, of course, most often pro-Confederate. Still, in the South as a whole, the loyalist minority probably did not differ greatly from the rebel majority in the distribution of wealth—except that the rebels held much more of their wealth in the form of human chattels. Otherwise, the two groups seem to have been pretty much alike in respect to economic and social status.

Unionists and Confederates seem to have been quite similar also in regard to ethnic composition. There were, to be sure, heavy concentrations of the foreign-born in certain of the loyalist units, though it is hard to know what nationalities the "secesh lady" could have had in mind when she described the Union soldiers from eastern North Carolina as "the offscouring of the people & foreigners." In polyglot New Orleans, Ben Butler enlisted large numbers of Germans, Irish, and what he called "French," who in all probability were native-born Cajuns. The members of Butler's First Louisiana Regiment were "generally foreigners," according to a New Englander on a U.S. government mission in New Orleans.[7]

Loyalists from Texas also were largely "foreigners." As the commander of a Union cavalry brigade once reported, "The enlisted men of nationality are about divided as follows: 433 Mexicans and 500 Americans (including in this designation Germans, Irish, &c.)." It has been estimated that "Anglos and Germans made up 46.3 and 13.1 percent of the Texas [Union] regiments, respectively," but "tejanos [Mexican-Texans] made up fully 40.6 percent, far above their share of the civilian population." Though *tejanos* "constituted a majority of the enlisted men in at least ten companies" of the First and Second Texas Regiments, the loyal *tejanos* were numerous only in proportion to the modest total of loyalists from the state. "Nearly three times as many Mexican-Texans served the Rebels as served the Yankees." [8]

Immigrants of various nationalities fought for the Confederacy, especially Irishmen, Germans, and Britons. An Irish battalion belonged to Robert E. Lee's Army of Northern Virginia, Germans filled several entire Confederate companies, and the British provided a Foreign Legion for the South. [9] It would seem that at least as high a proportion of rebels as of loyalists was born abroad. But the overwhelming majority of white Southerners in the 1860s were native Americans of British stock, and so were the overwhelming majority of both loyalists and rebels.

In some places the antagonism between the two groups was intensified by class conflict. This was likely to be true in areas where the local elite was pro-Confederate, as in coastal and Piedmont North Carolina.

A planter in coastal North Carolina said of his Unionist neighbors, "some have gone so far as to declare [that they] will take the property from the rich men & divide it among the poor men." Some of the Unionists certainly did aim to take property from the rich, as the sympathetic New Bern *Daily Progress* reported on October 6, 1862. According to this paper, loyal men in Washington and nine other counties were organizing "not only for self-protection against rebel guerrillas, but for the purpose of expatriating all the rebel families from their limits." The men were drawing up petitions to President Lincoln, asking him to authorize the formation of "a loyal regiment from each county," and proposing to "appropriate all the property, of every kind, belonging to rebels within these counties, to the support of this armed force."

When, on January 1, 1863, Lincoln issued his final Emancipation Proclamation and thus repudiated property in slaves, some of the Washington County Unionists took it as a warrant for attacking property of other kinds. Small landholders seized the land of large ones, and the landless went after the possessions of both farmers and planters.[10]

In the Piedmont, too, the more militant Unionists looked for a redistribution of property. At any rate, some of the well-to-do feared that the Unionist secret society, the Heroes of America, contained men of "the most ignorant classes" who were "induced to join the organization by the promise of a division here after among them of the property of the loyal Southern citizens." The main object of the Heroes, however, was to overthrow the Confederacy.[11]

That was also the main object of Unionists, high and low, in places where the elite classes themselves were mainly pro-Union. Indeed, that was the main object throughout the South, even after Lincoln had seemed to make the destruction of slavery as well as the destruction of the Confederacy a war aim.

If the war at times set Southerners of one class against those of another, it more often separated people of the same class. It turned neighbor against neighbor, friend against friend.

There were occasional exceptions, cases where friendships persisted after a parting of the ways. For instance, the Alabama loyalist John R. Phillips "took to the woods and went to Buck West's" to escape the Confederate draft. "Buck was a sort of a Secesh, had two boys, Lucien and Buddy, in the Rebel army," Phillips afterward recalled. "Buck was a good friend of mine and had sent me word if I got in a tight [place] to come to his house and he would care for me and keep me out of danger." [12]

Men who went off with the army, whether Union or Confederate, left their families at the mercy of their enemies. Enemies might be groups with private grudges, or guerrillas, or even regular troops. It was sometimes hard to tell friend from foe, and Unionists occasionally suffered at the hands of the Union army itself. "It has been represented to me that portions of your command have been committing the most outrageous excesses, robbing and burning houses indiscriminately," the commanding general once admonished the colonel of the First Arkansas Union Cavalry. "Hundreds of good Union people are left destitute and become a public charge." [13]

Men who joined or assisted the Union army had much more to fear than those who went willingly with the Confederates. Not only did loyalists run the risk of mistreatment or even execution if captured— as did the bridge burners in Tennessee and the alleged deserters in North Carolina. Loyalists also ran the risk of being killed instead of being captured—of being denied the right to surrender and be treated as a prisoner of war. Some loyalists who had the misfortune to be assigned to garrison duty at Fort Pillow, Tennessee, in the spring of 1864 suffered such a fate at the hands of their Confederate captors.

Fort Pillow, on the Mississippi River about fifty miles above Memphis, had been constructed by the Confederates in 1861 and was captured by the Federals the following year. With its earthworks and guns, its wooden barracks and other buildings, it was designed to guard the river passage, not to defend against an approach by land. In April 1864 it was garrisoned by 557 officers and men, 262 of them black and 295 (including all the officers) white. The black soldiers belonged to the First and Second U.S. Light Artillery and the Sixth U.S. Heavy Artillery; they had never been under fire. The white soldiers composed five companies of the Thirteenth West Tennessee Cavalry; these men also were raw recruits, and the members of the fifth company had not even been mustered into the U.S. service yet. Besides the troops, there were present a number of civilians who had sought refuge from Nathan Bedford Forrest.

Forrest, a native Tennesseean, had made a fortune before the war as a slave trader, land speculator, and cotton planter, with plantations in Mississippi and Arkansas. Early in the war he raised troops and provided horses and equipment for a cavalry battalion, which he commanded. He soon gained a name for himself as a daring, devilish, and adroit tactician. In April 1864, by then a major general, he was conducting raids in West Tennessee and southwestern Kentucky with a force of about 5,500 men. His objectives were to replenish his manpower through forcible conscription and to destroy the military potential of West Tennessee loyalists.

So far as Forrest was concerned, the war was not about some abstraction, such as state rights. It was about slavery. He commonly referred to the Union forces as "the Abolitionists"; he was fighting against slavery's abolition. He thoroughly agreed with his government's official policy of usually treating black captives as slaves and never accepting them as regular prisoners of war. (It was no historical accident that after the war he was to become the first Grand Wizard of the Ku Klux Klan.)

Forrest dispatched General James R. Chalmers with 1,500 men to attack Fort Pillow early on the morning of April 12. Later in the morning Forrest arrived to take personal command. His men, approaching the fort from the river bluff behind it, gradually closed in, amid heavy fire. The post commander, Major Lionel F. Booth of the Sixth U.S. Heavy Artillery, fell dead from a musket shot, and Major William F. Bradford of the Thirteenth West Tennessee Cavalry took Booth's place. During a midafternoon truce Forrest sent in the following communication: "I now demand the unconditional surrender of your forces, at the same time assuring you that you will be treated as prisoners of war. I . . . can take your works by assault, and if [I am] compelled to do so you must take the consequences." Bradford replied in a note to which he signed Booth's name (to conceal the fact of his death): "I will not surrender." Forrest's battle-hardened veterans finally overwhelmed the inexperienced and outnumbered defenders of the fort.

"The enemy carried our works at about 4 p.m.," one of the few surviving officers of the Thirteenth Tennessee remembered, "and from that time until dark, and at intervals throughout the night, our men were shot down without mercy and almost without regard to color." There was a "wholesale butchery of brave men, white as well as black." "The rebels were very bitter against these loyal Tennesseeans, terming them 'home-made Yankees,' and declaring they would give them no better treatment than they dealt out to the negro troops [along] with whom they were fighting." [14]

Actually, the black soldiers received even worse treatment than the white troops. Of the 295 whites, Forrest took 168 as prisoners; of the 262 blacks, only 58. That is to say, 127 white (or 43 percent) and 204 blacks (78 percent) were killed or wounded. Only about 60 of the wounded of both races survived long enough to be taken off on a U.S. gunboat. This means that approximately 270 men, or nearly half of the original garrison of 557, died as a result of the onslaught. And these figures do not include the uncounted civilians who were in the fort when the attack began.

One of the prisoners was the commanding officer, Major Bradford. Two companies of Forrest's troops set out with him and about thirty new conscripts for Forrest's headquarters at Jackson, Tennessee. Near dusk the procession halted. A lieutenant and a guard of five soldiers took Bradford off to the side of the road. Three of the soldiers aimed at him and fired, killing him instantly. "Major Bradford, before he was shot, fell on his knees and said that he had fought them manfully, and wished to be treated as a prisoner of war." So one of the conscripts at the scene testified under oath eleven days later, after eluding his captors. The Confederates said Bradford had been shot while trying to escape.[15]

From his headquarters at Jackson, Forrest sent reports to the government at Richmond, boasting of his recent successes, overestimating the Union casualties, and displaying his animus toward not only the black soldiers but also the loyalist whites. To the Confederate War Department he wrote with regard to the Fort Pillow garrison:

> The force was composed of about 500 negroes and 200 white soldiers (Tennessee Tories). The river was dyed with the blood of the slaughtered for 200 yards. There was in the fort a large number of citizens who had fled there to escape the conscript law. Most of these ran into the river and were drowned.
>
> The approximate loss was upward of 500 killed, but few of the officers escaping.
>
> It is hoped that these facts will demonstrate to the Northern people that negro soldiers cannot cope with Southerners. . . .
>
> My loss was about 20 killed and 60 wounded. . . .
>
> Large numbers of the Tories have been killed and made away with [in the course of the campaign], and the country is very near free of them.

Forrest assured Jefferson Davis that—with the killing, capture, and defeat of "Tory" officers at Fort Pillow and elsewhere—he had "broken up the Tennessee Federal regiments in the country."

Forrest's subordinate Chalmers reported that Forrest's "star never shone brighter" than in the recent West Tennessee campaign. His men had compelled the surrender of an entire regiment of "renegade Tennesseeans." Chalmers's men had also "stormed the works at Fort Pillow" and "taught the mongrel garrison of blacks and renegades a lesson long to be remembered." [16]

Six days after the attack President Lincoln gave a scheduled talk at the Sanitary Fair in Baltimore. He said: "A painful rumor, true I fear, has reached us of the massacre, by the rebel forces, at Fort Pillow, in the West end of Tennessee, on the Mississippi river, of some three hundred colored soldiers and white officers, who had just been overpowered by their assailants." He went on to say that the affair was being "thoroughly investigated" and that, if there proved to have been a massacre, the "retribution" would "surely come."

After investigating, the congressional Committee on the Conduct of the War issued a report that fully exposed and even exaggerated the atrocities against the black soldiers. Lincoln then instructed Stanton: "Please notify the insurgents . . . that the government of the United States has satisfactory proof of the massacre . . . of . . . white and colored officers and soldiers of the United States, after the latter had ceased resistance, and asked quarter of the former." Lincoln threatened to hold "insurgent prisoners" as hostages for "captured colored soldiers" in the future. But he could never bring himself to punish the innocent among the Confederates, and he came to realize that even to punish the guilty would only lead to an endless round of retaliation and reprisal.[17]

Lincoln was forgetting his Tennessee loyalists. Preoccupied as he naturally was with the Confederacy's anti-black policy, he treated the Fort Pillow affair as strictly a massacre of black soldiers and their white officers. Similarly, the congressional investigators, though receiving evidence of the massacre of white Tennesseeans too, gave them little attention in the committee's report. (Subsequent historians have given even less attention to the "Tennessee Tories" and the Confederate animosity toward them; Fort Pillow is still remembered for virulent racism alone.)

Forrest, of course, denied that he and his men had been guilty of any atrocities—or even the slightest impropriety. He attempted to turn the tables by charging that the loyalists, particularly Colonel Fielding Hurst and others of the Sixth Tennessee Union Cavalry, had been committing murder and other outrages upon the civilian population. Jefferson Davis's considered judgment: "Instead of cruelty, General Forrest, it appears, exhibited forbearance and clemency far exceeding the usage of war under like circumstances." [18]

Lincoln once mused about the "variety of motives" that, in their "combined effect," would induce a man to volunteer. "Among these motives would be patriotism, political bias, ambition, personal courage, love of adventure, want of employment, and convenience, or the opposites of some of these." Sometime in 1863 Lincoln concluded that he already had in the service "substantially all" who could be "obtained upon this voluntary weighing of motives." He must therefore resort to compulsion or the threat of it, that is, to the draft. [19]

His draft, necessary though it may have been in the North, had little to do with his recruiting in the South. After the passage of the Federal conscription act of 1863, a board of enrollment was appointed for each of the Northern states and for West Virginia. Men of military age were enrolled and some of them were drafted in that state. But no such board was set up and no men were enrolled or conscripted under the Federal law in any state of the Confederacy. Special, temporary, localized drafts were proposed in Tennessee, Arkansas, and Florida, but they affected an insignificant number of men.

A few Union recruiters in the South used overpersuasion or deception, like those in Arkansas who enlisted men for three years under the pretext of enlisting them for only one. A few even attempted something like compulsion. General John J. Peck called attention to cases of "virtual impressment and fraudulent enlistment" in coastal North Carolina. "It has been reported that some officers, availing themselves of the limited knowledge of some of the North Carolinians, have so worked upon their fears by threats of deeds of violence, which they had not the power to execute, as to compel men to enlist who preferred not to." A few Union officers in other states required destitute refugees to enlist in order to qualify for subsistence for themselves and their families. [20]

General W. S. Rosecrans noted that deserters from the rebel army had little choice but to join his own army in Chattanooga. "They cannot follow the avocations of peace nor have proper protection at home," he pointed out. Indeed, the Confederate policies of impressment and conscription did far more for Union recruiting than did the

U.S. conscription laws. Once a Unionist had been dragged into the rebel ranks, he was likely to desert at the first opportunity, thus finding himself in the predicament that Rosecrans described, with nowhere to go except to the relative security of the U.S. army.

This is not to say that the key motive for loyalists to join the Union army was monetary. "The inducements for enlisting men were the poorest," as the historian of the First Tennessee Union Cavalry wrote. "No magnificent bounties or 'big pay' were offered." In most cases the loyalist recruits could count on none of the generous state and local bounties that Yankee enlistees enjoyed. Loyalists could expect no more than the Federal bounty, and not always even that, as was the case with some of the Alabamians who enlisted in the First Alabama Cavalry, U.S.A. Soldiers from each of the Northern states had "a home government to look after them" and provide them with various kinds of care. Unionists from the Southern states generally had no such benefits.[21]

Loyalist recruits did, of course, obtain rations, clothing, and other necessities from the army. All this might seem like a great deal to poor men like the Alabamians who were the "raggedest, bare-footedest and most hatless set you ever saw" when, after eluding Confederate conscription officers, they finally made their way to the Federal lines, to enlist. "In uniform, mounted, and well armed, equipped with every thing we needed one cannot imagine how happy and brave we all felt," one of the Alabamian soldiers remembered. But these men could have obtained uniforms and equipment at much less risk and effort. They could have simply joined the Confederate army—if they had not preferred the war aims of the Union to those of the Confederacy.

Loyalists, like Yankees, generally put the preservation of the Union ahead of the destruction of slavery as a war aim. Forrest might call the Union forces "Abolitionists," and another Confederate officer might refer to them as "Abolition demagogues and demons." Pro-Confederate Arkansans might be inclined to believe that nobody "could be so bad as a 'Fed.' He's no better than a nigger." The fact remains that many (perhaps most) Southern Unionists were proslavery and antiabolitionist. With his emancipation program, Lincoln alienated such leaders as John S. Carlile of Virginia and Thomas A. R. Nelson of Tennessee.

A majority of the Unionists, whether antislavery at heart or not, were willing to accept emancipation, as Andrew Johnson was. Some, like Francis H. Peirpoint, had been opposed to slavery from the start. The North Carolinian Benjamin S. Hedrick thought he was expressing the feelings of many others when he addressed a letter to Lincoln on September 23, 1862, the day after the preliminary Emancipation Proclamation: "Permit me to thank you on behalf of myself, and such Southerners as have been for the Union first, last and all the time, for your Proclamation of yesterday," the former University of North Carolina professor wrote. "The Union or Slavery must perish." [22]

Loyalists shared with rebels the memory of past wars and heroes but viewed them as symbols of the nation, not of the South. Loyalists cherished another patriotic symbol that rebels utterly rejected—the U.S. flag. Again and again the Unionists displayed it and welcomed it at the approach of U.S. troops. Again and again they expressed their devotion to Old Glory, the Star-Spangled Banner, the Stars and Stripes.

"The inhabitants of this section," wrote an East Tennessee historian in the 1890s, "were mostly Whigs and the descendants of frontiersmen and Indian fighters. They were full of patriotism and had been taught from childhood to resent an insult, and especially one to the flag of their country, the emblem of liberty." They were "descendants of the brave men" who fought in the Revolutionary War, the War of 1812, and the War with Mexico. It was "not unnatural that they should be aroused by this great insult to their country's flag" when they heard the news that "Fort Sumter had been fired upon."

The Alabamian John Phillips recalled how some of his good friends had tried to persuade him to go with the Confederacy. "Now John, we have lost the Union and we cannot afford to fight against our homes and all we have," they argued. But Phillips held out against them. "It was firmly fixed in my mind," he remembered, "that I would never go back on 'Old Glory.' I had heard too much from my old grandparents about the sufferings and privations they had to endure during the Revolutionary War ever to engage against the 'Stars and Stripes.' " [23]

At the war's end a Georgian told how he had seen "the dear old flag go down to the dust by the hands of those whom Slavery had brutalized." His "love of country" caused him to remain "faithful to the spirit of the constitution and true to the flag" in secessionist Atlanta. "On the 4th of March 1862—Myself and family received a notice

from the Safety committee of Atlanta saying to us—that we sympathized with the enemies of the Confederate States—and therefore we
would have to leave the Country or be errested and imprisoned." With
his family he "safely reched the union lines" and went on to Cincinnati.

> I loved my country too well to stand edley by, and see it insulted
> without linding my ade in its suport. So I sholdred my gun and went
> forth to meet the cowards who had run me away from my native
> home be cause of my attachment to the government of my fathers.
> I was the first and probably the only Georgian who represented that
> state in the great contest for freedom and equal rights. I did not
> receive a cent of bounty for my services. I asked for none.[24]

This man had no way of knowing that a whole battalion of his fellow
Georgians also shouldered their guns for the United States.

Whatever the feelings that impelled a white Southerner to enlist in
the U.S. army, a strong sense of old-fashioned patriotism must have
been one of them. But, even in combination with other motives, patriotism could hardly have operated unless two conditions were present.
One of them was a high degree of both courage and independence.
The other was opportunity.

"It was easy to be a Union man in Ohio or Pennsylvania, but difficult and dangerous to be one in the South. In the one case the person
was in sympathy with his section; in the other, he stood in odious
array against it," wrote a Tennessee Unionist after the war. "Sympathy
and ties of kindred and association drew them [East Tennesseeans]
toward secession: patriotism and duty drew them the other way."

An Arkansan who had enlisted in the U.S. army, writing in the midst
of the war, gave a more revealing account of the loyalist dilemma:

> The loyal citizen in a rebel State is placed between two fires—and
> flanked beside. If he professes loyalty and manifests sympathy for
> the Union army, he does it at the sacrifice of his safety when they
> retire, which he has no assurance they will not do. In that case he is
> sure to be dealt with by the rebels. If on the other hand he appears
> unfriendly towards the Union troops, he is certain of nothing bet-
> ter, and often he finds but little favor arising from Union profes-
> sions. Thus it is that loyalty to the Government in a rebel State can

only be expected from men of uncommon nerve. Few men are pos-
sessed of moral courage enough to publicly commit themselves to a
cause surrounded with the dangers of Unionism in Rebeldom! It
costs our northern friends nothing, but rather they are well paid for
their loyalty. Not so with the loyal citizen who may at this unfortu-
nate time have his home in the "sunny south," it costs him his all
for the time being, and [he] is often but little rewarded for it.

To join the U.S. army, a Southerner of Union sympathies needed access
to it. He would be most inclined to enlist if the army were present in
force and if he had the "moral courage" to take a chance on its remaining in the vicinity.[25]

Opportunity might lead to opportunism. When the U.S. forces
seemed likely to hold their ground and, eventually, to win the war,
men of no previously apparent Unionism could be expected to align
themselves on the prospective victor's side. This consideration no
doubt accounted for many of the Confederate desertions and Union
enlistments in the very last days of the conflict.

Opportunism, though, was hardly an important factor with most of
the tens of thousands who not only braved the usual hazards of sol-
diering but also risked being denied the rights of a prisoner of war,
and who put their families in danger of harassment and even death at
the hands of vengeful neighbors or Confederate guerrillas. Probably
most of the loyalists responded to one or another of the motives for
volunteering that Lincoln listed—"patriotism, political bias, ambition, personal courage, love of adventure, want of employment, and
convenience"—but especially patriotism and personal courage.

From the Confederate point of view, the loyalists were lacking in sol-
dierly qualities. There may have been, indeed, a disproportionate
number of poor physical specimens in the loyalist ranks, since the men
were sometimes accepted with no medical examination at all, whereas
recruits in the North, with rare exceptions, received a detailed scru-
tiny.

Though sickness was common in both Union and Confederate army
camps, some of the Union troops from East Tennessee and eastern
North Carolina seem to have been unusually prone to diseases, scurvy
in particular. In 1863 a U.S. medical inspector reported, with regard

to the Fourth and Tenth Tennessee Infantry and the Third Cavalry, that "a more abundant supply of fresh vegetables, especially potatoes, lime juice & pickled cabbage," was needed, "the men being more scorbutic than those of most other regiments now in the field." Medical officers also noted "a strong scorbutic tendency" in the First North Carolina Cavalry.

But negative reports were offset by positive ones. As "fine a looking body of men as I have ever seen," Benjamin F. Butler said of his First Louisiana Regiment, and an investigator once described the First Texas Cavalry as being in "excellent serviceable condition." [26]

There were "no more loyal men in the country than the Union men of Texas," according to General N. P. Banks. "But it is impossible to get these men to participate in the struggle in which we are engaged excepting for a reclamation of Texas." Union men elsewhere in the South similarly preferred to fight for the redemption of their own particular state. Often they enlisted on the understanding that they would not be sent far away—despite a congressional act of February 13, 1862, providing that "no volunteers or militia from any State or Territory should be mustered into the service of the United States on any terms or conditions confining their services to the limits of said State or Territory or their vicinities." In a geographical sense, then, most of the loyalists committed themselves only to limited service.

But service in their home states made loyalists more rather than less valuable to the Union cause. As Lincoln said, if he could get a "fair share" of new troops in Tennessee he would "value it more highly than a like number most anywhere else," partly because these men would "be at the very place that need[ed] protection." A Tennessee Unionist argued, further, that "the Rebels in Tennessee" could "only be quelled by Tennesseeans." Native cavalrymen were "acquainted with the country and people, and could obtain such information as would enable them to operate effec[t]ually when it could not be done by strangers." [27]

In the mountains of northwestern Virginia, too, locally recruited troops had an advantage over outsiders, as both a Unionist and a secessionist in the area maintained. Regarding loyalist mountaineers, Francis H. Peirpoint thought it was "important to have them in the field as soon as possible, on account of their knowledge of the country." A secessionist advised the pro-Confederate state government that the Confederacy had erred in bringing in men from the flatlands of Middle and West Tennessee and central and southern Georgia:

> The Tennessee and Georgia troops, with many of whom I have talked, are very averse to serving in the mountains. The climate does not suit them, and toiling up the mountains on marches breaks them down directly. It is strange that they should be sent here to serve while many regiments raised in the mountains, accustomed to the inequalities of the surface of the earth, inured to the rigors of the climate, should be retained in Eastern Virginia, and the defense of their homes intrusted to strangers unaccustomed to so rough a country and so bleak a climate.

(One reason the Confederates used outsiders in strongly Unionist areas was a fear that local recruits might be disaffected.)[28]

Loyalists gained a reputation as particularly well qualified for such duties as scouting. A U.S. officer at Fort Smith, Arkansas, asked for authority to raise a cavalry company from the more than willing "union people" of that vicinity. "Such a company," he thought, "would be of valuable service to me as scouts and guides." An officer in northern Alabama wanted to enlist local Alabamians because they were "very useful men": "They are the best scouts I ever saw, and know the country well clear to Montgomery."

Butler, in New Orleans, thought his Louisianans were as well adapted to the swampy lowlands as northwestern Virginians were to the rugged heights. Of his first recruits, he said: "These troops would be very useful in manning the forts at Pontchartrain and down the river, which are fearfully unhealthy."[29]

The First Louisiana Cavalry certainly consisted of better soldiers than the Second Rhode Island Cavalry, though the Northerners of the latter looked down on the Southerners of the former and objected to being merged with them. General Banks gave the order for the consolidation on August 24, 1863, after the Second Rhode Island had dwindled, largely through desertion, to only a few hundred men. When Lieutenant Colonel Harai Robinson of the First Louisiana read Banks's order to the Rhode Islanders, none of them gave any sign of obeying it.

The next morning Robinson encircled the Rhode Island camp with one company of mounted men and faced the camp with a line of two companies on foot. "I then rode up to the mutineers, taking with me a German interpreter, who, after I had addressed them myself in English, Spanish, and French, and ordering them to join the companies to which they had been assigned, communicated the same order to them in German. Not a man of the mutineers stirred." Robinson saw that he had to act quickly and decisively. The men he confronted were "notorious for lawlessness and want of discipline. Nearly three of the companies present of the First Louisiana Cavalry were recruits who had not been a month in camp." Unless something drastic was done, the bad characters would "completely demoralize" the Louisianans. Robinson hastily arranged a firing squad, and in less than half an hour a couple of the mutiny's ringleaders were dead.

Governor James Y. Smith of Rhode Island was indignant when he received a copy of Banks's order. He protested that "the men who enlisted in a Rhode Island regiment [would] lose all their identity with their native State" and would be "disgraced by being torn from their own organization and placed in one which is in every way distasteful to them." The governor was still more offended when he heard that two men had been shot "for simply remonstrating against the order of consolidation." It was "an outrage to Rhode Island." The governor demanded that Secretary of War Stanton revoke the order and have the men transferred to another Rhode Island regiment.

Banks made a bit of a concession to Yankee sensibilities. "The Rhode Island cavalry was enlisted from New York chiefly," he explained to the War Department. It was "mostly composed of men entirely beyond control. Their depredations and robberies were frightful." So the "remnant of the regiment" had been "consolidated with a New York regiment for the purpose of bringing it into some discipline." [30]

As a rule, Yankees and loyalists probably got along as well as other men of the same race when associated in a regiment or company. There appears to be no other record of serious Yankee-loyalist conflict, at any rate.

There are a few indications of conflict between loyalists and black troops. The captain of a Florida company, stationed at Fort Myers, who was worried about the absence of two other white companies from a detachment of the Second Cavalry, reported:

> I am anxiously waiting the return of our companies, as it is almost impossible to get along with the colored troops. I am fully satisfied that each should be separate to accomplish anything. The ignorance of the one and the sensitiveness of the other tends to make every duty unpleasant. In fact the efficiency of the Second Cavalry has been seriously injured by this connection. . . . Our recruiting has been killed off almost entirely, and desertions have commenced, to end I do not know when. The small force now here (40 [white] men) apparently adds to their [the blacks'] impudence and insubordination.[31]

Soon after the war's end, William G. Brownlow's Knoxville newspaper reported that one black soldier had stabbed a member of the Ninth Tennessee Cavalry and another had shot and killed a veteran of the Eighth Tennessee Cavalry. "Our 8th, 9th & 13th Regiments are here to be mustered out," Brownlow, then the provisional governor, wrote to President Johnson from Knoxville, "and there is a bad state of feeling between them and the *colored troops*." [32]

Racial conflict, when blacks were present, may sometimes have been a cause of reduced efficiency on the part of loyalist units. But a much more frequent and more serious cause was the necessity of caring for the loyalists' families. Loyalist civilians often depended on the army both for sustenance and for protection from hostile neighbors or guerrilla bands. "The Western and Northern states are free from this pestilence," as a Virginian pointed out, "—their citizens when called into the service of the United States can leave their families and homes free from this danger." [33]

The U.S. army went to considerable trouble and expense to meet the needs of loyalists' dependents. In Louisiana the Union commander arranged for "liberal issues of provisions" to relatives of recruits. In Tennessee the Federal authorities made available the "Refugee House," a barrackslike building in Nashville, as a shelter for homeless women and children who flocked in not only from East Tennessee but also from western North Carolina and northern Georgia and Alabama.

Not all refugees were willing to accept the government's hospitality.

From his headquarters at Pulaski, the surgeon of the Twelfth Tennessee Cavalry appealed to Governor Johnson for help for those dependents who would not stay at the "Refugee House":

> Allow me to call your attention to the suffering families having husbands and fathers in the 10th and 12th Regts Tenn Cav. Those Regiments are composed principally of refugees from East Tenn. who were driven from their homes and families by the enemy of our country. . . . Their families were left behind to take care of themselves and work their way thro' the lines as best they could. And now here they are, suffering as I never supposed any American citizen would have to suffer. I saw two mothers with nine children a few days since near Nashville on the roadside without shelter, or money, a scanty supply of provisions and clothing and five of the children sick. This is only one case out of a thousand that has come under my observation. Many of those poor women follow their husbands into the field, carrying their children and walk when they cannot ride. It is inhuman to put them out of wagons, but our means of transportation justifies it. . . .
>
> I would gladly give my professional attention to these people did I have an oppertunity. I do hope his Excellency will devise some means by which these poor distressed women can be seen to by their husbands. They would rather go into the woods than the "Refugee House" at Nashville. Those women and children above referred to, were from said house.[34]

In North Carolina a New York cavalry major sent out an expedition "to bring in the families of some deserters from the rebel army who had enlisted in the Second North Carolina Volunteers." It was not an easy task. The lieutenant in charge found the Trent River unfordable. "He therefore had one of his men swim across and bring from the south side a small boat he saw there; with this he took across 10 men, and after great difficulty found a cart and ox team, with which he brought away the families and goods as directed, safely crossing them in his boat, making nearly a dozen crossings of the river in order to do so." The U.S. forces made several such expeditions, occasionally running into enemy fire.

This rescue work was not only dangerous and time-consuming; it burdened the army with the continuing presence of civilians who had to be protected, sheltered, and fed. By early 1864 the First North Carolina Regiment had accumulated some three hundred women and children as camp followers, and it continued to accumulate more. "The immense number of women and children with these troops is what perplexes us, for they must be provided for," the commanding officer at New Bern complained. "Some hundreds of refugees, poor people from Plymouth and vicinity [fleeing after the Confederate recapture of Plymouth], are to be here to-day. These will cause no little embarrassment, but they must be provided for, and I will endeavor to see that they do not suffer." The officer, sympathetic though he was, could only conclude that "these Carolina regiments," with all their human baggage, had become "a great drag upon us." [35]

In Arkansas the burden of caring for civilians was just as bad. From Elkhorn Tavern near the northwestern corner of the state, the lieutenant colonel of the First Arkansas Cavalry reported in 1862: "There is nothing in this immediate vicinity but scattered gangs of marauders. Several families, wives and children of Union men, came into camp this morning in a state of great destitution. If a small surplus of rations can be furnished to me to meet such an exigency our success will be very much enhanced." After an 1863 scouting trip from Fayetteville through the northern counties of Carroll, Marion, and Searcy, the captain of Company H of the same regiment noted: "The country is filled with refugee Missourians, who are committing all kinds of mischief, plundering the families of the soldiers who are serving in our regiment and the First Arkansas Infantry." [36]

In 1864 eighty-six citizens of Montgomery County and members of Company L, Fourth Arkansas Cavalry, petitioned the post commander at Little Rock to "urge the necessity of sending cavalry into our county for the relief of our families and friends." "The plundering of houses, breaking and burning of cotton cards, wheels, &c., belonging to Union citizens is of common occurrence." Company L was not yet armed, but its men offered to go as guides for the troops to be sent.

Later that year the captain of Company A of the same regiment noted that there were "a number of families at Dardanelle who were compelled to move there for protection while our troops were there," and that the vicinity was "infested with bushwhackers of the worst character" who were "committing depredations upon the families of loyal men daily." The captain, whose own family was among the victims, offered to do all he could to help the army drive out the bush-whackers.[37]

By early 1865 the problem was at its most extreme in the frontier area around Fort Smith, where the post commander reported:

> There are 200 families, nearly 1,000 persons, connected with the Second Arkansas Infantry, while the First Infantry, First and Second Cavalry, and First Arkansas Battery are almost equally as strong. Besides, there are many Arkansas men in other regiments whose families are here. Nearly all these people, besides a large number of citizens [unconnected with the army], are destitute and suffering, and without assistance from the Government will starve. While the Arkansas regiments remain here these people cannot be sent away, and as the troops have not been paid for a great length of time they have nothing to buy with. . . . The presence of such a large number of suffering people with the troops of this command is very embarrassing and destroys the efficiency of the troops to a great extent.[38]

Whether the relatives accompanied the army or remained at home, their plight did tend to destroy the efficiency of troops by impairing their morale. Prima facie, the dependability of troops on their home ground sometimes seemed doubtful at best. Even Butler, who became a most enthusiastic recruiter of Southern whites, originally had some misgivings about their trustworthiness. When raising his first Louisiana companies, he remarked: "They might have a company or two of Northern soldiers for instructors and for fear of possible accident." He thought that "while these troops would be proper to lead elsewhere upon the Southern coast, it would be a doubtful experiment to rely upon them solely here" in New Orleans, where they were being enlisted.[39]

How loyal were the loyalists? Those from Texas were clearly the least loyal. The commander at Brazos Santiago once complained:

> no dependence can be placed upon the detachment of the First Texas Cavalry left with my command. They desert at every opportunity. No less than nine deserted yesterday, taking with them their horses, arms, and accouterments. Three more deserted last night from a picket-post. Major Noyes informs me that among these men were some whom he considered the most reliable of the detach-

ment, and that he was unable to send after and arrest them, as he
dare not trust the First Texas, and the New York cavalry were un-
acquainted with the roads.

The Second Texas Cavalry was no better than the First. More than
two hundred *tejanos* left the Second Texas during the first half of
1864. Regarding his Mexican-Texan troops, Colonel Edmund J. Davis explained: "They soon become dissatisfied with our manner of
making payments, and being of Indian blood and nature, the discipline and nature of this camp; and the value of their horses, arms, and
equipments proving too much of a temptation, they take an opportunity to desert and carry them into Mexico, in some cases deserting
from off picket." General John A. McClernand thought the frequent
desertions from the Second Texas resulted, in part, "from the prox-
imity of the men of the regiment to their families," who were "constantly asking them to return home." [40]

Even less reliable were Adrian J. Vidal's partisan rangers. After they
had deserted from the Confederate army, most of them then deserted
from the Union army. "It is a great pity that the country ever accepted
these men for soldiers," Lieutenant Benjamin McIntyre commented in
his diary, "and still a pity that every *yaller belly* of them has not been
permitted to desert." But this kind of prejudice against *tejanos* was no
doubt as much a cause as a consequence of their disloyalty, for few of
the *tejanos* had a chance to rise in the ranks of the Union (or the Confederate) army, and few had much reason of any kind to devote themselves to the Union cause. [41]

To some extent the Mexicans, and to a greater extent other loyalists,
went absent without leave so they could protect and provide for their
families. Governor Johnson once intervened with General George H.
Thomas on behalf of some soldiers from East Tennessee who had gone
home without leave. These men, "hearing of the suffering and wants
of their families, have been induced to return to extend whatever relief
they could for the time; they did not intend to desert but to return to
the service, but fear of being court marshaled prevents many of them
from doing so." Johnson asked and Thomas agreed that the men be
allowed twenty days in which to return to their units without punishment.

Soldiers were inclined to leave the ranks and remain with their families if the army approached their home ground. Quite a few members of the Second Arkansas Cavalry came from the Batesville area. Ordered to move with the regiment from Springfield, Missouri, to Memphis, Colonel John E. Phelps objected: "I am afraid if I go by Batesville quite a number of my men will desert." Phelps received permission to take a long detour by way of Saint Louis and the Mississippi River.[42]

Loyalists were little affected by the conditions that presumably led large numbers of Yankees to decamp. According to a postwar report of the Provost Marshal General's Bureau, desertion from the Union army was "especially characteristic of troops from large cities," was "a crime of foreign rather than native birth," and was most frequent in troops from "those states which gave the highest local bounties." "The bounty was meant to be an inducement to enlistment," the report noted; "it became, in fact, an inducement to desertion and fraudulent re-enlistment"; and "the great mass of the professional bounty jumpers were Europeans."

Few loyalists came from large cities, few (except in Louisiana and Texas) were foreign-born, and few got any local bounty whatsoever. On the basis of these considerations, it would seem that the loyalists ought to have had a lower desertion rate than the Yankees. It has been estimated that approximately 25 percent of the Texans in the Union army deserted. Of the 2,066 enlisted in the First Alabama Cavalry, 279 were reported as deserters, that is, 13.5 percent. According to the Arkansas adjutant general, there were 1,026 deserters out of 8,789 Arkansas loyalists, or nearly 11.7 percent.

In comparison, one Wisconsin regiment of nine-month conscripts, mostly German immigrants, lost 283 out of 961 through desertion— 29.4 percent in less than a year! According to the U.S. provost marshal general, Connecticut had a desertion rate of 11.7 and New Jersey 10.7 percent, whereas the average for the "loyal States" as a whole was a mere 6.3 percent.

If all these figures were correct, the conclusion would seem to be that the desertion rate of loyalists was somewhat higher than that of Yankees, though in some cases comparable with that of a Northeastern industrial state. The calculations , however, are hardly more than guesses. The provost marshal general himself was inclined to believe that at least one fourth of those reported as deserters were "not deserters in fact"; many were "unavoidably absent . . . falling sick . . .

injured in action . . . overstaying their furloughs, &c." He adjusted his calculations accordingly, but he was proceeding on no more than a hunch.[43]

Tallying Confederate desertions is even more baffling, since the Confederacy kept far less complete records. Some historians have said that one of every seven Yankees and only one of every nine rebels deserted, but there is no good reason for accepting either of these ratios. According to Confederate law, a deserter was a soldier absent without leave and without intention of returning. But it was difficult if not impossible to prove intention. What really mattered was absenteeism, and this came to be, in the view of Confederate leaders themselves, an "evil of enormous magnitude." After the fall of Atlanta in September 1864, Jefferson Davis publicly stated: "two-thirds of our men are absent . . . most of them without leave." [44]

Such a statement was never made—and could never be truthfully made—of the Southerners in the Union army. All in all, they were at least as firmly loyal to the Lincoln government as Southerners in the Confederate army were to the Davis government.

Fighting by Southern Federals

$\mathcal{S}$OUTHERN FEDERALS, like their Northern counterparts, left a mixed record of service in the Civil War. As fighters, some proved to be excellent, some adequate, some poor. The same company or regiment might perform badly at times and quite well at other times.

Many of the loyalist troops spent most if not all of their time doing such quotidian duties as garrisoning, guarding, patrolling, foraging, recruiting, scouting, and raiding rather than engaging the enemy head-on in large-scale, spectacular battles. So, for that matter, did many other soldiers, both Union and Confederate. For the war consisted largely of routine or random, if often dangerous, activity; it was not entirely a great game of strategy.

Loyalist troops also took part in nearly all the major campaigns and battles of the war. They frequently played a heroic and significant part, even though they confined their service mostly to their home states. They faced much the same hazards of camp and combat as the Yankees did, and they suffered losses proportionally as large—if we count not only the number of men killed and mortally wounded in action but also the number who died in consequence of accident and disease.

President Lincoln, keeping an eye constantly on the course of battle, could not help noting the role his loyalists played in the war effort. On at least one occasion he gave credit for a tremendous Northern victory to the "Sunny South too." He was referring to the part that Louisiana troops had played in freeing the Mississippi River from the rebel grip.

By the spring of 1863 the Confederacy had lost its hold on all but two Mississippi River bastions: one at Vicksburg, Mississippi, and the other at Port Hudson, Louisiana. Ulysses S. Grant and his army, coming from the north, were about to close in on Vicksburg. N. P. Banks and his army, approaching from the south, were getting ready to attack Port Hudson.

Included in Banks's army were the First and Second Louisiana Infantry and the First Louisiana Cavalry, as well as the First and Second Louisiana (African American) Native Guards. The First Infantry contained some rather obstreperous though hard-fighting characters. Before the Port Hudson campaign, when one of its companies "returned from a scout" after "breaking up a small camp of guerrillas," the regiment's colonel heard reports of "depredations said to have been committed by some of the men." He indignantly responded: "Though the men of that regiment are not so careful about stepping on the toes of rebels as some others, yet I think that it is as free from the charge of plunder as any other in this department [the Department of the Gulf]."

After another successful raid, which netted seventy prisoners, the First Louisiana along with the Sixth and the Ninety-first New York set out on a two-day march to New Iberia in the Cajun country. Along the way they created "scenes of disorder and pillage," according to the brigade commander. "Houses were entered and all in them destroyed in the most wanton manner. Ladies were frightened into delivering their jewels and valuables into the hands of the soldiers by threats of violence toward their husbands. Negro women were ravished in the presence of white women and children." This time the colonel of the First Louisiana praised his officers and men for having "behaved admirably and with great gallantry" in a skirmish during the raid. He conceded, however, that on the subsequent march two of his captains had "allowed their men to loiter behind so much for the purpose of pillaging" that he was obliged to put the two under arrest.[1]

In front of Port Hudson the Louisiana regiments, even the First Infantry, demonstrated remarkable valor. After two costly and unsuccessful assaults, General Banks congratulated his troops on "the steady advance made upon the enemy's works" and proclaimed: "One more advance and they are ours!" He summoned the "bold men of the corps to the organization of a storming column of 1,000 men, to vindicate the flag of the Union." Among those volunteering were a couple of dozen men from the First Louisiana, a larger number from the Second Louisiana, and a still larger number from the African American Native Guards. This charge also failed, with terrible losses.

Banks then laid siege to Port Hudson. Its defenders held out for six weeks and finally surrendered on July 9, 1863, five days after the fall of Vicksburg. Later Banks honored the First and Second Louisiana Infantry and the participating companies of the First Louisiana Cavalry by including them among the units to "have inscribed upon their colors the names of the several actions" of the Port Hudson campaign in which they had "borne a distinguished part." [2] Lincoln averred:

> The signs look better. The Father of Waters again goes unvexed to the sea. Thanks to the great North-West for it. Nor yet wholly to them. Three hundred miles up, they met New-England, Empire, Key-Stone and Jersey, hewing their way right and left. The Sunny South too, in more colors than one, also lent a hand. On the spot, their part of the history was jotted down in black and white. [3]

After Port Hudson, the career of the white Louisiana troops was rather anticlimactic. The First and Second (Mounted) Infantry and the First Cavalry did accompany Banks on his futile Red River campaign (March–May 1864), in which they performed creditably enough, especially the Second Infantry. This regiment "met the enemy" (the Confederate Second and Fourth Louisiana Cavalry) near Alexandria, Louisiana, and "drove them 7 miles" to where the "Louisiana cavalry (rebel) were holding the hill." Advancing as skirmishers on the Shreveport road, the loyal mounted infantry again ran into the Second and Fourth Louisiana cavalry of the enemy and, along with the Sixteenth Indiana, showed "great coolness and gallantry." [4]

For most of the rest of the war the Louisiana loyalists had little to do except to protect positions that the Union already held. Yet the men did not always perform this duty to the satisfaction of their officers. "The Second Louisiana Mounted Infantry numbers [only] 185 for duty," an officer once complained, "and the outpost duty is at present very loosely performed." When Company K of the First Louisiana Cavalry went "out in search of guerrillas" and came back empty-handed, General Thomas W. Sherman characterized the captain's report as "unsatisfactory" and said "the failure to capture at least the horses" was "inexcusable." [5]

In the final weeks of the war, however, the First Louisiana Cavalry added notably to its exploits while accompanying a large expedition that moved from Pensacola Bay toward Mobile. "The charge at Bluff Springs [Florida] was headed by the First Louisiana Cavalry," General Frederick Steele reported. "Both officers and men behaved in the most gallant style." At Bluff Springs Private Thomas Riley of Company D captured the battle flag of the Sixth Alabama Cavalry and was later awarded a Medal of Honor, the highest U.S. military decoration. More important, Riley's comrades captured James H. Clanton, the general commanding the enemy brigade.[6]

Union soldiers from Texas, Florida, Mississippi, and Georgia had little or no opportunity to show what they could do in heavy combat.

The Texans spent most of their time in readiness to defend Union-held positions in Louisiana and on the Rio Grande. Navy transports shuttled the First and Second Cavalry back and forth between New Orleans and the Texas coast. Some members of the First Cavalry finally objected to being stationed in Louisiana—"they were enlisted to serve in Texas and are dissatisfied to serve elsewhere"—so they were ordered to "proceed by first boat to Brazos Santiago, Tex."[7]

In its earliest action the First Texas, together with the Sixth Michigan and the One Hundred Twenty-eighth New York, moved north from Baton Rouge up the Amite River in the spring of 1863. Their main object was to make the Jackson Railroad useless to the Confederates. After a raid, which entailed only light skirmishing, a long stretch of track was "effectually broken up," depots and stations along it were destroyed, and a "large car-manufactory," a shoe factory, and a tannery lay in ruins.[8]

The Texans reconnoitered only when, in the summer of 1863, they accompanied Banks's army in an attempt to move overland west from New Orleans. And they went along but were called upon to do no fighting when, in September, Banks sailed from New Orleans on the Sabine Pass expedition, which failed in its aim to take Beaumont and the Houston-Beaumont Railroad. But in October the Texan troops had to fight when Banks again tried to move westward from New Orleans by land. In this Têche campaign, Texan fought Texan when the First Cavalry ran into fierce resistance, which it finally succeeded in overcoming. The campaign itself proved another failure.

Soon the men of the First and Second Cavalry, again on navy transports, were heading along the coast toward the Rio Grande, to join in the quick and easy occupation of Brownsville in late October. In June 1864 they started back to New Orleans "with the exception of two companies, detained for picket duty." Before the end of the summer they found themselves on the Rio Grande once more. An army inspector then noted that there had recently been "a marked improvement in the discipline and general conduct" of the First. "No new desertions have occurred . . . and I am in hopes that all the disorderly and unreliable men of the command were those who have left."

Banks intended that Colonel Edmund J. Davis, whose First Texas Cavalry controlled the river from the mouth up to Rio Grande City, should "keep a close watch upon the river as far north as possible" and eventually join forces with General James H. Carleton, who commanded the U.S. troops in New Mexico, with an advance guard at Franklin, "the northwestern point of Texas." The combined forces would then control the river for its entire length. But Davis never acquired an army large enough to make possible such a result.[9]

Near the end of the war General Lew Wallace (who would author the best-selling novel *Ben Hur*) briefly aspired to achieve control over the Rio Grande and more. On Washington's Birthday 1865 he proposed to General-in-Chief Ulysses S. Grant an expedition to "initiate the organization of the Territory or new State of Rio Grande." "In selecting troops please send me Western men," he urged Grant. "I would also like the regiment of Texans now serving in the department. They know the region of Western Texas perfectly." But again the troops had no chance to show what they could do.[10]

The Floridians had even less opportunity than the Texans to distinguish themselves in combat. During the last year of the war the First Florida Cavalry was stationed at Fort Barrancas, near Pensacola, and the Second Florida was far away at either Fort Myers or Cedar Keys. Each regiment contained fewer than half the normal complement, which was one thousand, more or less. General Alexander S. Asboth, whose command included the First Florida, proposed to combine the Second with it, but his superior replied that consolidation of the two would be "impracticable." "It could not be done without moving one to where the other was. Both are at present needed in their present location."[11]

The First Florida was brigaded with the Second Maine, which depended on the Floridians for scouting. Some of these men professed to be able to "take boats to the head of navigation" on both the Apalachicola and Chipola Rivers, and the lieutenant colonel of the Second Maine once asked for the six men from the First Florida who were "best acquainted with the country between the Alabama River and the Choctawhatchee, and as far north as Montgomery." Detachments from the Florida and Maine regiments went on occasional, mostly uneventful excursions through western Florida and southern Alabama.[12]

Men of the Second Florida saw additional action when 186 of them, together with 200 of the Second U.S. Colored Infantry, made an incursion into peninsular Florida from Cedar Keys. Skirmishing with a rebel force, they took a few prisoners and horses and lost several men of their own. At the end of the war the Second Florida entered and occupied Tampa.[13]

Like the Floridians, Mississippians took part in no big battles. In January 1863 "a detachment of First West Tennessee Cavalry and the independent companies of the Tippah and Mississippi Rangers" proceeded to "scout the country between Bolivar, Tenn., and Ripley, Miss., to break up the guerrilla bands infesting that neighborhood." They scattered the guerrillas but did not capture any of them; they did capture two Confederate privates and two officers, one of them the lieutenant colonel of the Twenty-second Tennessee Infantry. The major of the loyalist Tennessee cavalry acknowledged in his report: "The independent rangers were of great service to us as guides, they being residents of the country I passed through."[14]

During Nathan Bedford Forrest's April 1864 raid, the First Mississippi Mounted Rifles assisted in the defense of Memphis by patrolling the roads running south and southeast from the city. That summer, on a foray into Mississippi, a detachment of the Mounted Rifle regiment was "attacked by a superior force of the enemy" and driven back, and later, a detachment accompanying the Nineteenth Pennsylvania Cavalry lost a couple of foragers who "straggled from the column." Still, the Pennsylvania officer in charge of the operation commended the Mississippians as well as the Pennsylvanians for having "conducted themselves in a very creditable manner."[15]

The First Mississippi Rifles went along on the raid that General Benjamin H. Grierson led from Memphis into Mississippi, December 1864–January 1865, to destroy the Mobile and Ohio Railroad. "I reached Vicksburg with my entire command in good condition with about 600 prisoners, 800 head of captured stock, and 1,000 negroes, who joined the column during the march," Grierson reported. He, too, included the Mississippi troops when he referred to the "uniform good conduct of the officers and men" of his command.

Before the end of the war, the Mounted Rifles were back at their more mundane duties. They were ordered to station themselves "at any important bridge, if needed," in the Memphis vicinity, "to prevent surprise and to capture any prowling bands of soldiers or thieves."

By this time the First Georgia Battalion of loyalists had come into being. They were stationed at Dalton, Georgia, with the brigade of General Henry M. Judah (who in April 1865 accepted the surrender of the Confederate forces in that area). In the opinion of General James B. Steedman, Union commander of the district, the First Georgia was "utterly worthless." [16]

The loyalist troops from eastern North Carolina, from Arkansas, and from Alabama had their moments of greatness—especially the troops from Alabama. Those from eastern North Carolina started out with considerable spirit, but many of them eventually were broken down. Those from Arkansas began with little promise; then some, at least, managed to win a couple of notable victories.

The First North Carolina, U.S.A., had not been in existence long when some of its men, occupying Plymouth, were called upon to help defend the town against the Seventeenth North Carolina, C.S.A. A detachment of the rebel regiment attacked before dawn on December 10, 1862, and drove the defenders into the customhouse, disabled a gunboat on the Roanoke River, and set fire to the town, leaving most of it in ashes. Still, the Union forces (from Massachusetts as well as North Carolina) succeeded in holding the town. "I do assure you our little North Carolina volunteers behaved most nobly," the lieutenant of Company C proudly reported. [17]

On November 25, 1863, a party of North Carolinians and Yankees accomplished what their commanding general, John J. Peck, lauded as "one of the most brilliant affairs of the war." Peck elaborated:

On the 25th instant, an expedition composed of details from the First North Carolina Volunteers, Twelfth New York Cavalry, and the Twenty-fourth [Twenty-third] New York Battery, under the command of Capt. George W. Graham, First North Carolina Volunteers (Capt. R. R. West, Twelfth New York Cavalry, having generously waived his rank in deference to Captain Graham's familiarity with the country to be traversed), attacked a camp of rebels near Greenville, and, after a brief and gallant contest, more than 50 prisoners, 100 stand of arms, and a considerable amount of subsistence and quartermaster's stores fell into our hands, while but 1 of our men was fatally wounded.

Peck announced to his officers and men: "The alacrity and intrepidity of Captain Graham's command are recommended as examples to other troops."

A month later General Peck had occasion to congratulate some of his men on "another affair near Greenville." While reconnoitering on the night of December 30, a detachment of North Carolinians and New Yorkers ran into a superior force of rebels. "After a hand-to-hand conflict the enemy retired" into the darkness. The general regretted "the death of Lieut. William K. Adams, of Company L, First North Carolina Volunteers, a gallant and dashing officer, who fell while making a charge at the head of his command." [18]

While reconnoitering and raiding, the U.S. troops faced the constant threat of counterattacks on their bases at New Bern, Plymouth, and elsewhere. When the Confederates made an attempt on New Bern in February 1864, they failed to take the place but did take a number of prisoners. And when, under the command of George E. Pickett, they tried twenty-two of the prisoners as deserters and hanged them at Kinston, the rebels achieved their aim of intimidating North Carolinians in the Union army.

The effect became apparent when, in April 1864, the Confederates again attacked Plymouth, this time with an overwhelming force from Lee's Army of Northern Virginia. After they had compelled General H. W. Wessells to surrender the post—and to surrender himself as a prisoner—the Union general wrote that "during the siege and in the night a considerable number of North Carolina soldiers (many of them deserters from the enemy, and all of them fearing bad treatment in the event of capture) left their companies without authority, escaping in canoes."

At Morehead City, Colonel E. H. Ripley was concerned lest other North Carolina soldiers would be inclined to skedaddle when under attack: "Since the arrival of the news from Plymouth the remainder of the Second North Carolina Volunteers are much excited. I cannot place the least dependence on them for the defense of Beaufort or any other place. They are utterly demoralized and will not fight." The colonel also feared that the North Carolinians would "inevitably, in case of a fight, become panic-stricken and have a bad effect on the rest of this slim command."

Similarly, from New Bern, General I. N. Palmer reported: "I have but little confidence in these North Carolina troops when they are menaced by a very superior force. They recollect the fate of those recently hanged at Kinston, and the wives, sisters, and children of those victims haunt us daily." [19]

The First Arkansas Cavalry began almost as ignominiously as the Second North Carolina ended. In the fall of 1862 the Arkansans were left in the vicinity of Pea Ridge. "These, I think, will be sufficient to take care of Southwestern Missouri, while the army advances into Arkansas," General John M. Schofield said with ill-founded optimism. Scouting to the south, they found rebel troops approaching in numbers too large for them to handle. The Arkansans were moved to the south of Fayetteville in time to meet the enemy in the battle of Prairie Grove on December 12, 1862.

> Just at daylight they [the Arkansan troops] were attacked by a heavy cavalry force, under [John S.] Marmaduke, and after several rounds were stampeded [Union General F. J. Herron reported]. They came back on me 6 miles south of Fayetteville, at 7 a.m., closely pursued by at least 3,000 cavalry. It was with the greatest difficulty that we got them checked . . . but after some hard talking, and my finally shooting one cowardly whelp off his horse, they halted.

When Herron finally repelled the Confederate attack, he did so with little help from the First Arkansas Cavalry. [20]

The men of the regiment soon began to redeem themselves. Ninety of them, along with forty members of the Tenth Illinois Cavalry, rode to Van Buren, skirmished with and dispersed a company of rebels on the opposite bank of the Arkansas River, and captured a Confederate steamer loaded with troops, horses, and arms. They seized more than three hundred prisoners. [21]

The colonel of the First Arkansas Cavalry, the New York native

M. La Rue Harrison, was proud of his men for that exploit. But he doubted whether his command as a whole was well enough equipped to defend Fayetteville, still less to move in force upon Van Buren and Fort Smith. In April 1863 the First Arkansas Cavalry numbered 1,032, perhaps 850 of them effective, but had only 154 serviceable horses. Many of the men lacked uniforms. The First Arkansas Infantry would "number in a few days an aggregate of 830 men; probably 700 of them effective."

> They are totally without transportation, clothing or tents, or equip-ments of any kind, except the arms picked up on the Prairie Grove battle-ground, which are of all patterns and calibers. The destitu-tion of clothing is very great, and much suffering and sickness pre-vails on account of it; besides, it would be a ruinous policy to place this undrilled, barefooted, butternut regiment in the field to be mixed up with and cut to pieces by rebels in the same dress.

The First Arkansas Light Artillery consisted of 110 men and no guns. Ammunition for the cavalry and the infantry was scarce.

Such was the entire force that Harrison, at Fayetteville, had at his immediate disposal after a battalion of the Tenth Illinois Cavalry was taken away. Harrison's superior, Colonel William A. Phillips, thought the three Illinois companies should have been allowed to remain, and he said as much to his superior, General Samuel R. Curtis: "The Ar-kansas force is very raw and ought not, I would respectfully suggest, be left without the countenance of other troops." [22]

Yet on April 18, 1863, Harrison telegraphed to Curtis: "Arkansas is triumphant. . . . The rebels, 2,000 strong, with two 6-pounder guns, attacked Fayetteville at daylight this morning, and, after four hours' desperate fighting, they were completely routed." Harrison added: "Every officer and man in my command was a hero; no one flinched."

In a long letter the next day, Harrison qualified his account of hero-ism a bit. He acknowledged that a quartermaster had "disgracefully" run away, thirty-five men had "stampeded" and were missing, and a lieutenant and eight privates had been "taken while absent without leave at a dance, 9 miles from town." Still, he could honestly say: "Every field and line officer and nearly every enlisted man fought bravely."

Harrison congratulated his men "that this battle was fought upon

Arkansas soil, and this victory won by Arkansians alone." Curtis added his thanks to the soldiers: "You have done nobly. Arkansas vindicates her own honor by repulsing the rebel flag with her own brave sons." If these tributes seem grandiloquent, there can be no questioning the sincerity of the testimonial that the commander of the attacking rebels, General William L. Cabell, gave in his report:

> The enemy all (both infantry and cavalry) fought well, equally as well as any Federal troops I have ever seen. Although it was thought by a great many that, composed as they are of disloyal citizens and deserters from our army, they would make but a feeble stand, the reverse was the case, as they resisted every attack made on them, and, as fast as driven out of one house, would occupy another and deliver their fire.

For the next year or so, Colonel Harrison and his First Arkansas Cavalry were mainly concerned with warding off rebel guerrillas, including those who menaced the construction of a telegraph line from Missouri to Fayetteville. "Your officers and men, from their knowledge of the country and the zeal inspired by their strong interest in restoring peace to Arkansas, are peculiarly fitted for this service," the commander at Springfield, Missouri, advised Harrison. "Posts and highways are not the places to find bushwhackers. The byways and mountain paths your men know so well are the real tracks to glory and honor. Night marches, sudden attacks, ambuscades, and untiring pursuit are the only cure for bushwhackers and guerrillaism." [23]

Then, in the late summer of 1864, Sterling Price with twelve thousand rebel cavalrymen undertook a daring incursion into Missouri with the desperate aim of recovering the state for the Confederacy. Joining in the Union pursuit was the Second Arkansas Cavalry under the command of Colonel John E. Phelps. "On the morning of October 8, while the enemy appeared to be in full force in front of Jefferson City, he [Phelps] moved out with a portion of his regiment, charged the enemy's line and broke it . . . settling the question as to whether the enemy was about to attack or was retreating." As Price retreated to the west and then to the south, Phelps and his Arkansans made one "gallant" and telling charge after another.

A part of Price's army returned to Arkansas by way of Fayetteville. Frustrated in the attempt to retake the state of Missouri, the rebels thought they could at least retake this Arkansas town. "Fayetteville was attacked this morning by a strong force, who posted themselves at sunrise on the almost inaccessible bluffs of East Mountain, about 1,000 yards east of town, and opened a brisk fire on my camp," Colonel Harrison reported on October 28, 1864. "Captain Hopkins and Captain Harrison led their men, less than 100 strong, up the mountain in the face of a galling fire from 700 rebels, charging the topmost bluff three times, and the third time driving the enemy from their position." After a ten-day siege, Fayetteville was finally rid of the rebel threat.[24]

While the First and Second Arkansas Cavalry regiments were giving a good account of themselves, the Third and Fourth were making no better than mediocre records. The Third was on "outpost duty" at Lewisburg for a time. "Since it has been there," an army inspector learned in January 1864, "in different skirmishes the regiment has killed about 500 of the enemy" (a typical example of a body count in the Civil War). As for the Fourth Arkansas Cavalry, one officer had "no confidence" in its men. "They have not been under fire enough to stand the burning of villainous saltpeter," he said in February 1864. But another officer declared only a few months later that, as scouts, his troops were the best that could be found anywhere. In November 1864 General Herron recommended that "the worst cavalry regiments be dismounted," among them the Fourth Arkansas, but by January 1865, the army inspector said this regiment was "steadily improving."[25]

From the Confederate point of view, the Second Arkansas Infantry was the worst. In early 1865 some men of this regiment, along with Kansas cavalrymen and members of the "U.S. Colored Troops," were stationed at Clarksville, on the Arkansas River about midway between Fort Smith and Little Rock. Civilians in that neighborhood complained of "wrongs to our helpless women committed indifferently by black and white." According to the complainants, the Union soldiers, after stealing everything in sight, had tortured the women with hot coals to find out where their money was hidden. Confederate General M. Jeff Thompson subsequently lodged an official protest.[26]

Alabamians in the Union army were much fewer than Arkansans, but no loyalist Arkansas regiment saw more action than the First Alabama Cavalry did. "From the first formation the regt. has been engaged in scouting in N. E. Miss. and owing to the acquaintance, thorough and minute, which a large portion of both officers and men have with the country, they have been almost universally successful," the regiment's own "record of events" for March 1863 stated. "The first Cos. were formed in Nov. & Dec. 1862 and all have been engaged in continual service, since that time."

In the spring of 1863, while two of the companies joined Abel D. Streight's ill-fated expedition to destroy railroads in northern Alabama, the rest of the First Alabama accompanied Grenville M. Dodge on his more successful expedition raiding in the Tennessee Valley and collecting horses and mules. Dodge was impressed by the willingness of his Alabama troops to attack whenever Confederates offered resistance. "The charge of the Alabamians with muskets only, and those not loaded," he reported, "is creditable, especially as they were all new recruits and poorly drilled." 27

The First Alabama went on its first big solo raid soon after George E. Spencer took command of it. The youthful Spencer, a New York native and Iowa lawyer, was then promoted from captain to colonel. At Corinth, Mississippi, he received the following orders, dated October 3, 1863, from his corps commander, Lincoln's South Carolina–born friend Stephen A. Hurlbut: "You will take all the available and well-mounted men of your command and proceed rapidly through Jasper, Ala., to Montgomery, or to some point east of Montgomery on the West Point railroad. Arriving there you will proceed to destroy effectually the Montgomery and West Point Railroad in its rolling-stock, track, and depots, doing the most thorough amount of damage possible." Both Hurlbut and Spencer were sanguine of success. "They have been in several engagements and behaved well," Hurlbut wrote of the Alabamians. "Spencer is certain that he can get through the center cordon without observation, and if he does so, I am satisfied he will make his way to Montgomery."

But Spencer, with about 650 cavalrymen and six engineers who could "either run or destroy railroads or steamers," had barely got into Alabama when his troops ran into a force of some two thousand mounted Confederates. "The woods was so dense and the fight kept up for so great a distance that many killed and wounded were not found," the Confederate commander, General Samuel W. Ferguson, said. He estimated the Federal losses to be at least a hundred, not counting a large number of prisoners, horses, mules, and weapons. "I have succeeded in effectually destroying the First Alabama Tory Regiment," the general boasted.[28]

Though badly hurt, the First Alabama was by no means destroyed. During the winter of 1863–64 the regiment, with Spencer still in command, was busy again with reconnaissances and patrols, which occasionally resulted in skirmishes with Confederates on similar errands.

From April to September 1864 the First Alabama then took part in William T. Sherman's campaign for Atlanta, acting as scouts (whose value Sherman himself acknowledged) and as rear guards for the supply line.

And from September to December the Alabamians joined in the march from Atlanta to the sea. Carrying out Sherman's order to "burn the countryside within fifteen miles" of their route, they destroyed the depot at Milledgeville and a long stretch of the Atlantic and Gulf Railroad. "Had slight skirmish every day until the 9th, when we came to the enemy's outer works at Savannah," the regiment's scribe recorded in December. "We drove them two miles over a road where torpedoes [mines or booby traps] were buried, which exploding mortally wounded Adjutant Tupper and six men slightly, also killing six horses. We drove the enemy to their main works." [29]

During January–March 1865 Spencer led the Third Cavalry Brigade as Sherman's army moved from Savannah up through the Carolinas. The Third Brigade—consisting of the First Alabama, the Fifth Kentucky, and the Fifth Ohio, and accompanied by the Tenth Wisconsin Battery of artillery—drew the praise of the overall cavalry commander, General Judson Kilpatrick, and of Sherman himself for its exploits along the way.

As Spencer's brigade approached Williston, South Carolina, the First Alabama "having the advance," the Alabamians "struck a force of the enemy" and "had no difficulty in driving them in and through the town." But when Spencer and his men prepared to camp there, they were fired upon, the "firing in the advance becoming quite heavy." He ordered the Alabamians to "crowd the enemy" and his Kentuckians to go to the Alabamians' support.

> Then commenced one of the most thorough and complete routs I ever witnessed [Spencer recounted]. The ground was completely

strewn with guns, haversacks, &c. Five battle-flags were captured, including the brigade and four regimental flags, and a large number of horses and over thirty prisoners. After a charge of about seven miles from this point the enemy dispersed and went in every direction through the woods and swamps. . . . The force we had the encounter with proved to be the Alabama brigade . . . consisting of the First, Third, Fifth, Ninth, Twelfth, and Fifty-first Regiments Alabama Cavalry.

After advancing into North Carolina, Spencer's brigade fought off another Confederate attack in what developed into the battle of Monroe's Cross Roads. One morning at reveille his men awoke to find the enemy charging their camp from opposite directions—under the lead of two of the most famous rebel cavalry commanders, Wade Hampton and Joseph Wheeler. The rebels overran almost the entire camp before Spencer's men, "by desperate fighting behind trees," succeeded in driving them off. For two and a half hours the Federals stood up against repeated charges, until finally "the enemy retreated in confusion," leaving behind more than a hundred of their men killed, a larger number wounded, and a few dozen captured. "Our loss . . . was 18 killed, 70 wounded, and 105 missing," Spencer reported; among those were eight officers from the First Alabama and one from the Fifth Kentucky.

Near Averasborough Spencer's brigade, coming upon rebels entrenched on a ridge, "advanced skirmishing quite heavily up to within 200 yards of their works" and then helped to dislodge them. At Bentonville, in the concluding battle of Sherman's march through the Carolinas, Spencer's men again played a supporting role, "guarding part of the time the left flank" of the Union army. On March 24, 1865, three days after the battle, they "went into camp after a campaign of fifty-five days" during which they had "marched over 700 miles, crossing seven large rivers on pontoon bridges and an innumerable number of smaller streams and swamps that under ordinary circumstances would be considered impassable." Over all that distance they had "subsisted almost entirely upon the country." [30]

In proportion to their numbers, the Union troops from Alabama contributed as much to the war's outcome as did those from any other Southern state. But the Alabama numbers were quite small in comparison with those of Virginia/West Virginia and those of Tennessee. The Virginians and the Tennesseeans, who together made up more than half of all the loyalists, did more than half of all the loyalist fighting.

Volunteering early in the war, Unionist Virginians fought in the very first battle after the attack on Fort Sumter. When General George B. McClellan ordered his Ohio soldiers to "enter upon the soil of Virginia" in May of 1861, the First Virginia Infantry and four companies of the Second Virginia were ready to join them at Wheeling. "You are to act in concert with the Virginia troops," McClellan told the Ohioans, "and to support their advance." With Virginians leading the way, Unionists hoped to attract other Virginians to the Union cause.

After McClellan had occupied Grafton and secured the Wheeling and Parkersburg branches of the Baltimore and Ohio Railroad, he "learned that the insurgents had retreated to Philippi and received very considerable accessions to their numbers." So he "directed an immediate movement to dislodge and disperse them from their new position." His troops marched all night through mud and rain and, with the Virginians out in front, attacked at dawn on June 3, 1861. The rebels, McClellan reported, "were surprised in their camp, routed, and in great confusion driven before our troops for several miles." He proclaimed to the inhabitants of the region: "The army of this department, headed by Virginia troops, is rapidly occupying all Western Virginia." [31]

Months later the Confederates still held the Baltimore and Ohio at Romney, a strategic point where the railroad crossed the main branch of the upper Potomac. President Lincoln and his general in chief, Winfield Scott, had their eyes on the place. Scott sent orders regarding Romney to Benjamin F. Kelley, originally the colonel of the First Virginia, now a general in command of a brigade, having been promoted on the basis of his performance at Philippi.

With elements of the Third, Fourth, and Seventh Virginia and the Fourth and Eighth Ohio, Kelley approached Romney from the west on October 26, 1861. He found that "the artillery of the enemy was strongly posted on the east side of the river, in a cemetery lot, on an eminence commanding the entire western approaches to the town, and the infantry and dismounted cavalry occupied intrenchments on the heights, commanding the bridge and the ford." When his own artillery failed to silence the enemy's after an hour-long cannonade, he ordered his infantry to charge across the bridge and his cavalry to advance across the ford. "The enemy, after firing a few rounds, now gave way and fled from their works," Kelley later reported.

Kelley soon heard from the War Department: "Your late movement upon and signal victory at Romney do you great honor in the opinion of the President and of Lieutenant-General Scott." [32]

While, for the time being, Union forces controlled the Baltimore and Ohio line through Virginia, they had a very insecure hold on some of the western counties of the state. Rebel guerrillas were continually on the prowl, even harassing counties that bordered on the Ohio River. On October 10, 1861, the Ninth Virginia was "a new regiment just forming at Guyandotte, Va.," across the river from the southernmost tip of Ohio, and there were "only 150 men yet in camp." That evening the fledgling regiment was "completely surprised by 700 cavalry, under command of [Albert G.] Jenkins, the guerrilla chief, and cut to pieces and captured."

The next morning "the steamboat Boston came up with about 200 of the Fifth Virginia Regiment." They were "joined by a number of the Home Guards of Lawrence County, Ohio, who had assembled at Proctorville, opposite, to prevent the rebels from landing in Ohio, which they had threatened to do." After the rebels withdrew, "the armed citizens of Ohio set fire to the town."

On December 29, 1861, guerrillas roving the mountains east of Charleston attacked Suttonville, which was garrisoned by one company of the First Virginia Cavalry. "The company retreated to Weston, and the guerrillas burned the town and what commissary stores were there." The next day "three companies of the First Virginia Cavalry and three of the Third Virginia Infantry marched to punish the marauders and pursued them into the Glades of Webster County, killed 22 and burned 26 houses, thus breaking up their nest." [33]

Commanding the Mountain Department in the spring of 1862, John C. Frémont had to contend not only with guerrillas but also with the army of Stonewall Jackson. Frémont's command included elements of the Second, Third, Ninth, and Tenth Virginia Infantry and the First and Second Virginia Cavalry. Jackson was moving up the Shenandoah Valley in the hope of drawing McClellan's Army of the Potomac away from Richmond. After crossing the main Appalachian range, he took up a position on Bull Pasture Mountain near the hamlet of McDowell. The Federals attacked and were repulsed. Union General Robert H. Milroy—on whose head the Confederates put a price because of his rigorous suppression of guerrillas—praised the Third Virginia along with the Ohio regiments of his brigade for having "proved themselves true representatives of the American citizen soldier."

When Lee's and John Pope's armies met in the second battle of Bull Run, in August 1862, the Second, Third, and Fifth Virginia Infantry and three companies of the First Virginia Cavalry were with Pope. They performed about as well as other Union regiments in what proved a disastrous defeat for all of them. Just before the climax of the campaign Herman Haupt, in charge of U.S. military railroads, reported from Alexandria on August 28: "Company A, Sixteenth Virginia, sent on guard duty at some point on the railroad between this place and Manassas, were all captured some time last night." [34]

The Seventh Virginia Infantry was with McClellan and the Army of the Potomac at the battle of Antietam, September 17, 1862. "We succeeded in driving the enemy back with great slaughter," Colonel Joseph Snider of the Seventh reported. "Our colors were shot down three times, but were promptly hoisted each time." McClellan gave the Virginians credit in his report. Referring to the desperate struggle in the cornfield, he said: "The enemy attempted to turn the left of the line, but were met by the Seventh Virginia and the One Hundred and thirty-second Pennsylvania Volunteers and repulsed." At Antietam the Seventh suffered 145 casualties: 29 officers and men dead, 116 wounded, none missing.

The Seventh distinguished itself again on December 13, 1862, when Ambrose E. Burnside ordered the Army of the Potomac to make repeated charges up an exposed hillside against the Army of Northern Virginia, which was "concealed under good cover," near Fredericksburg. Colonel Snider having been wounded, Lieutenant Colonel Jonathan H. Lockwood assumed command of the Virginia regiment. "We moved up briskly over a distance of some 80 rods, under a most galling fire from the enemy's rifle pits and batteries in front," Lockwood reported. "My officers and men behaved with admirable coolness and bravery, and deserve well of their country." [35]

At Gettysburg, on July 2, 1863, the Seventh Virginia (renamed the

Seventh West Virginia) went to the support of Battery L, First New York Artillery, on Cemetery Ridge. "We found the battery about to be taken charge of by the enemy, who were in large force," Lockwood recalled three days afterward. "We immediately charged upon the enemy, and succeeded in completely routing the entire force and driving them beyond their lines, capturing a number of prisoners." One of the prisoners was the colonel of the Confederate Seventh Virginia Regiment. The Seventh Virginia, U.S.A., had gotten the better of the Seventh Virginia, C.S.A.

Also involved in the Gettysburg campaign was the First (West) Virginia Cavalry, under Major Charles E. Capehart. Moving north from near Frederick, Maryland, the First Virginia "met and repulsed the enemy at Hanover, Pa.," on June 30. Then, on July 2, at Gettysburg, Capehart's men "made one of the most desperate charges during the present rebellion," as he asserted. The defensive position of the enemy was "the worst for a cavalry charge—that is, behind stone fences so high as to preclude the possibility of gaining the opposite side without dismounting and throwing them down."

> The whole ground over which we charged was very adverse in every particular, being broken and uneven and covered with rock. This regiment here charged upon infantry, and still did not falter in any of its movements until it had scaled two stone fences and had penetrated some distance the enemy's lines, which had kept up a continual fire of musketry. The entire regiment was entirely surrounded, when they received an order to return. The First Texas Regiment having occupied the ground over which we advanced . . . an order was given for the officers and men to cut their way through, which they did, and brought with them quite a number of prisoners.

Then, pursuing Lee's army on its retreat, Capehart's men, "with a whoop and a yell," dashed upon a wagon train in "inky darkness" on the night of July 4. A "hand-to-hand conflict" ensued. "The road was interspersed with wagons and ambulances for a distance of 8 miles, and the whole train was taken—300 wagons, 15 ambulances, together with all the horses and mules attached. The number of prisoners taken was 1,300, including 200 commissioned officers." [36]

In August 1863 General William W. Averell led an expedition consisting mostly of West Virginia troops from Moorefield, West Virginia, far to the south to dispose of a Confederate force under Colonel William L. Jackson. Averell and his troops succeeded in driving Jackson out of Pocahontas County, but the enemy would return. (Averell continued to refer to his regiments by their original names—the Second, Third, and Eighth Virginia—even after West Virginia had been a separate state for more than two months.)

Approaching White Sulphur Springs, after filing through a gorge with a column of horses four miles long, Averell's men met a superior force under General Samuel Jones at Rocky Gap. They withdrew "in good order," leaving behind more than a hundred dead and wounded. At the conclusion of his campaign, Averell could not help expressing his "high commendation" of the soldiers of his command. They had "marched over 600 miles through a rugged, mountainous region, fighting the enemy almost daily; had one severe battle; destroyed the camps of the enemy; captured large amounts of supplies and 266 prisoners."

By November 1863 the Confederates under William L. Jackson were back in Pocahontas County. Averell went after them again, this time with the Second, Third, Eighth, and Tenth West Virginia Infantry (the first three of these regiments mounted) plus a regiment and a company of Ohio troops. Jackson withdrew to the summit of Droop Mountain, where he dug in and received reinforcements but to no avail. "I turned the enemy's left with infantry, and when he became disturbed made an attack direct with four regiments of dismounted cavalry," Averell reported. "The victory was decisive and the enemy's retreat became a total rout."

The next month Averell led a raid over the Alleghenies and into the Shenandoah Valley. There he "succeeded in cutting the Virginia and Tennessee railroad at Salem, in Roanoke County." He destroyed not only water stations, bridges, and tracks but also large quantities of flour, wheat, corn, oats, meat, salt, leather, clothing, shoes, saddles, tools, oil, tar, and other stores. "This," his superior declared, "is undoubtedly one of the most hazardous, important, and successful raids since the commencement of the war." [37]

Troops from West Virginia engaged in even more large-scale raiding in the Shenandoah Valley in September 1864. Seven of the state's regiments took part in Philip H. Sheridan's campaign to devastate the valley and render it unusable as a route for Confederate movements on Washington, such as the recent one by Jubal A. Early. The West Virginians helped Sheridan to win his victories at Winchester (September 19), Fisher's Hill (September 22), and Cedar Creek (October 19). At Winchester the Tenth West Virginia suffered especially heavy losses. "This was owing to the fact that it occupied the left of my line," the brigade commander explained, "and was exposed to a heavy enfilading fire at close range from a wood on my left as it advanced." Another Union officer commented: "I have never witnessed more zeal and daring than was here displayed."

While the Tenth and several other Virginia/West Virginia regiments distinguished themselves in the course of the war, the Seventh Infantry received—and deserved—the greatest honor. According to an order of March 7, 1865, the Seventh Infantry was one of the regiments in the Army of the Potomac that were to have inscribed upon their colors or guidons the names of the battles in which they had "borne a meritorious part." Its battles, in the order in which they were listed, consist of "Romney, Antietam, Fredericksburg, Chancellorsville, Gettysburg, Bristol Station, Mine Run, Wilderness, Spotsylvania, Totopotomoy, North Anna, Cold Harbor, Petersburg, Strawberry Plains, Deep Bottom, Reams' Station, Boydton Road." And the Seventh was yet to participate in the Appomattox campaign—along with the First, Second, Third, Tenth, Eleventh, Twelfth, and Fifteenth West Virginia regiments.[38]

The Loudoun Rangers—or Independent Virginia Rangers—had a special relationship with the Lincoln government. Their captain, Samuel C. Means, could report directly to Lincoln's war secretary, Edwin M. Stanton, who had personally given Means his commission and instructed him to organize the company. The task of the Loudoun Rangers was to help protect the capital by hunting down rebel guerrillas in Loudoun County, Virginia, to the west of Washington and on the other side of the Potomac.

Captain Means, a native Virginian, already had a bad reputation among Confederates when he took command of his rangers, having previously guided Yankee troops on raids into Loudoun County. Confederates called him a renegade, and according to rumor, the Richmond government offered a large reward for his capture.[39]

Means soon acquired a bad reputation also among U.S. officers who resented his independence. This was particularly true of the commander of U.S. forces in Means's area, Dixon S. Miles, whose headquarters were at Harpers Ferry, near the edge of Loudoun County. Miles, an old veteran of the regular army, was easily disgusted by the kind of recruits that were being sent to him—men who "never had a gun in their hands until the boxes were opened and muskets issued to them" and whose officers did not "know how to drill or anything about the drill." Very quickly he found reason to be even more disgusted with Means and his rangers.

Means had been leading his company for only a couple of months when he made one of his many hairbreadth escapes. At daybreak on August 27, 1862, while sleeping in a Waterford church, he and his men were "attacked by at least 500 guerrillas," as he telegraphed to Miles (grossly exaggerating the number). "They will kill all if I cannot get help." He got no help but managed to get away from the rebels, leaving a number of dead and wounded at the church. Miles expostulated:

> Means' company, lately raised, without discipline, has committed all kinds of depredations on the inhabitants, living on them, taking what he pleased and when it suited him, until the arrival of his men in any vicinity was a dread and terror. The company was never placed under my command or I should have removed him from Loudoun County long since. In my last interview with him I warned him, from the loose, straggling manner he encamped and marched, he would be surprised and cut to pieces.

But Miles, not Means, was about to be surprised and completely done in.[40]

Lee, moving north in the campaign that was to culminate in the bloody battle of Antietam, divided his army on the way to Sharpsburg and sent a large part of it, under Stonewall Jackson, to dispose of Miles at Harpers Ferry.

By September 2, 1862, Confederate Colonel Thomas T. Munford and his Second Virginia Cavalry were advancing through Loudoun County ahead of Lee's main force. They headed for Leesburg, where they planned "to capture the party of marauders under Means, which so long had infested the country and harassed the inhabitants." Means was in the neighborhood with his own company and a small detachment of the First Maryland Cavalry when Munford caught up with them. "I succeeded in surprising Means' party, Means himself escaping," Munford reported. "Without halting in the town I pressed heavily upon him, and soon succeeded in routing his command after a heavy skirmish, and pursued them as far as Waterford, 7 miles." Edward, a slave belonging to one of Munford's men, followed his master in the charge, gun in hand, and "shot Everhart, one of the most notorious ruffians of Means' party," leaving him badly wounded.

The captain of the First Maryland Cavalry, on reaching the (temporary) security of Harpers Ferry, told Colonel Miles: "Captain Means and his company broke and ran." Miles had the satisfaction of repeating this to his superior, General John E. Wool, and to Lincoln's military adviser and general in chief, Henry W. Halleck. Wool then sent the same message directly to Means's sponsor, Secretary Stanton.[41]

According to Means, "The day after we had the skirmish in Leesburg—not a skirmish either, but a pretty hard fight—Colonel Miles sent me back to Leesburg to learn the truth of the forces coming there." Miles would have done well to pay more attention to what Means told him, as Means testified a little later: "I could not go to Leesburg, but I got on a mountain near by, within a mile of it, and I had a good spy-glass and saw everything distinctly. I saw forty regiments coming into Leesburg and sixty-odd pieces of artillery. I went back and reported it to Colonel Miles. He turned around to me and said, 'It is a damned no such thing,' just in that way."

Miles then sent Means to Point of Rocks, on the Maryland side of the Potomac about a dozen miles downriver from Harpers Ferry. Near Point of Rocks, Means hid and watched Confederate troops cross the river during the night—he estimated there were at least ten thousand of them. Next morning he went back to Harpers Ferry to report to Miles. "I went up and saw Colonel Miles, but he would not believe anything I said, or that there were any soldiers over the river, or any danger."

Within a week or so the Confederates, with a force several times larger than Miles's, had surrounded Harpers Ferry, occupying Bolivar Heights at the west of the town, Loudoun Heights across the Shenandoah River, and Maryland Heights on the other side of the Potomac. By Sunday night, September 14, Means believed there was no longer any hope of holding out against the besiegers. "And I knew I would be hanged if I was caught," he said not long afterward. "I thought if I could get out I would, and I invited all who wished to follow me to follow me; and there were a great many that did." Thus he and his Loudoun Rangers, eluding the rebels, guided some fifteen hundred cavalrymen to safety.

The next day, after a bombardment from the heights, Miles surrendered the rest of his army. Mortally wounded, he did not live to face the consequences. "What was the matter with Colonel Miles?" a military commission shortly inquired. Means, one of those testifying, thought the colonel had been drinking too much. Other witnesses agreed, at least, that something must have been wrong with him. The commission's verdict was that "Colonel Miles' incapacity, amounting to almost imbecility, led to the shameful surrender of this important post." [42]

After Lee's retreat from Sharpsburg, Union forces recovered Harpers Ferry, but they still had to contend with rebel raiders for control of Loudoun County. Early in 1863 two battalions of Jeb Stuart's cavalry began to cause serious trouble for Means's Loudoun Rangers and other Union cavalrymen associated with them from time to time. Elijah V. White headed one of the Confederate battalions and John S. Mosby the other and (in the Confederacy) more celebrated one, known as the Virginia Partisan Rangers.

In February 1863 General Benjamin F. Kelley, in command at Harpers Ferry, "sent two expeditions after White's cavalry, in Loudoun County," where White's men were going about "in small detached portions, for the purpose of enforcing the conscript act and stealing horses." Kelley looked to Means for information as to where White could be found.

Rebel cavalry were said to be near Leesburg in May, and Means at Point of Rocks was instructed to "keep a sharp lookout on and across the river." General Julius Stahel "sent out a force of 400 of the First Michigan Cavalry to try and intercept Mosby." Colonel A. T. McReynolds of the First New York Cavalry thought "a concerted movement of the cavalry of General Stahel, with the First New York and Captain Means' company, moving from the direction of Harpers Ferry, sweeping the shole country from the line of Fauquier [County] to the Potomac, would clear that section pretty effectively." But Mosby's partisans were hard to find; after a raid, they could easily melt away among sympathetic civilians. As McReynolds pointed out, "Mosby's men don't wear uniforms, but appear like citizens."

White's cavalrymen were equally elusive and just as destructive. In June they drove the Loudoun Rangers away from Point of Rocks, captured a railroad train loaded with troops and supplies, and set fire to the cars. A Baltimore and Ohio telegraph operator erroneously reported that "they also captured and carried off Captain Means, with his entire company of cavalry." White's men did make off with some of Means's horses.[43]

Means recuperated quickly enough from his losses to be of service when Lee again moved north to invade Pennsylvania in June 1863. Means then received the following orders directly from General-in-Chief Halleck: "You will, as soon as you have a sufficient number of your men remounted, proceed to the region threatened by the rebel forces, and take possession of and drive off into the nearest depot all horses suitable for cavalry, artillery, or baggage trains which are in any danger of falling into the hands of the enemy." Within a few days Means and his men were ranging widely through northern Maryland to collect horses, particularly those belonging to "disloyal citizens."

And during the battle of Gettysburg Means again heard from Halleck, this time with orders to "move across the front of the Washington fortifications, scouting the country, and reporting whether you find any parties of the enemy." Obviously the Lincoln administration still depended on him.[44]

Means certainly had confidence in himself. Later in the summer of 1863 he reported from Point of Rocks that about four hundred rebel cavalry were camped a few miles away, on the opposite bank of the Potomac. "The river is now fordable, and, if you will send me one battalion of cavalry, we can rout them," he telegraphed (July 23) to General Robert C. Schenck in Baltimore, and he dispatched the same message to Halleck in Washington. But, as Schenck explained to Halleck, he had no cavalry to send to Means.

"White and Mosby were at Leesburg yesterday, several hundred strong, threatening the Baltimore and Ohio Railroad in Frederick County," General Lockwood noted (August 1) at Harpers Ferry. "There seems to be a want of co-operation on our part, which enables this contemptible body of irregulars to exist, notwithstanding the presence on our part of four times their force."

The lack of cooperation was not Means's fault. "I know that there is a large [rebel] force in Loudoun waiting an opportunity to make a raid into Maryland," he reported (August 8) to General S. P. Heintzelman, who was commanding the Department of Washington, D.C. "Send me the [adequate] force [of Union troops], and I will clean them out. Strangers cannot find them." He also dispatched a telegram to Stanton.

In response, Halleck's chief of staff, J. H. Taylor, communicated with Colonel C. R. Lowell, commanding a brigade of cavalry in Washington. "It is reported that White is in the vicinity of Dranesville with a body of some 350 men," Taylor wrote. "Can you make any expedition in that vicinity with sufficient force to attack if you succeed in finding the party? Captain Means, Independent Rangers, stationed at Point of Rocks, says he knows all the country from Dranesville to Aldie, and wishes to co-operate with you." [45]

No such cooperation came about, so the Loudoun Rangers kept on being overtaken and routed. White sent "50 men on scout in the direction of Harper's Ferry," as he informed Jeb Stuart (October 2). "Encountered Captain Means, with 75 men, about 5 miles from that place. Charged and drove him to the ferry; wounded 3, and captured 5 prisoners and 8 horses."

A couple of weeks later the Loudoun Rangers and a contingent of Maryland troops were cooperating to the extent of jointly fortifying and garrisoning the courthouse square in Charles Town (where John Brown had been hanged in 1859). A Confederate force under General John D. Imboden suddenly appeared. "The surprise was complete, the enemy having no suspicion of our approach until I had the town entirely surrounded," Imboden related. After he began to shell the square, its occupants fled toward Harpers Ferry. Means reported his losses as "17 men prisoners and 1 wounded; also 19 full sets of arms and horse equipments, 1 wagon, 4 sets of harness, and 23 horses." [46]

When Means was finally removed from command, the reason was not his habit of being taken by surprise. The problem was his anomalous position between the secretary of war and the commanders in the field.

On April 1, 1864, General Averell, commander of the cavalry division, Department of West Virginia, with his headquarters at Martinsburg, directed one of his colonels to "send 200 men under a reliable officer to Point of Rocks to arrest and bring to these headquarters

Captain Means and his battalion." Means's misdeed: he had disregarded Averell's orders to join the general's division and proceed to Charleston, West Virginia. General Max Weber, in command at Harpers Ferry, told Averell that Means's men, now comprising two companies at Point of Rocks, were "known as the Independent Virginia Rangers. It seems they are acting in accordance with their name."

Weber soon heard from Averell's superior, General Franz Sigel, commander of the Department of West Virginia: "Captain Means has been dismissed from the service for not obeying orders."

Instead of reporting to Charleston, Means and his rangers went to Waterford, Loudoun County, on another of their forays. Sigel wanted to know why, and Weber explained: "Means crossed the river into Virginia by the orders of the Secretary of War."

Once the Loudoun Rangers had returned to Point of Rocks, Weber undertook to carry out Averell's and Sigel's program. "Means' battalion, under command of Lieut. D. M. Keyes, will move without delay via railroad to Parkersburg, thence to Charleston," he ordered. "If any refuse to go, put them in irons and forward."

But, after hearing from the War Department, Weber had to issue a new order the following day. He now directed Keyes and the rangers to stay where they were for the present, "the order for their movement having been countermanded." The information was passed on to General George Crook, who, from his headquarters in Charleston, was planning raids on the railroad between East Tennessee and Lynchburg, Virginia. "The orders directing Captain Means' companies to proceed to Charleston have been revoked under instructions from the Secretary of War, they having been recruited for provisional service." In other words, Means and his men had signed up to serve only in Loudoun County and its environs.[47]

Though he countermanded the order for moving the battalion to Charleston, Stanton let stand the order for removing Means from its command. Means continued to scout for Stanton, sending him information about enemy movements in and around Loudoun County. Occasionally Means also accompanied scouting parties of his former rangers as their guide.

Under the command of Daniel M. Keyes, who was promoted from lieutenant to captain, the Loudoun Rangers persisted in trying to clear Loudoun County of guerrillas—with no greater success than they had realized under Captain Means. Mosby and his partisans raided almost at will during the summer and fall of 1864. They burned trains, robbed passengers, and tore up tracks. On one occasion Mosby reported that his men, "coming upon a portion of the enemy's cavalry which was engaged in burning houses, attacked and routed them. Such was the indignation of our men at witnessing some of the finest residences in this portion of the State enveloped in flames that no quarter was shown, and about 25 of them [the Union cavalrymen] were shot to death for their villainy."

The Union commander at Harpers Ferry complained that he had at his disposal "Loudoun County Rangers, 100 strong; total, 400 men," most of them infantry. "This is my entire force; I think wholly insufficient." And the rangers remained rather inefficient as well. "On the 6th of April [1865]," General Winfield Scott Hancock recorded, "a body of Mosby's guerrillas surprised the camp of the Loudoun County Rangers near Charlestown [Charles Town], capturing a number of men and nearly all of their horses." That was just three days before Lee's surrender at Appomattox.[48]

During the winter of 1861–62 the First and Second East Tennessee regiments—"most desirous of driving the rebels from East Tennessee in the quickest possible time," as their Tennesseean brigade commander, Colonel Samuel P. Carter, said—waited impatiently in Kentucky for a chance to move to and through Cumberland Gap. At first, Carter thought the enemy force at the gap was so small that his own men would "meet with but little opposition." But after making a large-scale reconnaissance in March 1862, he discovered that the Confederate presence there was rather formidable.

In April the Carter brigade, as part of George W. Morgan's army, reached Cumberland Ford, Kentucky, fourteen miles from the gap, but the army did not move on until June. By this time, Carter was a brigadier general, and his brigade consisted of the First, Second, Third, and Fourth East Tennessee, in addition to an Indiana and two Kentucky regiments.

Even without much resistance from the rebels, it was a struggle for Carter's men to get over Pine Mountain and up the Cumberland slope. "To one who has not passed over the route it would be hard to imagine the difficulties to be overcome in transporting artillery and a heavy baggage train over it," Carter wrote. "But officers and men, eager to meet their rebel enemies and to gain an entrance into long-looked-for East Tennessee, went to work with the greatest energy, and by main strength carried wagons and artillery over a road which many would pronounce impassable to either."

Before Morgan's army reached Cumberland Gap, on June 18, the Confederates had abandoned the place. Then Morgan, too, abandoned it after Kirby Smith invaded Kentucky. One of Smith's cavalry brigades attacked the Third Tennessee near London, Kentucky, and compelled it to retreat to the gap. "The enemy gained our rear and cut off our supplies," Morgan finally had to acknowledge. So, on the night of September 17, after occupying the gap for only three months, he marched his army away from it.

Afterwards, Morgan (a Pennsylvania-born veteran of the Mexican War) characterized the Tennesseans in his army: "The First Tennessee is well drilled and well commanded; the Second not in quite so good condition; the Sixth has an excellent colonel, with good officers. The Tennessee troops would be equal to any in the service; they are brave, enduring, and anxious to learn, but are very clannish, and imagine slights when none are intended; they should not be brigaded together."[49]

Not all the loyalist Tennessee soldiers proved themselves "equal to any in the service" when seven Tennessee regiments took part in the Stones River campaign from December 26, 1862, to January 5, 1863. In the battle near Murfreesboro, Tennessee, the First Tennessee Infantry particularly distinguished itself. Its men twice charged the rebels and "drove them from the field." But the Second Tennessee Cavalry did not do as well.

The adjutant of the Second Tennessee afterwards reported that on December 27, 28, 29, and 30 the regiment "put the enemy to flight," "drove the enemy," "started in pursuit," and engaged in "skirmishing with the enemy during the entire day." The adjutant said nothing about what the regiment did the following day, December 31.

But officers not connected with the regiment did say something about its performance at that time. The commander of the Second Cavalry Brigade told how his men had been guarding a long wagon train on the Nashville road when the enemy came "charging up the pike in our rear." "A short time before we were attacked a large number of the Second Tennessee came running by my column, running away from the front, stating that our forces were in full retreat. I placed a company in the road, halted every one of them, but at the breaking out of the skirmish they ran again like sheep." [50]

Four Tennessee regiments participated in the Chickamauga campaign and two others in the Knoxville campaign during the late summer of 1863. Then, during the fall and winter of 1863–64, Tennesseeans helped to fight off the rebels who attempted to recover control of East Tennessee.

The Second East Tennessee Mounted Infantry ran into bad luck while camping on November 6 near Rogersville, northeast of Knoxville. The rebels captured most of the officers and men, who, according to one of the officers, "performed their duty with the most gratifying coolness and courage, and were only induced to surrender to greatly superior numbers." Men of the First Tennessee Cavalry were equally courageous and more fortunate. Advancing from New Market toward Dandridge, on Christmas Eve they followed orders to "charge with sabers, which they did most nobly, driving the enemy's line over a fence." These words of commendation came not from their own colonel but from the Second Michigan's.

A Kentuckian commanding the Union force at Cumberland Gap (after its occupation by Burnside's army) had a low opinion of the Tennessee troops he happened to see. "When I passed through the country here, previous to my arrival here, I met an almost continuous stream of stragglers, principally belonging to Tennessee regiments." Of the Thirty-fourth Kentucky and the Ninety-first Indiana Infantry, which were under his command, he said: "These two regiments are composed of good material." But he added: "The other two regiments, the Second North Carolina Mounted Infantry and the Eleventh Tennessee Cavalry, are without discipline, especially the latter regiment, and with their present organization are of but little value." [51]

While contending with rebels in East Tennessee, the loyalist troops still had to confront rebels from time to time in the middle and western sections of the state. The Third Tennessee Cavalry, "surrounded by a greatly superior force," yielded the post of McMinnville, in central southern Tennessee, in October 1863. "The rebels robbed the citizens of pretty much all they had," the colonel of the Nineteenth Michigan reported. "And after they left the First Tennessee Cavalry were sent here, and from what I learn were a nuisance hardly inferior to the rebels. They stabled their horses in public buildings and quartered in the houses."

During Nathan Bedford Forrest's expedition into West Tennessee and Kentucky in the spring of 1864, not only was the Thirteenth Tennessee Cavalry decimated at Fort Pillow, but the Seventh Cavalry was compelled to surrender the post at Union City and allow most of its officers and men to be taken captive. After a later Forrest raid, however, the commander of the Tenth and Twelfth Cavalry could boast, "My command was in the saddle eight days and nights, and marched 230 miles, with frequent skirmishes with the enemy . . . demonstrating to the world that there are no braver or better soldiers than Tennesseeans." [52]

The Tennesseeans had their greatest opportunity to show their quality as soldiers—and to gain at least a measure of revenge against Forrest—when the Confederates under John Bell Hood made a rash attempt to retake Nashville and invade the North in the autumn of 1864. The campaign culminated in the battle of Nashville, December 15–16, during which the forces of George H. Thomas managed not only to repel but practically to destroy the army of Hood. Sharing in the defense of Nashville were four Tennessee Union regiments of infantry and six of cavalry, plus two batteries of light artillery.

Once again some of the units performed better than others. The Tenth Cavalry was not one of the better performers. On the way from Columbia to Nashville, on November 14, General Jacob D. Cox noted in his journal when he came to Lynaville: "It was formerly a village of about thirty houses, most of which were burned a week ago by the Tenth Tennessee Cavalry in revenge for being fired upon by some rebel guerrillas in the neighborhood." The Tenth Tennessee's colonel was placed under arrest, not because he had torched the village but because he had "grossly neglected his duty and disobeyed positive orders to give his personal attention to equipping his regiment." [53]

In the climactic battle at Nashville the Third Infantry "moved forward, driving the enemy in confusion." The Sixth Infantry, enfiladed by musketry fire from behind a stone wall, "charged the wall and captured about 150 prisoners." The Eighth Infantry, together with the

One Hundredth Ohio, "captured four pieces of artillery, which, or at least two of them, were being loaded by the gunners, but they were so closely pressed that they were compelled to abandon them, leaving the charges in the muzzles of the guns."

The First Cavalry scored an even more spectacular coup. When they were engaging some of Forrest's cavalry—troops from the division commanded by Forrest's subordinate James R. Chalmers—a First Cavalry corporal captured one of the Confederate division's battle flags. "The corporal saw the rebel standard bearer, under the direction of a rebel major, trying to rally his men. He determined to have the flag; led a charge, killed the major, routed his men, and secured the flag." 54

But the Twelfth Cavalry, garnering not one but three battle flags, outdid all the loyalist Tennessee units in dramatic deeds. On the first day of the big battle, the Twelfth "captured the headquarters train of General Chalmers, consisting of fourteen wagons with records, clothing, forage, and safe." On the second day, at nightfall, the Twelfth again met cavalry of Chalmers's division, "charged the enemy, broke his lines, scattered them in all directions, and captured Brigadier-General [E. W.] Rucker, then in command of the division."

> Brigadier-General Rucker was captured by Capt. Joseph C. Boyer, Twelfth Tennessee Cavalry, who received a severe blow on the forehead from the hand of the rebel general. In this personal contest Captain Boyer wrenched the rebel general's saber from his hand, who in turn seized and took his, when a Federal soldier, name unknown, shot the general in the arm, causing him to surrender. It was in this mêlée, amidst intense darkness, that the two regiments of Twelfth Tennessee Cavalry, Federal and Confederate, met and mixed in mad confusion, neither knowing the other save by the usual challenge, "Halt, who comes there?" . . . Majors Kirwan and Bradshaw, of the Twelfth Tennessee, charged entirely through the rebel lines with their battalions, and afterward returned by passing themselves as belonging to the Twelfth Tennessee Confederate Cavalry, and in great anxiety to meet the Yankees.

Actually, Rucker was only a colonel, not a general, and he had no Twelfth Tennessee in his brigade, though he did have a Seventh, Fourteenth, Fifteenth, and Twenty-sixth Tennessee.55

While some Tennessee loyalists were helping to drive Hood's army out of the state, other loyalists were similarly disposing of the army of John C. Breckinridge, the Kentuckian who had run against Lincoln for the presidency in 1860. Opposing Breckinridge was Alvan C. Gillem, a native Tennesseean and West Point graduate, with a command that consisted of three Tennessee regiments of cavalry and a battery of light artillery.

On October 28, 1864, Gillem attacked a rebel detachment near Greeneville, Andrew Johnson's hometown. Praising all his men for their gallantry, Gillem reported: "The forces engaged in this battle were about equal on each side and were exclusively Tennesseeans, except the Sixteenth Georgia (rebel) Regiment." The enemy's loss was "not less than 500 in killed, wounded, and captured." Gillem's loss was "8 killed and 18 wounded." But Breckinridge was soon to avenge this defeat.

On November 8 Gillem "sent the Ninth Tennessee Cavalry to Greeneville to insure quiet and give confidence to the people to attend the Presidential election." (The local people voted for Lincoln, but the Tennessee vote was not counted in the electoral college that year.) Breckinridge "collected together all the force at his disposal" and took the offensive. On November 13 Gillem felt compelled to fall back to Knoxville with his entire brigade. "My loss in this retreat," he confessed, "was 6 pieces of artillery with caissons complete, 61 wagons, 71 ambulances, about 300 horses, and probably about 150 men." [56]

"General Gillem was endeavoring to reorganize and refit his command," General George Stoneman observed upon arriving in Knoxville "to take the direction of affairs in that region." Stoneman planned, after accumulating a larger army than was available to Breckinridge, to move into the southwestern corner of Virginia "and thus cut him off from Saltville, and force him across the mountains into North Carolina, and maybe to destroy the salt-works" (an indispensable resource for the salt-poor Confederacy). Gillem was to cooperate in the movement.

On December 10, 1864, Gillem set out from his Knoxville camp with "1,500 picked men and horses" belonging to the Eighth, Ninth, and Thirteenth Tennessee Cavalry. They rode on through snow, freezing rain, and ice to seize one position after another from the retreating enemy. At Wytheville, Virginia, they destroyed railroad tracks and an arms depot. "Among the buildings destroyed was one church, used as a magazine and ordnance store-house, it being considered that its sacred character did not protect its warlike contents." At Saltville, Virginia, "all the buildings in any way connected with the salt-works were burned; the engines and pumps at the wells were destroyed"; and men worked "with sledge hammers breaking the kettles." So Gillem related, and he added:

> Since the occupation of East Tennessee by the Federal forces, upper East Tennessee has been constantly harassed by raids from Southwestern Virginia. It was my aim to prevent a repetition of these raids. . . . I regretted the necessity of giving orders that may cause suffering to non-combatants, but regard this as the most effectual means of protecting the people of East Tennessee . . . and I unhesitatingly gave the orders to desolate the route of the invader.
>
> The conduct of the command, officers and men, has been above praise. For eleven days our horses were not unsaddled; we marched day and night, halting only when it was absolutely necessary to rest and feed; more than 300 of the command were frost-bitten; yet during the entire march not a murmur of complaint was heard from these men.[57]

During the final months of the war, loyal troops under the command of Stoneman and Gillem completed the task of subduing the rebels in East Tennessee and western North Carolina. Involved in these missions were the Eighth, Ninth, Tenth, and Thirteenth Tennessee Cavalry; the First, Second, Fourth, and Seventh Tennessee Infantry; the First Tennessee Light Artillery; and the Second and Third North Carolina Mounted Infantry.

In preliminary operations, the Second North Carolina kept busy looking for guerrillas in the vicinity of Cumberland Gap. One scouting party "killed 12 rebel guerrillas, wounded a number, and captured 10, besides having captured from the rebels 40 horses, some of them saddled," Lieutenant Colonel W. C. Bartlett reported on January 28, 1865. He did not approve of bringing in the ten captured men. "My orders are to shoot a guerrilla whenever and wherever he is found, and not to take prisoners on any account," he said. Meanwhile, east of Knoxville the Third North Carolina, George W. Kirk's regiment, was "scouting to the front most of the time."

On March 22, 1865, the Tennessee and North Carolina troops, together with units from other states, started a general advance to the east. After Union forces reached Boone, North Carolina, Kirk's men remained in occupation there, while Gillem's cavalry went along with Stoneman's raiders and penetrated as far east as Salisbury. At the end of the war Stoneman sent the Eighth and Thirteenth Tennessee, with other troops, to Asheville "to intercept Jeff. Davis and his party" who were erroneously thought to be "on their way west with $5,000,000 or $6,000,000 of treasure, specie, loaded in wagons."[58]

How do Southern Federals compare with Northerners in regard to the number of lives they sacrificed toward winning the war? Surely this is one measure of the Southerners' contribution to the Union's final victory.

More than eight hundred Union regiments lost fifty or more men killed and mortally wounded in action. Only nineteen of the eight hundred regiments came from the South, four of them from Tennessee and the other fifteen from Virginia/West Virginia. This was only about half of a proportional share. Of all the white troops who served in the Union army, around 5.3 percent died in or as a direct result of combat. In the Southern regiments, that figure is half as large.

But these figures are somewhat misleading. They do not take into account the men in Texas, Tennessee, North Carolina, and other Southern states who never joined the Union army and yet died fighting for the Union cause. Consider the example of Texas. Only twelve Texans in the Union army were killed or mortally wounded in action, according to the official records. The records ignore the thirty-two loyalist German-American militiamen who were killed by the pro-Confederate Texas Mounted Rifles while trying to get to Mexico to join the Union army. Also uncounted are the dozens of Unionists who died in Texas at the hands of pro-Confederate military or civilian authorities or mobs.

The records attribute to Northern states the deaths of thousands of Tennesseans, Arkansans, and other Southerners who fought in regiments from those states. So the number of Lincoln's loyalists who died in action or from action is larger than the records indicate.

If total losses are considered—deaths from battle, disease, accident, and all other causes—the Southern Federals sacrificed somewhat more than the Northern. To cite extremes, 15 percent of the loyalists credited to Arkansas, 14.7 percent of those credited to Florida, and 13.1 percent of those credited to Tennessee died from disease, but only 3.3 percent of those credited to Rhode Island did so. Fatalities from all causes amounted to 14.4 percent of the Union army as a whole and 15.1 percent of the white Southerners who served in it.[59]

8   The Unknown Soldiers

*T*HEY HAVE been forgotten, those white Southerners who fought on the Union side. They are the unknown soldiers of the Civil War. In the vast and growing literature of that conflict they remain practically unmentioned. There are historic reasons why this has been so, but it has not been because the men are historically unimportant or undeserving of remembrance. Not at all. They made a difference in the outcome of the war: without them, it would not have ended when and as it did.

The direct military value of the loyalist units varied from one to another, as has been seen. Some regiments fought very well—such as the First Alabama Cavalry, the First Tennessee Cavalry, and the Seventh Virginia Infantry, to mention only a few. But even such erratic performers as the Loudoun Rangers made themselves useful not only by scouting for other Union troops but also by helping to keep Mosby's raiders busy. And the Second North Carolina Infantry weakened the Confederacy by occupying Plymouth and drawing a part of Robert E. Lee's army away from the defense of Richmond, even though Lee's soldiers badly defeated the outnumbered and demoralized North Carolina loyalists.

The Union cause was aided by men who did nothing more heroic than garrison posts or guard bridges at some distance behind the lines—or by men who did their fighting, if any, against Indians on the far frontier. Men of that kind at least made it possible for other soldiers to be released for combat with the rebels. Indeed, anyone who joined the Union army, or who served with loyalist state troops instead, or who merely resisted the Confederate draft helped the cause by depriving the Confederacy of its most desperately needed resource—military manpower.

Lee stated the Confederacy's need for men forcefully in a letter he wrote to the Confederate secretary of war on January 10, 1863. "I have the honor to represent to you the absolute necessity that exists, in my opinion, to increase our armies, if we desire to oppose effectual resistance to the vast numbers that the enemy is now precipitating upon us," Lee said; ". . . every man who remains out of service increases the danger to which the brave men, who have so well borne the burden of the war, are exposed." What provoked Lee to these remarks was the "savage and brutal policy" that President Lincoln had recently proclaimed. Lee was referring to the Emancipation Proclamation; he dreaded the "vast numbers" of freed African Americans whom Lincoln had begun to recruit from the rebel states.[1]

Having issued the proclamation, Lincoln became more interested in recruiting blacks than in recruiting whites in the South. He seemed to think that, in comparison with the black manpower resource, the white loyalist one was approaching exhaustion. "The colored population is the great *available* and yet *unavailed* of, force for restoring the Union," he wrote to Andrew Johnson on March 26, 1863, hinting that it was time for Johnson to start enlisting black as well as white Tennesseeans. "The bare sight of fifty thousand armed and drilled black soldiers on the banks of the Mississippi would end the rebellion at once."

Thereafter Northern governors looked to the South for black recruits who would help fill the quotas of troops and thus enable the states to escape the draft. Lincoln eagerly signed an act of Congress authorizing the states to send their own recruiting agents into areas that Union armies had occupied. This arrangement displeased William T. Sherman while he was carrying on his Atlanta campaign. "I have seen your despatches objecting to the agents of Northern States opening recruiting stations near your camps," Lincoln wrote Sherman on July 18, 1864. Asking him for his "hearty co-operation," Lincoln said he hoped the state agents "would get out substantial additions to our colored forces, which, unlike white recruits, help us where they come from, as well as where they go to."[2]

Lincoln meant that black recruits from the South, unlike white recruits from the North, constituted a double loss for the Confederacy. Their numbers would be subtracted from the enemy's strength and added to the strength of the Union. But Lincoln was overlooking his loyalists, his white recruits from the South. They represented a double loss for the Confederacy even more surely than black recruits did, since the whites composed a part of the Confederacy's *military* potential and the blacks did not: the war was over before the Jefferson Davis government got around to employing blacks as soldiers.

Looking back on the war from the perspective of later years, East Tennesseans were convinced that their region alone, by furnishing as many loyalist soldiers as it did, had had a significant effect on the outcome. "Had its territory been friendly ground for . . . Southern armies," an East Tennesseean suggested in an 1888 book, "and had the ranks of those armies been recruited with the thirty thousand East Tennesseeans who volunteered in the service of the United States . . . the war [might have] been prolonged, to the hurt of the whole country." Two other authors, publishing in 1903, elaborated on the theme: "If the 30,000 East Tennessee troops . . . had been transferred to the Southern army, making a difference . . . of 60,000 men, then add to this difference 10,000 Confederate troops whose services were required to keep the Union people of East Tennessee in subjection and guard the mountain passes, and we find a difference of 70,000 men— a vast army." This expanded army would, indeed, seem to be vast enough that—in augmenting the forces that the Confederates succeeded in raising—it could have enabled the rebels to hold out much longer than they did.[3]

But Tennessee as a whole produced many more loyalist troops than East Tennessee alone claimed credit for, and the total from all the Southern states came to at least 100,000!

The question arises: Should not the number of loyalists be offset by the number of Northerners who fought for the Confederacy? There were, of course, those Federal soldiers who were captured and who, to escape the horrors of Andersonville and other prisons, enlisted in the Confederate army. But they were comparatively few, not more than a few thousand at most, and the majority of them only awaited an opportunity to desert the rebels and rejoin their Union comrades. There were also Confederate regiments that originated in Maryland, Kentucky, and Missouri, though they were not nearly so numerous as the Union regiments that derived from those border slave states.

As for the free states of the North, only a stray individual here and there went to the South to enlist as a rebel soldier. Northerners did not go in groups to augment the Confederate army as regiments, battalions, companies, or even squads. The Confederacy could boast nothing like a First Wisconsin Cavalry, C.S.A.; a Second New Jersey Infantry, C.S.A.; or a battalion of Massachusetts Rangers, C.S.A. The Confederacy had nothing to compare with the dozens of Union regiments that came from Southern states.

Neither could the Confederacy claim a disproportionate number of army officers from the North. Of the 425 men who attained the rank of general in the Confederate army, only 26—or 6 percent of the total—were born and brought up in the Northern (as distinct from the border) states. Nearly all of the twenty-six generals were West Point graduates and career officers who had been stationed in the South, or soldiers or civilians who had married into Southern families, or business or professional men who had relocated to one of the Southern states. Very few Confederate generals had had no Southern connection before 1861. As for the Southern-born officers in the antebellum army, more of them stayed with the U.S. service than resigned to assist the Confederacy.[4]

The South provided approximately as many black as white soldiers for the Union. When those of both races are taken into account, one may note that Louisiana furnished more Federal troops than Rhode Island, Virginia more than Minnesota, and Tennessee more than New Hampshire. The grand total of Lincoln's soldiers from the "Sunny South too, in more colors than one," exceeds 200,000.[5]

The total number of loyalists is at least a fifth as many Southerners as fought for the Confederacy. Confederate troops numbered altogether perhaps 900,000. If 20 percent of that figure is counted twice—both as a loss for the Confederacy and as a gain for the Union—the human potential of the Confederacy, limited enough to begin with, is drastically reduced. Surely that loss in manpower is an important, though overlooked, reason for the defeat of the Confederacy and the preservation of the Union.

Why have historians missed the contribution of Lincoln's loyalists to this result? Part of the explanation lies in the fact that the U.S. government neglected the loyalists, and many of them afterward played down their own roles in the war. To see how this came about, it is helpful to look at the fate of the loyalist veterans in the postwar years.

Throughout the spring, summer, and fall of 1865 the future of the loyalist veterans remained uncertain. They could no longer look to President Lincoln for encouragement and support. Still, they could hope for assistance from President Johnson, who they assumed was just as good a friend. And they could expect help from Ulysses S. Grant, the army's general in chief, who usually gave a sympathetic hearing to appeals from Southern Unionists.

Though the war was over, hostility—if not hostilities—continued between the loyalists and their late enemies. To one of the ex-rebels, it looked as if the war that had "terminated between organized armies" was to be "carried on indefinitely between private citizens."

Some of the loyalists remained in uniform as occupation troops for several months. For instance, four companies of the First Alabama Cavalry, along with the Fourth Alabama Colored Infantry, were assigned to duty in Huntsville, where they policed their fellow Alabamians from May to October. The presence of occupation troops, especially black ones, was a constant irritant to former Confederates.[6]

At times the troops preyed upon the people they were supposed to protect, motivated either by greed or by grudges. "The men who are employed about Chattanooga as scouts, guides, and spies are, as a rule, thieves, and accompany troops who go out from there simply for the chances of plunder," General Lewis Merrill reported in May. "They have most of them been residents of the country, and constantly mislead officers in regard to the character of citizens with whom they are brought in contact by allowing some private wrong or quarrel to influence their statements in regard to them." At about the same time that Merrill made his complaint, General William Jackson Palmer, in command at Athens, Georgia, recommended that Colonel George W. Kirk "be recalled to East Tennessee to prevent his men from pillaging and committing excesses, now that hostilities have ceased."

Some ex-Confederate soldiers were behaving no better. In mid-May there were "still several mounted bands of rebel desperadoes, with their principal camps near Marianna, Fla., and Elba, Ala.," who continued "in arms against the United States Government," according to

General Alexander S. Asboth. In western Florida there were also "lawless bands of deserters from our army, robbing indiscriminately the people of both parties," according to General Andrew J. Smith. As late as the end of June, "deserters from both armies" were still "committing depredations upon the property of both loyal and disloyal men" along the Florida-Alabama border.[7]

"In East Tennessee they are having some trouble," Robert Johnson, in Nashville, informed his father, the President, on May 31. "The Union men will not permit the leaders and others who have persecuted their families to live in that section. A few have been killed—and others badly beaten—but things are getting more quite [quiet] there, and I think will settle down in a short time."

Unionists, however, were not having things entirely their own way even in East Tennessee, as the veterans of the Tenth Tennessee Infantry found while they were waiting to be mustered out in the President's hometown of Greeneville. The men were "pretty badly treated" there, and their colonel requested that they be "ordered to some place" where they would "not be harassed by their *personal* enemies and the enemies of the *State of Tennessee*."[8]

Conditions were still worse for Unionists in West Tennessee. "In Memphis, at the present time," one of them wrote to Johnson on May 29, "there are *three* rebels to *one* Union man, and it is as much as we can expect to be allowed to remain in the State. I tell you the fact, that I am now on my good behavior to the returned rebels, and have to shape my course not as I would, but as may be *expedient*."

Unionists begged Johnson, in vain, to do what he could to compensate them for their wartime losses and punish the ex-Confederates who were responsible. "The conscript officers tracked us with bloodhounds, shot us in the swamps like wild beasts, and when they had decoyed refugee soldiers by a flag of truce gave no quarter," a Floridian wrote. He asked that the secessionists' property be confiscated and that the Unionists be reimbursed for the property they had lost. A North Carolinian who had been drafted into the Confederate army advocated the restoration of "the estates of loyal men" that the Confederates had confiscated and the seizure of the estates of "disloyal men." An Alabamian recalled how loyal men were "hunted down with dogs for the rebel army," were "violently torn from their allegiance and, in effect, rammed like the Sepoys into the cannon of treason and shot like waste powder at the Constitution, the Flag, and the Life of their country." He thought the survivors, including widows and orphans, should be enabled to sue for damages.[9]

The state of West Virginia did allow Unionists to sue. "There is a law here in West Virginia authorizing Loyal Citizens who have lost property or sustained damage by the war to institute suit & recover damages from any one who has aided abet[t]ed or sympathized with the rebellion," a returning Confederate veteran complained to Grant in September 1865. "Under this law I presume there have been at least forty suits against persons living in Hampshire Co." Grant apparently did not bother to reply.

Forty-two other ex-rebels from West Virginia also appealed to Grant without success, though they protested that according to his surrender terms to Lee they should be allowed to return to their homes "and remain there *unmolested.*" "We never in any instance took horses or any other property from union men unless ordered to do so by our commanding officers," they pleaded. Yet suits for "exhorbitant damages" were being "instituted by men who were never in the regular service of the United States—who under the assumed name of State troops or Home Guards received their pay in safety."

Some Unionists in West Virginia, like those in East Tennessee, tried to prevent ex-rebels from returning at all. At a public meeting in Parkersburg they resolved that former residents of the area who had gone "off to the Rebel Army not forgetting generally to clean their Loyal neighbors of horses and such other necessaries as they wanted," and who later had made "raid after raid . . . till there is scarcely a good horse in our county," should not be allowed to "have homes amongst us and . . . be treated as gentlemen." [10]

Though Unionists obtained favorable legislation in West Virginia, they were unable to do so in other Southern states. These, under Johnson's restoration plan, had fallen into the hands of ex-Confederates for the most part during the summer of 1865. "The secessionists are very strong here," an "original Union man" protested to Johnson from Alabama, "& are still disposed to run over the Union men, and are recieving [*sic*] all the offices from the federal officers, & the Provisional Governor [a Johnson appointee]. They make their boasts that, so soon as the Federal soldiers leave, they will kill the Union men." "This State is not now in the hands of Union men," a Pennsylvania-born longtime resident of North Carolina cautioned the Pennsylvania Representative Thaddeus Stevens just before Congress met in December 1865. Disillusioned with Johnson, Unionist veterans found life in the South becoming more and more uncomfortable for them and their families.[11]

Grant personally intervened to provide safety for the family of Henry T. Dixon, whom he described as "a loyal Virginian who was driven out of the state at the beginning of the rebellion, on account of his loyalty. He took service in the Union Army, as paymaster, and continued in it until the close of hostilities." On November 10, 1865, after having resettled in Virginia, "he was murdered by a Virginia ex-rebel officer." He left "a widow and eight children who found their home so unpleasant for them, even dangerous," that Grant arranged for them to move to Washington.[12]

For more than two years after the war ended the seceded states remained under the governments that Johnson had authorized. When Congress met in December 1865, the Republican majority refused to accept representatives and senators from the seceded states, which were left in a kind of limbo. Still, those state governments continued to function. They granted no political rights to blacks, though Lincoln had suggested giving the suffrage at least to black veterans of the Union army. As for white veterans of the Union army, they had political rights but no political power in the South.

Ex-Confederate leaders regained both rights and power once they had received pardons from Johnson, and he issued pardons at a rapid rate. Johnson did not require evidence of past favor to Unionists, but Grant made such evidence the main consideration when he recommended P. D. Roddey, "late a General in the Southern Army," for amnesty. "Gen. Roddey has high testimonials from radically loyal men of Alabama for his humanity and kindness to the families of Union refugees whilst the War was in progress," he wrote to Johnson. "I will also add that whilst I commanded in the West, and when Gen. Roddey was in command of troops about Decatur, I was told that his course towards Union families within his lines, the heads of many of them within our lines and some actually serving in our Army, was most kind and courteous." Johnson promptly pardoned Roddey.[13]

Since they could no longer consider Johnson a friend, and since they certainly could expect no favors from the state governments, loyalists looked to Congress for help. Charles H. Foster, formerly lieutenant colonel of the Second North Carolina Union Volunteers, complained to Vermont Congressman Justin S. Morrill about what the North Carolina government was doing. "The Legislature of this State has passed an act providing for the furnishing of artificial legs & arms to Confederate soldiers of this State who have lost limbs in the Rebel service; and the Governor ([Jonathan] Worth) has officially called upon the Sheriffs of the several counties to make diligent inquiry for such cases," Foster wrote. "How do you imagine Union soldiers feel when they see these gratuities to the Confederates whom they fought while they are themselves 'severely let alone.'"

Foster had been doing what he could for these men, especially by preparing, without charge, their "applications for pensions and arrears of pay & bounty," but the men were "scattered over nearly the whole State," and he was unable to help all of them. So he proposed to Morrill that Congress provide for the appointment of pension agents in all the Southern states—"as a means of discriminating, to some extent, between at least the *fighting portion* of the loyal men of the South and the rebels," because those fighting men had defended the Republic with "constancy and heroism."

> History will do them justice, [Foster continued,] when it shall come to be fairly & fully written.
>
> But their present lot is one of local dishonor & infamy. They are stigmatized as renegades and traitors to the South. . . . The rebellion which they fought to overcome has succumbed, and the Union which they fought to maintain has reasserted its imperial authority. But what recognition or reward have they?
>
> The Republic owes these brave loyalists, or their surviving relatives, a debt not only of gratitude & honor, but of pecuniary compensation. They need immediate relief.

Congress never got around to providing special compensation for the loyalists, though it did allow them the ordinary veterans' benefits, and it finally arranged for pension agents in the South.[14]

"Western North Carolina furnished a quota of officers and soldiers to the Federal army, amounting to about four thousand, amongst whom I was one," the "Late Surgeon 3 Regt N.C. Mt. Inftry (Federal)" wrote to Congressman Stevens from Asheville. After the war these Unionists were being persecuted while former rebels held all the government jobs in the state, he said. Though this veteran wanted no job for himself, he did want to see justice done to the Union veterans.[15]

Witnesses from various Southern states testified before a congressional committee in 1866 to the effect that "without the protection of United States troops, Union men, whether of Northern or Southern origin, would be obliged to abandon their homes." At about the same time a Northerner asked Grant to send troops to the vicinity of Warrenton, Virginia, because he had been cursed as a Yankee and threatened by ex-Confederate soldiers, including "some Mosby's men."

In September 1866 a convention of Northern-born and Southern-born Unionists from the South met in Philadelphia. They denounced the President in a formal address, declaring: "since Andrew Johnson affiliated with his early slanderers and our constant enemies, his hand has been laid heavily upon every earnest loyalist in the South." Most of the delegates also demanded that Congress provide for Negro suffrage in the late rebel states. Especially insistent was an Ohio-born delegate from North Carolina, Albion W. Tourgee. "He argued that it was absolutely necessary in order to protect Union men at the South," the *New York Times* reported. Black enfranchisement would assure "justice, liberty, protection and salvation for the white men of the South as well as for the black men." [16]

"Union men are ostracized and proscribed socially in all parts of these [Southern] States," Tourgee maintained on a speech-making tour after the Philadelphia convention. "Soldiers of the Federal armies are compelled to discard the blue which they have worn with honor, to protect themselves from insult and violence."

It was certainly true that, by the fall of 1866, Johnson had "affiliated with his early slanderers" and gone completely over to what had been the Confederate side. Ex-Confederates considered him their advocate. Supporters of his administration held a "soldiers' convention" in Cleveland soon after the loyalist convention in Philadelphia. The object was to give the impression that Union veterans, too, recognized Johnson as their friend, though most of the delegates turned out to be Democratic politicians. They received a telegram of sympathy and congratulation from ex-rebel officers assembled in Memphis, among them Nathan Bedford Forrest. The Cleveland conventioneers then adopted a resolution thanking Forrest and his colleagues for their "magnanimity and kindness." [17]

Arkansas loyalists appealed to both Grant and Congress to see that the state adjutant general's report was published. Grant told the chairman of the Senate committee on printing that he thought it "due to the troops from that state who served in the Union Army that their services should be placed on record and their history preserved." Senator Henry Wilson of Massachusetts made the following statements when introducing a resolution for the Government Printing Office to issue the report:

> All the loyal States have prepared rosters of the men who served in the loyal army, and they have been published, with the reports of the adjutants general of the various States.
>
> The State of Arkansas furnished over ten thousand men to the loyal army. The adjutant general presented his report, with a roster of those names, to the legislature of that State, which is now under disloyal control, and they have refused to publish it, so that there is no record whatever of the services of these gallant men.

The Government Printing Office duly printed the Arkansas report, and the state of Tennessee published its loyal adjutant general's report, but the loyalists from other Southern states were left without such record and recognition.[18]

Some loyalists faced still other handicaps and hazards in the Southern states as restored by Johnson. Ex-rebels could sue Union veterans for alleged wartime offenses and could win verdicts in sympathetic local courts. An East Tennessee court, deciding against a former U.S. quartermaster, ordered the sale of 320 acres of his land to compensate a man whose bacon he had confiscated to feed Union troops during the war. The former U.S. quartermaster protested to Grant: "Many union soldiers have been prossacuted for acts done under orders & while in the service of the U.S. & the Courts have caused them to pay large costs." Grant asked the attorney general to take charge of the matter, telling him: "The attention of this Department is not unfrequently called to cases of persons against whom suits are brought for alleged trespass while in the performance of public duties under orders from their superior officers of the United States, in States where force was used in the suppression of the rebellion." The attorney general replied that his office referred such cases to the appropriate Federal district attorney "to appear for the defendant." [19]

In 1865 ex-rebels had been held legally accountable for their wartime actions in West Virginia. By 1867 the loyalist veterans were facing and losing lawsuits in other parts of the South, even in East Tennessee. The victors were becoming the victims.

Congress responded to loyalist demands when it passed the Reconstruction Act of 1867. This gave black men the right to vote and hold office (and temporarily deprived leading ex-Confederates of the right) in all the Southern states except Tennessee, which alone among them had ratified the Fourteenth Amendment and consequently had regained full statehood in 1866. The Southern states then had to remake their constitutions and reestablish their governments in conformity with the act.

Congressional Reconstruction brought no lasting good to the wartime Unionists of the South. Some of them combined with recent slaves and with Union veterans from the North to form new branches of the Republican party, which at first controlled the reconstructed states. Other Unionists refused to join the new party and, of those who did join it, many sooner or later turned against it. The opposition, recovering control of one state after another, could boast of a Solid South, completely Democratic, by 1877. What had divided and weakened the Unionists was, in a word, racism.

The division had begun when Lincoln issued his Emancipation Proclamation. Johnson, as military governor of Tennessee, went along with Lincoln's policy, but not all Unionists did so; some even switched their allegiance from Lincoln to Jefferson Davis. Then Johnson, as President, objected to congressional Reconstruction (Congress repassed the act of 1867 over his veto), and many of the remaining Unionists followed Johnson's lead. These people, while grudgingly accepting emancipation, could not stand the idea of political rights for blacks.

The Unionists' internecine conflict came rather dramatically to a head in Texas when the two leading wartime loyalists, Alexander J. Hamilton and Edmund J. Davis, ran as opposing candidates for governor of the reconstructed state. Hamilton, as Johnson's appointee, had been provisional governor under the Johnsonian restoration plan, and at that time he assured Johnson that the Union men of the state were a "unit." In fact, the "unit" was already splitting, since Davis and his followers were accusing Hamilton of pro-rebel leanings. During the Davis-Hamilton campaign Davis's supporters said Hamilton was the candidate of the ex-Confederates. Davis defeated Hamilton for the governorship but rapidly lost the support of white Texans who thought his administration too dependent on black votes.[20]

From the beginning, Republicans throughout the South faced the threat of violence. When some of them became fearful of the former rebel partisan John S. Mosby, Grant requested that a scout be sent into Virginia to investigate. "Mosby lives at Warrenton—his farm, four miles from Warrenton in the mountains," the scout reported on March 10, 1868. "Mosby declares he intends to prevent 'all d———d niggers and yankees' from reenforcing the friends of Congress if any trouble should occur at Washington." (There were rumors that a new civil war was about to break out between the adherents of Congress and the followers of the President.) The scout also told Grant: "Colored men think Mosby is reorganizing his command. His men say colored men shall not vote."[21]

As things turned out, Mosby did not reorganize his command, but Forrest helped to reorganize a rebel army of another sort—the Ku Klux Klan, of which he became the first overall commander, or Grand Wizard. The Klansmen, who pretended to be the ghosts of the Confederate dead, were mainly flesh-and-blood veterans of the Confederate army. In a newspaper interview Forrest said of the Klan: "Its objects originally were protection against Loyal Leagues and the Grand Army of the Republic."[22]

Loyal Leagues were Republican clubs organized in the North during the war and in the South after the war. In the South a number of white Unionists joined the Loyal Leagues, but most of them left the organization during Reconstruction, when the membership became predominantly black. The Grand Army of the Republic was a Union veterans' association that originated in Illinois and spread throughout the country. According to its constitution, it aimed to provide for the "defense of the late soldiery of the United States, morally, socially, and politically." By 1868 there were GAR posts in Tennessee, Alabama, Louisiana, Virginia, West Virginia, Florida, Mississippi, and Texas. In Louisiana and Mississippi the members were mostly black.

In the South, as in the North, the GAR often served as an auxiliary of the GOP, but the members also carried on nonpolitical activities. In Athens, Tennessee, for example, members and their Northern comrades contributed to the support of Grant Memorial University, which the Methodist church established in 1867 for the education of members of loyalist families who "suffered more or less ostracism in the schools of the Old South." [23]

The Ku Klux Klan, in its first major operation under the command of Forrest, went after a Republican leader who was a Georgia native and a Union veteran. State Senator George W. Ashburn had just returned from the state constitutional convention in Atlanta to his home in Columbus, Georgia. On the doors of local Republicans the KKK had affixed posters with threats, among them a sketch of a coffin with Ashburn's name on it. On March 31, 1868, Ashburn was shot and killed. The local authorities made no attempt to "ferret out the guilty," as General George Gordon Meade reported to Grant. Neither "had the people of Columbus evinced or felt any horror of the crime" nor "co-operated in any way in detecting the perpetrators." [24]

The largest postwar confrontation between ex-rebels and ex-loyalists occurred in North Carolina during the state election campaign of 1870. To win the election for the Democrats, the Klan was carrying terrorism to extremes, especially in the counties of Caswell and Alamance. Governor W. W. Holden proclaimed those two counties to be in insurrection and called out the militia, which consisted not of local men but of mountaineers from western North Carolina who had served in the Union army. The governor put the militia under the command of George W. Kirk, the former colonel of the Third North Carolina Mounted Infantry. With his two companies, Kirk pacified Caswell and Alamance and arrested a number of Klansmen. But he had to let them go when they got a writ of habeas corpus from a Federal judge. [25]

In 1871 Congress finally did something for those Unionists who sought reimbursement for property taken or destroyed by Federal armies during the war: it set up the Southern Claims Commission, which spent ten years sifting through thousands of petitions and making awards. But Congress never made any comparable gesture on behalf of those Unionists who had risked or given their lives instead of their property. As Tourgee said in his best-selling novel *A Fool's Errand* (1879), the U.S. government made no offer of encouragement or reward to those who had stood the fast friends of the nation in the hour of its peril. The ingratitude of republics is the tritest of thoughts, but there never was a more striking illustration of its verity. Perhaps no nation ever before, after the suppression of a rebellion which threatened its life, quite forgot the claims of those who had been its friends in the disaffected region.[26]

Many of the loyalist veterans could not even obtain the solace of belonging to the Grand Army of the Republic, which lobbied for pensions and other benefits and provided comradeship and a measure of self-esteem. The GAR refused to admit a single man among the tens of thousands who, after being pressed into the rebel service, had borne arms against the Union only until they could manage to bear arms for it. As the historian of the GAR has written,

> Southern Grand Army members were disposed to be more tolerant than their northern comrades toward those who had deserted from the Confederate forces to join the Union. From time to time they suggested that these men be made eligible for Grand Army membership. The [GAR] Department of Tennessee and Georgia, for example, suggested to the national encampment in 1885 and again in 1888 that the word "voluntarily" be prefixed to the clause banning those who bore arms against the Union. But the majority always vehemently opposed any such concession.

James G. Blaine sagely commented on the fate of the loyalists—and the fate of the Republican party—when writing his survey of national politics from 1861 to 1881. Blaine had been a Republican congressman and senator from Maine and secretary of state; he was about to be the party's unsuccessful candidate for president in 1884. He said:

> The Republicans lost in many of the Southern States a valuable support upon which they had counted with confidence. Union men whom no persecution could break and no blandishment could seduce, were to be found in the South at the outbreak of the rebellion. They were men who in a less conspicuous way held the same faith that inspired Andrew Johnson and William G. Brownlow during the war. It was the influence and example of this class of men which had contributed to the Union Army so large a number of white soldiers from the rebellious States,—numbering in the aggregate

more than one hundred thousand men. Tennessee alone furnished at least thirty-five thousand white troops as brave as ever followed the flag. The Carolinas, Virginia, Georgia, Alabama, all furnished loyal men from their mountain districts; and beyond the Mississippi a valuable contingent came from Arkansas and Texas.

The men who had the courage to stand for the Union in time of war should not have separated from its friends in time of peace. If Reconstruction had been completed according to the first design, on the basis of the Fourteenth Amendment, these men would have remained solidly hostile to the Southern Democracy. But as the contest waxed warm, as negro suffrage become a prominent issue, many of them broke away from their associations and became the bitterest foes of the Republican party. If the whole number had proved steadfast, they would have formed the centre of a strong and growing influence in the South which in many localities would have been able—as in East Tennessee—to resist the combined rebel power of their respective communities.

Blaine overlooked Louisiana, Florida, and Mississippi in listing the Southern states that had provided Federal troops. Still, he gave a valuable clue to the effect that postwar politics had on the later reputation of the wartime loyalists.[27]

It would seem that, in the public mind both North and South, the loyalists who became Republicans were discredited by their association with the so-called Negro-carpetbag-scalawag state governments, which came to be generally (but unfairly) viewed as a national disgrace. Many of the rest—those who followed Johnson and the Democrats in resisting Reconstruction—eventually identified more or less with the ex-Confederates and gave some credence to the myth of the Lost Cause. Men of this kind would not have wished to be remembered as one-time comrades of men whom in retrospect they looked upon as nigger-loving Yankees.

Hatred persisted for many years. As late as 1895 the Tennessee commander of the GAR found that in some localities the Union veteran was still "a stench in the nostrils of his unrepentant neighbors." A little later the Unionist author of *East Tennessee and the Civil War* (1899) declared that, "all over East Tennessee," the mutual hostility had finally disappeared. "Brave Union soldiers and equally brave Confed-

erate soldiers dwell together in peace." With the aging and passing of
veterans of both sides, it is probable that some degree of reconciliation
gradually developed throughout the South.[28]

How this came about is a story that remains to be told.

Except for the East Tennesseans, loyalists received little notice from
contemporaries who wrote books about the war. Loyalists themselves
wrote few, while Yankee veterans published numerous accounts of
their regiments. East Tennesseans produced regimental histories of
the First and Thirteenth Tennessee Volunteers and general histories
such as *East Tennessee and the Civil War* and *The Loyal Mountaineers
of Tennessee* (1888). Former Virginians recounted the experiences of
the West Virginia Second and Fifth Cavalry and Fourth Infantry, all of
which originated as *Virginia* regiments. Two veterans of the First Alabama Cavalry left folksy recollections that appeared in a rather ob-
scure newspaper, and an Alabamian who served in a Northern regiment told his story in a seldom read book.[29]

William T. Sherman acknowledged but did not elaborate on the services of the First Alabama in his *Memoirs* (1875). Very seldom did any
other former Civil War officer, either Federal or Confederate, do as
much for a loyalist unit. Don Carlos Buell, in *Battles and Leaders of
the Civil War* (1887–88), recalled how Unionists had rallied around
his army when it arrived in northern Alabama in the spring of 1862.
In the same series, the one-time Union commander in eastern North
Carolina devoted a long footnote to the execution of North Carolina
loyalists who had fallen into the hands of George E. Pickett. But in
those four big volumes of generals' reminiscences, which became
some of the most cited works in Civil War literature, there is hardly
the slightest hint of the role of Southern Federals in the war.[30]

John G. Nicolay and John Hay, as Lincoln's former private secre-
taries, must have been aware of the President's interest in recruiting
white (as well as black) troops in the South. Yet in all the ten volumes
of Nicolay and Hay's *Abraham Lincoln: A History* (1890) the two
authors said not a single word about the subject. They did not even
mention Lincoln's authorizing Ward Hill Lamon to enlist Virginia refugees. They did mention his sending William Nelson to Kentucky, but
they assumed that Nelson's mission was to recruit only Kentuckians;
they made no reference to Lincoln's and Nelson's expectation of re-

cruiting Tennesseeans. In telling of Lincoln's early preoccupation with East Tennessee, Nicolay and Hay failed to catch the significance, for Lincoln, of recruiting as an objective there.[31]

Benjamin F. Butler personally saw to the enlistment of thousands of Louisianans in his army. At the time, as his official correspondence shows, he looked upon this as an important and praiseworthy accomplishment. When he wrote the autobiographical *Butler's Book* (1892), however, he gave only one sentence to his raising of white troops in New Orleans: "I had gone as far as I could get in enlisting the former soldiers of the rebel army to strengthen the regiments I then had." Having disposed of them (referring only to the deserters he had enlisted), he proceeded to devote several pages to his success in raising black troops; he claimed credit for organizing the very first regiment of them anywhere during the Civil War.[32]

When Thomas L. Livermore, a former New Hampshire colonel, recorded his calculations in *Numbers and Losses in the Civil War* (1900), he paid no attention to the numbers of loyalists except for the Tennesseeans. He asserted: "Those [Southerners] joining the Union army were, with unimportant exceptions, all from Tennessee." He did not take those from West Virginia into account because, like other writers, he viewed West Virginia as a border state rather than a Union fragment of a Confederate state. And he was simply unaware of the numbers who had originated elsewhere in the South. Livermore's book became a standard reference, one cited by practically all Civil War historians who had occasion to deal with numbers and losses.[33]

Since the most influential authorities of the war generation considered them so few and so insignificant, it is not surprising that subsequent historians have paid very little attention to Lincoln's loyalists.

Appendix: The Question
of Numbers

*I*T TAKES a lot of guesswork to arrive at the number of soldiers who fought for the Confederacy. There are no official statistics. It is a little easier to derive a figure for white Southerners who fought for the Union, since the U.S. government tried to keep count of the troops furnished by all the states. But the official count shows only the numbers presumed to have enlisted in units from Alabama, Arkansas, and so on; it ignores those Southerners who enlisted in Northern regiments.

To find out how many did so, the researcher could go to the National Archives in Washington and examine, name by name, the manuscript "cumulative service records" for all the Northern regiments that ever operated in the South. This method would hardly be feasible until those records had been computerized. Even then, a certain amount of extrapolation would be necessary, for on many of the dossiers the soldier's birthplace is not recorded. In the meantime, the only option is to proceed on the basis of such evidence and estimates as are available.

Reporting at the end of the war, the U.S. provost marshal general credited the Southern states for white troops as follows: Alabama 2,576, Arkansas 8,289, Florida 1,290, Louisiana 5,224, Mississippi 545, North Carolina 3,156, Tennessee 31,092, Texas 1,965, and West Virginia 31,872. The provost marshal general did not credit either Virginia or Georgia with any white troops. The official figures come to a total of 86,009.[1]

These numbers refer to *enlistments*. The number of individual soldiers was a bit smaller, since some men enlisted more than once and hence were counted more than once. There were proportionately fewer reenlistments from the South than from the North for a couple of reasons. First, men from the Southern states—except Virginia—did not begin to enlist in the Union army until some time after the outbreak of the war; they did not form three-month regiments in response to Lincoln's very first call. Hence they were less likely to serve out either a three-month or a three-year hitch and thus have occasion to reenlist. Second, Southern enlistees were offered no such munificent bounties as many Northerners were, so they had much less temptation to enlist again and again as bounty jumpers.

When adjustments are made for duplications, the provost marshal general's aggregate of 86,009 will have to be reduced somewhat; yet his figure is much too low to begin with.

The earliest writer on "Southern Federals" went far to the opposite extreme. Charles C. Anderson proclaimed on the title page of *Fighting by Southern Federals* (1912): "the author places the numerical strength of the armies that fought for the Confederacy at approximately 1,000,000 men, and shows that 296,579 white soldiers living in the South, and 137,676 colored soldiers, and approximately 200,000 men living in the North that were born in the South, making 634,255 southern soldiers, fought for the Preservation of the Union."

To arrive at 296,579 white and 137,696 black soldiers, the author included men from the border states of Maryland, Kentucky, and Missouri. He gave no evidence whatsoever for the 200,000 supposedly born in the South and living in the North. His book, the title of which is a complete misnomer, is not about fighting by Southern Federals at all. It is merely a compilation of data on the military careers of Union generals ("and some other southerners who notably aided the Federal cause") who were born in one of the slave states, the vast majority of them in Maryland, Kentucky, Missouri, and the District of Columbia.[2]

The following calculations on the number of Southern loyalists will take into account only the Union soldiers recruited in or from the states of the Confederacy: Tennessee, Virginia and West Virginia, Arkansas, Louisiana, North Carolina, Alabama, Texas, Florida, Mississippi, and Georgia. Also considered will be the rebel prisoners, not identified with any particular state, who enlisted in the Union army.

Tennessee furnished much the largest number of loyalist troops, a number considerably larger than the 31,092 that the U.S. provost marshal general credited to the state. The "Federal roster" in *Tennessee in the Civil War* (1964) lists alphabetically the names of more than 39,000 men, including members of the National Guard. The guard, militia, and other miscellaneous groups served for periods of less than a year, but practically all the thirty-three regiments of regular infantry and cavalry were three-year units. As impressive as the numbers on the Federal roster are, it still falls short of being a complete list.

What the historians of one Tennessee regiment said in 1903 remains true today: "East Tennessee [alone] furnished between 30,000 and 40,000 troops to the Federal army. The exact number could not be ascertained for the reason that before any regular Tennessee organizations were formed many who went through the lines volunteered in the first Federal regiments they found and served to the end of the war in Northern and Western regiments." In January 1865 the Tennessee adjutant general reported, with reference to the "number of Tennesseeans in the [U.S.] army not in Tennessee Regiments," that "7000 would not be an overestimate." If this 7,000 is added to the more than 39,000 on the Federal roster, the sum is more than 46,000. Deducting for a small number of Northerners who enlisted in Tennessee units, for a somewhat larger number of reenlistments, and for a certain amount of exaggeration, a reasonable estimate would seem to be about 42,000.[3]

Virginia and West Virginia together probably furnished slightly fewer than the 31,872 that the provost marshal general attributed to West Virginia (he did not attribute any to Virginia itself). This figure includes some reenlistments. At least a few members of the First Infantry Regiment undoubtedly signed up again at the end of their three-month term. Others, enough of them to form two veteran regiments, reenlisted at the end of their three years. Allowing for reenlistments, West Virginia historians have conjectured: "In all probability the total did not exceed 25,000." But it is hard to believe that more than, say, 2,500 reenlistments took place. This would leave a balance of more than 29,000.

From this balance a further subtraction must be made for men who were credited to West Virginia but who actually came from Pennsylvania or Ohio. Of these, there was the equivalent of somewhat more than two regiments. This deduction is offset, however, by the number of Virginians—somewhat more than two regiments of them—who were recruited by Ward Hill Lamon and then distributed among units from Maryland and Pennsylvania and credited to those states.

Besides Lamon's recruits, there were other Virginians enlisting from counties that were never incorporated in the state of West Virginia. The Loudoun Rangers and others in identifiable Virginia units numbered perhaps 500. Probably another 500, at least, enlisted in Northern units. Add these 1,000 men to the 29,000 net allotted to West Virginia, and the revised total is 30,000.[4]

Arkansas furnished considerably more than the 8,289 troops that the U.S. provost marshal general credited to the state. This figure may be a misprint for the 8,789 that the Arkansas adjutant general accounted for. According to him, the actual total was still larger: "The State of Arkansas furnished more than ten thousand men to the loyal army." This is entirely credible. As a Unionist refugee from the state wrote in 1863, "There is scarcely a regiment from Missouri in which there is not a number of Arkansians, and many are to be found in regiments from other States." Even allowing for reenlistments, which appear to have been very few in Arkansas, the loyalist total would surely amount to 10,000 and more.[5]

Louisiana received credit for 5,224 white troops. This figure, again, includes only those who belonged to Louisiana units. As early as September 1862, Benjamin F. Butler reported from New Orleans that he already had "more than 1,200 men enlisted in the old regiments to fill up the ranks." Later, additional Louisianans undoubtedly filled up the ranks of other regiments from the North. Reenlistments were negligible. Thus a fair estimate for Louisiana would be a total of at least 6,500 and probably 7,000.[6]

North Carolina was credited with 3,156, all of them three-year enlistees. But uncounted numbers from the Piedmont and the mountains made their way to the Union lines and joined regiments from Tennessee, Kentucky, and other states. One contemporary Unionist declared that more than 4,000 did so. Another Unionist estimated that western North Carolina provided all together "about four thousand," including the members of the two North Carolina regiments from that part of the state (and there were, of course, two regiments from eastern North Carolina). Not counting the North Carolinians who joined Tennessee units—and were counted with the Tennessee total—very likely there were 2,000 or more troops in addition to the 3,156 credited in the official records, making an aggregate of at least 5,000.[7]

For Alabama the official figure was 2,576. Some 2,000 of these men served at one time or another in the First Alabama Cavalry. Only about half of the 2,000 were native Alabamians, but almost all the rest were born somewhere in the South. Several hundred other Alabamians enlisted in Northern regiments—among them were approximately 400 who joined the Fifty-first Indiana in July 1862 and 20 who joined the Fourth Indiana in August 1863. All these would bring the Alabama total from 2,576 to well over 3,000.[8]

Texas got credit for 1,965 soldiers in the provost marshal general's report, but the index to the compiled service records of soldiers in the Texas units contains a large number of names—2,164. An estimate of 2,200 would therefore be very conservative, taking into account the Texans who enlisted in Northern regiments.[9]

Florida was credited with 1,290 and Mississippi with 545 loyalists, not counting those credited to Northern states. Only Georgia and South Carolina (besides Virginia) were omitted from the provost marshal general's list of states. Georgia actually furnished a battalion, which numbered perhaps 200, and probably furnished at least another 200 to Northern regiments. Of the members of the First Alabama Cavalry, 271 were born in Georgia, 98 in South Carolina, and 65 in Mississippi, but these, of course, were counted as Alabama troops. The net addition from Florida, Mississippi, and Georgia (including men who enlisted in Northern regiments) would probably amount to more than 2,300.

As for the recruited rebel prisoners, a few hundred of them served in regiments from Illinois and other Northern states and were credited to those states. About 5,000 others were organized as U.S. Volunteers before the end of the war and were sent to the Western frontier. Not all the 5,000 should be counted as additions to Union manpower in the Civil War. Nevertheless, the prisoner recruits relieved Northern troops from frontier duty and made it possible for Northerners to be transferred to the South. The Galvanized Yankees, then, may be considered the equivalent of 2,000 or 3,000 Union troops. If these are added to the prison recruits who fought in Northern regiments, the sum surely would be at least 2,700.

To recapitulate, the estimated contributions of the Southern states to the Union army are as follows: Tennessee 42,000, Virginia and West Virginia 30,000, Arkansas 10,000, Louisiana 7,000, North Carolina 5,000, Alabama 3,000, Texas 2,200, Florida 1,500, and Georgia 400. In addition, about 2,700 rebel prisoners were recruited. The grand total, nearly 104,000, does not include the thousands who belonged to military or paramilitary Unionist organizations that were never mustered into the U.S. service.

Assuming that, at the very least, 100,000 white Southerners served in the Union army, how does this compare with the number who served in the Confederate army? Estimates of Confederate numbers have varied from 600,000 to 1,500,000.

Thomas L. Livermore, in his *Numbers and Losses* (1900), assumed: "Substantially the whole military population of the Confederate States was placed under arms in the War of the Rebellion." This meant "substantially every male white from seventeen to fifty . . . excepting the 87,863 exempts, and those who were in hiding or had joined the Union army." According to Livermore, "Those joining the Union army were, with unimportant exceptions, all from Tennessee," but the number of Tennessee loyalists was offset by the number of Confederate troops from the border states. Making these and other dubious assumptions, Livermore concluded that there were possibly as many as 1,406,180 enlistments in the Confederate army and that the equivalent in three-year men was 1,082,119.[10]

Few if any experts nowadays would agree with Livermore. Albert B. Moore, in *Conscription and Conflict in the Confederacy* (1924), concluded: "The number actually enrolled . . . will probably total 850,000 to 900,000." James M. McPherson, in *Battle Cry of Freedom* (1988), came to exactly the same conclusion: "it seems safe to estimate that somewhere in the neighborhood of 850,000 to 900,000 men fought for the Confederacy."[11]

If as many as 900,000 fought for the Confederacy, the 100,000 who fought for the Union represented a loss of 10 percent of the Confederacy's military manpower. In reality the Confederacy suffered a double loss, since the 100,000 loyalists must not only be subtracted from the strength of the Confederacy but also be added to the strength of the Union.[12]

Notes

1. Virginia Volunteers

1. *The War of the Rebellion: A Compilation of the Official Records of the Union and Confederate Armies*, 128 vols. (Washington, D.C.: Government Printing Office, 1880–1901), series 3, volume I, pages 67–69, 72, 76, 81, 91–92, 99. This compilation is hereinafter cited thus: *OR* 3, I, 67–69, etc.

2. James M. McPherson, *Battle Cry of Freedom: The Civil War Era* (New York: Oxford, 1988), 293.

3. Roy P. Basler, ed., *The Collected Works of Abraham Lincoln*, 9 vols. (New Brunswick: Rutgers University Press, 1953–55), IV, 426–29, 437. Hereinafter cited as *Works of Lincoln*.

4. Richard O. Curry, *A House Divided: A Study of Statehood Politics and the Copperhead Movement in West Virginia* (Pittsburgh: University of Pittsburgh Press, 1964), 50, 58; Warren W. Hassler, Jr., *General George B. McClellan, Shield of the Union* (Baton Rouge: Louisiana State University Press, 1957), 6–7.

5. G. R. Latham to Cameron, May 8, 1861, *OR* 1, II, 630.

6. F. M. Boykin to Lee, May 10, 1861, *OR* 1, II, 827.

7. G. A. Porterfield to R. S. Garnett, May 16, 1861, *OR* 1, II, 855.

8. C. P. Stone to E. D. Townsend, June 19, 1861, *OR* 1, II, 112–13.

9. Peirpoint to McClellan, July 3, 1861, enclosing article dated Columbus, July 1, from the *Cincinnati Gazette*, *OR* 2, II, 15.

10. McClellan to B. F. Kelley, May 26, 1861; to E. D. Townsend, May 27, 1861; and to W. Scott, June 29, 1861, *OR* 1, II, 44–46, 731.

11. Wise to Lee, July 17, Aug. 1, 1861, *OR* 1, II, 292, 1011–12.

12. Burton to Cameron, Apr. 25, 1861, and Patterson to Cameron, Apr. 25, 1861, *OR* 3, I, 114, 110.

13. Lincoln to Scott, May 4, 1861, and editorial note, *Works of Lincoln*, IV, 355.

14. D. M. Shriver to T. J. Jackson, May 19, 1861, *OR* 1, II, 864.

15. Frederick H. Dyer, *A Compendium of the War of the Rebellion* (1908; Dayton, Ohio: National Historical Society, 1979), 1660.

16. *Works of Lincoln*, IV, 353–54.

17. Order to Anderson, May 7, 1861, *OR* 1, LII (1), 140–41.

18. McClellan to Scott, June 6, 1861, and Carlile to Cameron, June 19, 1861, OR 1, II, 666; 3, I, 280.

19. McClellan to Scott, June 29, 1861, and Patterson to E. D. Townsend, July 4, 1861, OR 1, II, 158, 731; Curry, *House Divided*, 53.

20. Lamon to Mrs. George Lamon, May 6, 1861, Lamon Papers, Huntington Library, quoted in Lavern M. Hamand, "Ward Hill Lamon: Lincoln's 'Particular Friend'" (Ph.D. diss., University of Illinois, 1949), 230.

21. Lamon to Lincoln, May 27, 1861, Robert Todd Lincoln Collection, Library of Congress; Lincoln, testimonial for Lamon, June 5, 1861, *Works of Lincoln*, IV, 395; Hamand, "Lamon," 231–33.

22. Lamon to Lincoln, June 18, July 4, 1861, R. T. L. Collection; Lincoln to Lamon, June 25, 1861, *Works of Lincoln*, IV, 416.

23. Lamon to Lincoln, Nov. 20, 1861, R. T. L. Collection; Hamand, "Lamon," 237–51.

24. Curry, *House Divided*, 71–72; Charles H. Ambler, *Francis H. Pierpont, Union War Governor of Virginia and Father of West Virginia* (Chapel Hill: University of North Carolina Press, 1937), 1, 74–76, 117–30.

25. Peirpoint to Lincoln, June 21, 1861, and Cameron to Peirpoint, June 25, 1861, OR 1, II, 11, 723–24.

26. Curry, *House Divided*, 34, 73; Cameron to Carlile, June 25, 1861, OR 1, II, 723.

27. *Works of Lincoln*, IV, 428–29.

28. Carlile to Lincoln, July 8, 1861, OR 3, I, 323–24; Lincoln to Cameron, July 8, 29, 1861, *Works of Lincoln*, IV, 443, 464.

29. OR 3, I, 383–84.

30. Peirpoint to Carlile, Aug. 1, 1861; G. D. Ruggles to Rosecrans, Aug. 1, 1861; J. Lesley, Jr., to Peirpoint, Aug. 3, 1861, OR 3, I, 378, 387.

31. Cameron to the governors, Aug. 19, 1861, and Peirpoint to Cameron, Aug. 19, 1861, OR 3, I, 425, 431.

32. Peirpoint to Rosecrans, Oct. 8, 1861, and W. H. H. Russell to P. B. Stanberry, June 19, 1862, OR 1, V, 615; XII (3), 412.

33. Peirpoint to T. A. Scott, Sept. 9, 1861, and to Cameron, Sept. 9, 1861; Cameron to Peirpoint, Sept. 10, 1861; J. Lesley, Jr., to Peirpoint, Sept. 17, 1861, enclosing a note from J. W. Ripley, Sept. 11, 1861, OR 3, I, 494–95, 497, 524–25.

34. H. J. Samuels to Cameron, Oct. 26, 1861, and to L. Thomas, Jan. 11, 1862; Cameron, annual report, Dec. 1, 1861; Peirpoint to Stanton, Mar. 20, 1862; U.S. adjutant general's report, June 30, 1862, OR 3, I, 600, 698–99, 788–89, 937; II, 183.

35. Francis S. Reader, *History of the Fifth West Virginia Cavalry, Formerly the Second Virginia Infantry* (New Brighton, Pa.: F. S. Reader, 1890), 25, 41–42, 71, 94.

36. Joseph J. Sutton, *History of the Second Regiment West Virginia Cavalry Volunteers* (Portsmouth, Ohio, 1892), 48, 50; Thomas H. Barton, *Autobiography, Including a History of the Fourth Regt. West Va. Vol. Inf'y* (Charleston, W.Va.: Print Co., 1890), 75.

37. J. G. Randall, *The Civil War and Reconstruction* (Boston: D. C. Heath, 1937), 409.

38. Peirpoint to L. Thomas, May 19, 1862, and to Stanton, July 17, 1862, *OR* 3, II, 46, 232.

39. U.S. Constitution, Article IV, Section 3; *Works of Lincoln*, VI, 26–27; Curry, *House Divided*, 6, 10, 46, 111, 122–24, 136–37.

40. Randall, *Civil War*, 410–11.

41. J. Darr to J. B. Fry, May 25, 1863; H. J. Samuels to Darr, May 28, 1863; Fry, endorsement on letter of Darr to Fry, May 28, 1863, *OR* 3, III, 224–25, 235–36.

42. Boreman to Fry and Fry to Boreman, Mar. 4, 1864; Boreman to Stanton, July 23, 1864; Fry to Boreman, July 29, 1864, *OR* 3, IV, 153, 557, 560.

43. Boreman to Fry, Feb. 11, 1865, and to Lincoln, Feb. 25, 1865, with endorsement by J. G. Nicolay, Mar. 9, 1865, *OR* 3, IV, 1166–67, 1198–1200.

44. Lincoln to B. F. Butler, Aug. 9, 1864, *Works of Lincoln*, VII, 487.

45. L. Thomas to McDowell, June 23, 1861, *OR* 3, I, 291.

46. Underwood to Lincoln, Feb. 17, 1862, with endorsement by Lincoln, Feb. 19, 1862, John Curtiss Underwood Papers, Library of Congress; L. Thomas to Underwood, Feb. 15, 1862, *OR* 3, I, 891.

47. Briscoe Goodheart, *History of the Independent Loudoun Virginia Rangers, U.S. Vol. Cav. (Scouts) 1862–1865* (Washington, D.C.: McGill & Wallace, 1896), 1, 9, 23, 24, 26–27, 232.

48. H. Stevens to L. Thomas, Jan. 7, 1863, Hazard and Isaac Stevens Family Papers, microfilm, Library of Congress; Mark M. Boatner III, *The Civil War Dictionary* (New York: David McKay, 1959), 796–97.

49. Undated circular; Stevens to L. Thomas and to "the Public," undated drafts, Stevens Papers.

50. Throckmorton to Stevens, Jan. 4, 1863, Stevens Papers.

51. H. H. Wells to J. H. Taylor, Nov. 19, 1864; F. J. White to W. Hoffman, Jan. 18, 1865; E. D. Townsend, Circular No. 54, Dec. 19, 1865, *OR* 1, XLIII (2), 646; XLVI (2), 174; 3, V, 578.

52. E. Merton Coulter, *The Confederate States of America, 1861–1865* (Baton Rouge: Louisiana State University Press, 1950), 84–85.

53. For the April 1865 report of the provost marshal general, see *OR* 3, IV, 1269. On the organization of West Virginia regiments, see Dyer, *Compendium*, 1655–66.

2. Tennessee Troops

1. Hans L. Trefousse, *Andrew Johnson: A Biography* (New York: W. W. Norton, 1989), 142–43.

2. Cameron to Scott, June 27, 1861; endorsement by Lincoln, June 29, 1861, in Samuel W. Scott and Samuel P. Angel, *History of the Thirteenth Regiment, Tennessee Volunteer Cavalry, U.S.A.* (Knoxville, 1903), 61.

3. LeRoy P. Graf, Ralph W. Haskins, and Paul Bergeron, eds., *The Papers of Andrew Johnson*, 8 vols. (Knoxville: University of Tennessee Press, 1967–89),

IV, 549–50n; V, 13n; Nelson to Seward, June 9, 1861, *Works of Lincoln,* IV, 398 and n.

4. Lorenzo Thomas to Nelson, July 1, 1861; Nelson to Thomas, July 16, 1861, *OR* 1, IV, 251–53.

5. *Johnson Papers,* IV, 518n; Johnson to Cameron, July 6, 1861; Cameron to Johnson, July 8, 1861; Nelson to Johnson, July 11, 16, 17, 1861; Carter to Johnson, July 15, Aug. 2, 1861; G. M. Adams to Johnson, July 23, 1861, ibid., 546, 557, 581–82, 586–89, 594–95, 659.

6. Ibid., 659n; S. P. Carter, manuscript biography, 3–5, microfilm, Library of Congress.

7. Letters to Johnson from B. T. Staples, Aug. 16, 1861; J. T. Shelley, Dec. 28, 1861; and C. L. Johnson, Aug. 8, 1862, *Johnson Papers,* IV, 681; V, 84–85, 599–600; William R. Carter, *History of the First Regiment of Tennessee Volunteer Cavalry* (Knoxville: Gaut-Ogden Co., 1902), 19.

8. Johnson to Welles, Sept. 30, 1861, *Johnson Papers,* V, 12–13; Robert Anderson, Special Orders No. 3, Sept. 10, 1861; Thomas to Anderson, Sept. 22, 1861, *OR* 1, IV, 257, 268.

9. S. P. Carter, manuscript biography, 19; Scott and Angel, *Thirteenth Regiment,* 59–65; Johnson and W. B. Carter to Lincoln, Aug. 6, 1861, *Johnson Papers,* IV, 669–70 and 670n.

10. G. H. Thomas to McClellan, Sept. 30, 1861; L. Thomas to Sherman, Oct. 10, 1861, and to Cameron, Oct. 21, 1861, *OR* 1, IV, 284, 299–300, 313–14.

11. W. B. Carter to G. H. Thomas, Oct. 22, 27, Dec. 23, 1861, *OR* 1, IV, 317, 320; VII, 513–14.

12. G. H. Thomas to Sherman, Oct. 23, Nov. 5, 1861, to Schoepf and to Johnson, Nov. 7, 1861; McClellan to Buell, Nov. 7, 1861, *OR* 1, IV, 321, 339, 342–43.

13. S. P. Carter to G. H. Thomas, Nov. 16, 1861, *OR* 1, IV, 359–60.

14. L. C. Haynes to Walker, July 6, 1861; Harris to Walker, Aug. 16, and to J. Davis, Nov. 12, 1861, *OR* 1, IV, 240–41, 364–65, 389.

15. S. A. M. Wood to Braxton Bragg, Nov. 17, 1861; W. B. Wood to Benjamin, Nov. 20, 1861; D. Leadbetter to S. Cooper, Dec. 8, 1861, *OR* 1, IV, 249–50; VII, 700–701, 747–48; W. G. Brownlow, *Sketches of the Rise, Progress, and Decline of Secession* (Philadelphia: George W. Childs, 1862), 311, 420–21.

16. W. H. Carroll, General Orders No. 4, Nov. 20, 1861; J. C. Ramsay to Benjamin, Dec. 7, 1861; Leadbetter to Cooper, Dec. 8, 1861; H. C. Young to D. M. Currin, Dec. 19, 1861, *OR* 1, VII, 720–21, 744–45, 747–48, 777–79.

17. J. G. M. Ramsey to Benjamin, Nov. 29, 1861; W. G. Swan to Davis, Dec. 7, 1861; S. B. Buckner to W. J. Hardee, Dec. 11, 1861; Leadbetter to Cooper, Dec. 24, 1861, *OR* 1, VII, 721–22, 742–44, 758, 791–92.

18. S. P. Carter to G. H. Thomas, Nov. 20, 24, 1861, *OR* 1, VII, 440–41, 446–47.

19. S. P. Carter to Maynard, Nov. 21, 25, 1861; endorsements by Lincoln, Dec. 3, 1861; McClellan to Buell, Dec. 3, 1861; Johnson and Maynard to Buell, Dec. 7, 1861, *OR* 1, VII, 468–70. See also *Works of Lincoln,* V, 54 and n.

20. McClellan to Buell, Dec. 29, 1861, and Jan. 6, 1862; Lincoln to Buell,

Jan. 4, 6, 1862; Buell to Lincoln, Jan. 5, 1861, *OR* 1, VII, 480, 530–31, 926–28.

21. Trefousse, *Johnson,* 153; Boatner, *Civil War Dictionary,* 586.

22. Stanton to Thomas A. Scott, Mar. 8, 1862, *OR* 1, X (2), 20.

23. E. D. Morgan and A. G. Curtin to Johnson, June 30, 1862, *Johnson Papers,* V, 522–23; Lincoln to Johnson, July 3, 1862, *Works of Lincoln,* V, 302–3; Johnson to Lincoln, July 10, 15, 1862, and Stanton to Johnson, July 16, 1862, *OR* 1, XVI (2), 118–19, 159.

24. Letters to Johnson from Houk, Feb. 18, 1862; Robert Johnson, Apr. 9, 1862, and Daniel Stover, Jan. 12, 1863, *Johnson Papers,* V, 146–47, 280–81; VI, 115–17.

25. Morgan to Fry, July 30, 1862; Buell to Morgan, July 31, 1862; Johnson to Rosecrans, Apr. 11, 1863, *OR* 1, XVI (2), 235, 240; XXIII (2), 228; Trefousse, *Johnson,* 168.

26. Letters to Johnson from L. C. Houk, Dec. 7, 23, 1861; W. R. Tracy, Feb. 6, 1862; W. B. Carter, Feb. 19, 1862; D. W. Trewhitt, Apr. 5, 1862; David Fry, July 2, 1863; and O. W. Keith, Aug. 7, 1863, *Johnson Papers,* V, 40–43, 75, 140–41, 149, 269–71; VI, 258n, 283n, 314.

27. Letters to Johnson from G. A. Gowin, Dec. 21, 1861; Stanton, Apr. 17, 1862; and Maynard, Apr. 26, 1862; Johnson to Stanton, Apr. 10, 1862; to Buell, Apr. 17, 1862; to Morgan, Aug. 7, 1862; and to Lincoln, Nov. 18, 1862, *Johnson Papers,* V, 73–75, 290, 307, 335–36, 398; VI, 64.

28. Gillem to Johnson, Apr. 27, May 14, 1862, *Johnson Papers,* V, 337, 390–91.

29. R. L. Stanford to Johnson, Dec. 31, 1861; Gillem to Johnson, Jan. 10, 1865, *Johnson Papers,* V, 88n; VII, 388; W. Gwin to A. H. Foote, Feb. 23, Mar. 5, 1862; Halleck to Grant, Mar. 1, 1862; Grant to N. H. McLean, Mar. 15, 1862, *OR* 1, VII, 421–22, 674; X (2), 8, 39.

30. Johnson to C. T. Larned, July 17, 28, 1862, and to Stanton, Jan. 10, 1863; Larned to Johnson, Aug. 18, 1862; W. H. Sidell to Johnson, Aug. 28, 1862, *Johnson Papers,* V, 564, 577, 620, 635; VI, 111.

31. J. T. Shelley to Johnson, Dec. 28, 1861; R. L. Stanford to Johnson, Dec. 31, 1861, *Johnson Papers,* V, 84–85, 86–87; S. P. Carter to J. B. Fry, Mar. 9, 1862; Johnson to Stanton, Apr. 23, 1862, *OR* 1, X (2), 23, 118.

32. D. Stover to Johnson, Jan. 12, 1863; D. Fry to Johnson, July 2, 1863, *Johnson Papers,* VI, 115, 283n; Oliver P. Temple, *East Tennessee and the Civil War* (Cincinnati: R. Clarke Co., 1899), 426–27; Scott and Angel, *Thirteenth Regiment,* 423 ff.

33. J. T. Boyle to G. H. Thomas, Dec. 10, 1861; D. Stuart to Halleck, Feb. 25, 1862; Kirby Smith to S. Cooper, Mar. 15, 1862, *OR* 1, VII, 490, 665; X (1), 20–21.

34. Kirby Smith, proclamation, Apr. 18, 1862, *OR* 1, X (2), 640–41.

35. Kirby Smith to R. E. Lee, Apr. 16, 1862, and to T. A. Washington, Apr. 20, 1862; H. L. Clay to J. C. Vaughn, Apr. 18, 1862; G. W. Morgan to O. D. Greene, Apr. 19, 1862; E. Cunningham to C. L. Stevenson, Apr. 21, 1862; W. M. Churchwell, announcement, Apr. 23, 1862, *OR* 1, X (2), 114, 424, 429, 432, 454, 641.

36. McCown to Kirby Smith, Sept. 16, 1862, and to Randolph, Sept. 17, 1862; S. Jones to Randolph, Sept. 24, Oct. 17, 1862, *OR* 1, XVI (2), 836, 841, 868–69, 953.

37. Jones to Randolph, Sept. 19, Oct. 17, 1862, and to S. Cooper, Oct. 18, 1862; C. S. Stringfellow to W. O. Cain, Sept. 21, 1862, and to L. M. Allen, Sept. 30, 1862; S. Cooper to Jones, Oct. 10, 1862, *OR* 1, XVI (2), 851, 858, 930, 953–55, 961.

38. Nelson, address, Oct. 3, 1862; Jones to Randolph, Oct. 4, 1862; Jones to Nelson, Oct. 17, 1862, *OR* 1, XVI (2), 908–11, 957–58.

39. "A Peace Democrat" to Johnson, Nov. 17, 1862; Johnson to Lincoln, Jan. 11, 1863, *Johnson Papers,* VI, 55, 114.

40. Johnson to J. W. Ripley, Dec. 3, 1862, *Johnson Papers,* VI, 83–84; Johnson to Rosecrans, Apr. 11, 1863, *OR* 1, XXIII (2), 228; Trefousse, *Johnson,* 166–67.

41. Johnson to Lincoln, Oct. 29, 1862, *OR* 1, XVI (2), 651; Lincoln to J. N. Fleming and R. Morrow, Aug. 9, 1863, *OR* 1, VI, 373.

42. J. L. Williams and N. G. Taylor to Lincoln, Oct. 15, 1863; Lincoln to Williams and Taylor, Oct. 17, 1863 (emphasis added); Lincoln to Burnside, Oct. 17, 1863, *OR* 1, XXX (4), 401, 448–49.

43. Burnside, General Field Orders No. 10, Sept. 15, 1863; Burnside to Stanton, Oct. 6, 1863, *OR* 1, XXX (3), 660; XXX (4), 143; Burnside to Lincoln, Oct. 22, 1863, *Works of Lincoln,* VI, 521–22; Burnside, Special Field Orders No. 56, Oct. 22, 1863; C. H. Taylor to W. C. Walker, Nov. 1, 1863, *OR* 1, XXXI (1), 235.

44. Rosecrans to Stanton, Sept. 11, 1863; Stanton to Rosecrans, Sept. 11, 1863; E. D. Townsend to Rosecrans, Sept. 14, 1863, *OR* 1, XXX (3), 529–30, 623.

45. R. M. Edwards to Johnson, Sept. 30, 1863, *Johnson Papers,* VI, 389–91.

46. Edwards to Stanton, Jan. 29, 1864; Lincoln to Stanton, Feb. 5, 1864, *Works of Lincoln,* VII, 169–70.

47. Johnson to Rosecrans, Oct. 1, 1863, *OR* 1, XXX (4), 10; Johnson to R. A. Crawford, Aug. 14, 1864, and to Stanton, Nov. 29, 1864, *Johnson Papers,* VII, 95, 321–22.

48. Meagher, General and Special Orders No. 1, Dec. 3, 1864, *OR* 1, XLV (2), 39–40.

49. Hurlbut to Johnson, Sept. 15, 1863, *Johnson Papers,* VI, 368–69.

50. Forrest to J. Davis, Apr. 15, 1864; Johnson to N. J. T. Dana, Feb. 7, 1865; Dana to Johnson, Feb. 19, 1865, *OR* 1, XXXII (1), 611; XLVIII (1), 911–12.

51. Gillem to Johnson, Mar. 11, 1864; Johnson to Stanton, Oct. 7, 1863, and to G. D. Ramsay, Mar. 20, 1864; Stanton to Johnson, Oct. 8, 1863, and Jan. 20, 1864, *Johnson Papers,* VI, 409, 412, 573, 643, 656.

52. Nashville *Dispatch* and *Press* quoted in *Johnson Papers,* VII, 123n.

53. Brownlow to Johnson, Aug. 18, Sept. 7, 1864; Johnson to G. H. Thomas, Aug. 25, 1864, *Johnson Papers,* 101–2n, 139–40 and n; Trefousse, *Johnson,* 170–75.

54. Dyer, *Compendium,* 1643–47.

55. E. S. Richards to Johnson, Jan. 10, 1865, *Johnson Papers,* VII, 385–91.

56. *OR* 3, IV, 1269. Approximately forty thousand names of men in Tennessee Federal units of one kind or another are listed in *Tennessee in the Civil War: A Military History of Confederate and Union Units with Available Rosters of Personnel* (Nashville: Civil War Centennial Commission, 1964), II, 453–608. A total of 33 white Union regiments is mentioned in I, vii–viii.

3. Carolina and Arkansas Recruits

1. John G. Barrett, *The Civil War in North Carolina* (Chapel Hill: University of North Carolina Press, 1963), 39–47; J. E. Wool to E. D. Townsend, Sept. 6, 1861, *OR* 1, IV, 606; Lincoln to Cameron, Aug. 31, 1861, *Works of Lincoln*, IV, 504 and n.

2. Hawkins to J. E. Wool, Sept. 7, 11, 1861; Lincoln to Scott, Sept. 16, 1861; L. Thomas to Hawkins, Sept. 17, 1861, *OR* 1, IV, 607–11, 613; Barrett, *Civil War in North Carolina*, 59.

3. Foster to Seward, Nov. 11, 1861; Seward to McClellan, Nov. 12, 1861, *OR* 3, I, 630–31. For an account of Foster's Civil War career, see N. C. Delaney, "Charles Henry Foster and the Unionists of North Carolina," *North Carolina Historical Review*, XXXVII (July 1960).

4. Hawkins to J. E. Wool, Sept. 19, 1861; R. C. Gatlin to S. Cooper, Sept. 13, Oct. 7, 1861; H. T. Clark to J. P. Benjamin, Sept. 24, 25, 1861, *OR* 1, IV, 617–19, 648–50, 657, 671–72.

5. Wayne K. Durrill, *War of Another Kind: A Southern Community in the Great Rebellion* (New York: Oxford University Press, 1990), 43–44, 53–56, 67; S. C. Rowan to G. Welles, Sept. 5, 1861, and to L. M. Goldsborough, Mar. 29, 1862, *Official Records of the Union and Confederate Navies in the War of the Rebellion*, 30 vols. (Washington, D.C.: Government Printing Office, 1894–1922) VI, 175 hereafter cited as *ORN*; VII, 178; Burnside to Stanton, May 5, 1862, *OR* 1, IX, 385.

6. Flusser to Rowan, May 19, 1862, and Rowan to Goldsborough, June 12, 1862, *ORN* VII, 391, 476; Rush C. Hawkins, "Early Coast Operations in North Carolina," in *Battles and Leaders of the Civil War*, 4 vols., ed. R. U. Johnson and C. C. Buel (New York: The Century Co., 1887–88), I, 658–59.

7. Burnside to Stanton, May 30, June 9, 1862; Stanton to Burnside, June 9, 1862, *OR* 1, IX, 394, 397–99.

8. Benjamin to Clark, Sept. 23, 1861, *OR* 1, IV, 655; John Pool to Vance, Sept. 18, 1862, Frontis W. Johnston, ed., *The Papers of Zebulon Baird Vance, Vol. I: 1843–1862* (Raleigh: N.C. State Department of Archives and History, 1963), 199–200; Durrill, *War of Another Kind*, 186–87.

9. Stanton to Stanly, June 3, 1862, and Stanly to Stanton, June 12, 1862, *OR* 1, IX, 395–96, 399–402; Norman D. Brown, *Edward Stanly: Whiggery's Tarheel "Conqueror"* (University: University of Alabama Press, 1974), 224, 242–49; Barrett, *Civil War in North Carolina*, 127–28, 173 and n; Durrill, *War of Another Kind*, 105–8, 118.

10. J. G. Foster, Return of the Eighteenth Army Corps, Jan. 31, 1863, *OR* 1, XVII, 533; J. A. Hedrick to B. J. Hedrick, Oct. 13, 1862 [1863?], quoted in Barrett, *Civil War in North Carolina*, 174n.

11. J. J. Peck to R. S. Davis, Apr. 14, 1864, *OR* 1, XXX, 870–71.

12. Flusser to Rowan, May 18, 1862, *ORN* VII, 384.

13. This account of Piedmont Unionism is derived from William T. Auman and David D. Scarboro, "The Heroes of America in Civil War North Carolina," and William T. Auman, "Neighbor against Neighbor: The Inner Civil War in the Randolph County Area of Confederate North Carolina," *North Carolina Historical Review,* LVIII (October 1981): 332–34, and LXI (January 1984), 64, 66–67, 77–78, 81, 87, 89–90, 92.

14. C. S. Stringfellow to G. N. Folk, Oct. 13, 1862; Schofield to Stanton, Feb. 12, 1864; Henry Curtis, Jr., Special Orders No. 44, Feb. 13, 1864; Stanton to Schofield, Feb. 15, 1864; organization of troops, Apr. 30, 1865, *OR* 1, XVI (1), 940; XLIX (2), 538; LII (1), 517; *OR* 3, IV, 96, 101.

15. J. W. McElroy to Vance, Apr. 12, 1864, *OR* 1, LIII, 326–27.

16. C. N. Allen to P. Mallett, June 29, 1864; Mallett to T. H. Holmes, July 1, 1864; J. B. Palmer to Holmes, July 4, 1864; J. C. Merrill to J. A. Seddon, July 13, 1864, *OR* 1, XXXIX (1), 235–37; *OR* 2, VII, 465–66.

17. Schofield to Sherman, July 21, 1864, and Sherman to Schofield, July 21, 1864, *OR* 1, XXXIX (1), 232–33.

18. J. K. Miller to Andrew Johnson, Jan. 30, 1865, *Johnson Papers,* VII, 446–47 and n.

19. J. G. Martin to W. H. Taylor, Mar. 6, 1865; Lee to Seddon, Mar. 19, 1865; D. Tillson to G. M. Bascom, May 18, 1865, *OR* 1, XLIX (1), 338–39, 1034–35.

20. *OR* 3, IV, 1269; Philip S. Paludan, *Victims: A True Story of the Civil War* (Knoxville: University of Tennessee Press, 1981), 58–59.

21. Rector to Davis, Nov. 28, 1861, and to J. P. Benjamin, Dec. 3, 1861; Benjamin to Rector, Dec. 5, 1861, *OR* 2, II, 1399, 1402–3.

22. Curtis to W. S. Ketchum, May 5, June 16, 24, 1862; Halleck to Curtis, May 12, 1862, and to Stanton, June 8, 1862; Stanton to Halleck, June 8, 1862, *OR* 1, XIII, 369, 378, 423, 433–34, 447.

23. [James W. Demby], *Mysteries and Miseries of Arkansas; or, a Defence of the Loyalty of the State,* by a Refugee (St. Louis: the Author, 1863), 11, 36–41; Dyer, *Compendium,* 999.

24. White to Yates, May 25, 1862; Yates to Lincoln, June 6, 1862; Lincoln to Stanton, June 11, 1862, *OR* 3, II, 70–71.

25. L. Thomas to Harrison, June 16, 1862; to Morgan, June 30, 1862; and to Brown, July 14, 1862, *OR* 3, II, 958–59.

26. Brown to J. M. Schofield, June 22, 27, July 5, 14, Aug. 10, 17, 1862, *OR* 1, XIII, 444–45, 451–52, 463, 470–71, 554, 580–81.

27. Stanton to Phelps, July 19, 1862; Halleck to Phelps, Aug. 21, 1862, *OR* 3, II, 233, 429; [Demby], *Mysteries and Miseries of Arkansas,* 42–48; Dyer, *Compendium,* 998.

28. Troops in the Department of the Missouri, Nov. 20, 1862; Volunteer Forces of the United States, Nov. 21, 1862, *OR* 1, XIII, 812; *OR* 3, II, 859.

29. Schofield to Phelps, Jan. 2, 1863; Harrison to Phelps, Jan. 27, 1863, *OR* 1, XXII (2), 8, 78.

30. Albert W. Bishop, *Loyalty on the Frontier, or Sketches of Union Men of the South-West; with Incidents and Adventures in Rebellion on the Border* (St. Louis: R. P. Studley and Co., 1863), 9–10, 210.

31. [Demby], *Mysteries and Miseries of Arkansas*, 35, 43.

32. W. H. Pierre to Curtis, Jan. 13, 1863, and W. A. Phillips to Curtis, Mar. 9, 1863, OR 1, XXII (2), 36–37, 149.

33. Cloud to J. McNeil, Sept. 20, 1863; Holland to Sanborn, Feb. 17, 1864, OR 1, XXII (1), 602–4; XXXIV (1), 89; XXXIV (2), 387.

34. This account is based on testimony and reports in 41st Congress, 2d session, *House Executive Document No. 244* (Washington, D.C.: Government Printing Office, 1870), 1–46.

35. *Report of the Adjutant General of Arkansas, for the Period of the Late Rebellion, and to November 1, 1866* (Washington, D.C.: Government Printing Office, 1867), 5, 250.

36. J. Stuart, report of expedition to Huntsville, Dec. 21–23, 1862, OR 1, XXII (1), 165.

37. Murphy to Lincoln, Mar. 22, 26, 1864; J. B. Fry to F. Steele, Apr. 18, 1864; Stanton to Murphy, Mar. 30, 1864, OR 3, IV, 204, 232–33, 210.

38. Murphy to Lincoln, June 29, 1864 (two letters), OR 3, IV, 460–63.

39. W. R. Judson, General Orders No. 4, Apr. 8, 1864; E. A. Carr, General Orders No. 28, Aug. 19, 1864, OR 1, XXXIV (3), 162–63; XLI (2), 770–71; *Report of the Adjutant General of Arkansas*, 6.

40. Flanagin to Davis, Aug. 11, 1864; Davis to J. A. Seddon, Sept. 10, 1864; Seddon to S. Cooper, Oct. 10, 1864, OR 1, XLI (2), 1054–57.

41. J. W. Orr to Murphy, Feb. 25, 1865; Harrison to Murphy, Mar. 15, 1865; Harrison to Sanborn, Mar. 29, 1865, OR 1, XLVIII (1), 931–33, 1177–79, 1293–94.

42. OR 3, IV, 1269; *Report of the Adjutant General of Arkansas*, 1, 6, 256.

4. Enlistees from Other States

1. John D. Winters, *The Civil War in Louisiana* (Baton Rouge: Louisiana State University Press, 1963), 58, 73, 84, 86, 101–2.

2. Butler to Stanton, May 16, Aug. 14, 1862, and to Halleck, Aug. 27, 1862; L. Thomas to Butler, June 23, 1862; Stanton to Butler, June 23, 1862, OR 1, XV, 424, 493–94, 548–49, 555; Winters, *Civil War in Louisiana*, 142–43.

3. Butler to J. W. Phelps, Aug. 2, 1862, and to Halleck, Aug. 27, 1862, OR 1, XV, 536, 556; Benjamin Quarles, *The Negro in the Civil War* (Boston: Little, Brown, 1953), 115–16.

4. Butler to Stanton, Sept. 1862 (received Sept. 11, 1862), OR 1, XV, 559.

5. Banks, General Orders No. 70, Sept. 28, 1863; Banks to Halleck, Oct. 16, 1863, OR 1, XXVI (1), 740–41, 766–67.

6. C. P. Stone to W. B. Franklin, Oct. 28, 1863, OR 1, XXVI (1), 778.

7. Hurlbut to Hahn, Dec. 1, 1864, OR 1, XLI (4), 737.

8. B. B. Campbell to J. G. Clark, Feb. 10, 1865, OR 1, XLVIII (1), 802–3.

9. OR 3, IV, 1269.

10. W. H. Brewin to J. S. Ford, Nov. 7, 1861; Ford to D. C. Stith, Nov. 11, 1861, *OR* 1, IV, 131–32, 137; James Marten, *Texas Divided: Loyalty and Dissent in the Lone Star State, 1856–1874* (Lexington: University Press of Kentucky, 1990), 122–23.

11. Claude Elliott, "Union Sentiment in Texas, 1861–1865," *Southwestern Historical Quarterly,* L (April 1947), 453–55, 459–60, 462–66.

12. H. E. McCulloch to S. B. Davis, Mar. 25, 31, 1862; C. D. McRae to E. F. Gray, Aug. 18, 1862, *OR* 1, IX, 614–16, 704–6.

13. L. Pierce to Seward, Mar. 1, May 5, 1862; C. B. H. Blood to Seward, May 23, 1862; Seward to Stanton, July 11, 18, 1862, *OR* 1, IX, 674, 684–86; XV, 522.

14. On Davis and Hamilton, see Marten, *Texas Divided,* 76; Frank H. Smyrl, "Texans in the Federal Army, 1861–1865," *Southwestern Historical Quarterly,* LXV (October 1961), 235, 239–40; D. W. C. Baker, comp., *A Texas Scrap-Book* (New York: A. S. Barnes, 1875), 295–97.

15. Lincoln to Stanton, Aug. 4, 1862, and editorial note, *Works of Lincoln,* V, 357.

16. G. S. Denison to Chase, May 15, Sept. 19, 1862, *Diary and Correspondence of Salmon P. Chase (Annual Report of the American Historical Association for the Year 1902,* vol. II, Washington, D.C.: Government Printing Office, 1903), 298–301, 314–15.

17. Quoted in John R. Adkins, "The Public Career of Andrew Jackson Hamilton" (M.A. thesis, University of Texas, Austin, 1947), 39–40.

18. Chase diary, Oct. 5, 6, 1862, *Diary and Correspondence,* 101–2; Ludwell Johnson, *Red River Campaign: Politics and Cotton in the Civil War* (Baltimore: Johns Hopkins Press, 1958), 14–17, 19–22; Fred H. Harrington, *Fighting Politician: Major General N. P. Banks* (Philadelphia: University of Pennsylvania Press, 1948), 85–87.

19. Denison to Chase, Oct. 27, 1862, *Diary and Correspondence,* 328.

20. Butler to L. Pierce, Oct. 30, Nov. 8, 1862, *OR* 1, XV, 588, 591–92.

21. Banks to Burrell, Dec. 1862, and to Halleck, Jan. 7, 1863, *OR* 1, XV, 201–2; Johnson, *Red River Campaign,* 26–28; Marten, *Texas Divided,* 66.

22. Burt to Banks, Jan. 7, 1863, and L. Bach to Banks, Jan. 7, 1863, *OR* 1, XV, 202–4.

23. Hamilton to Banks, Jan. 19, 1863; Bee to A. G. Dickinson, Mar. 11, 15, 1863, *OR* 1, XV, 658, 1013–14, 1016–17.

24. Bee to E. P. Turner, Oct. 28, 1863, and to M. Ruiz, Oct. 28, 1863, *OR* 1, XXVI (1), 447–51; Marten, *Texas Divided,* 126.

25. Dana to C. P. Stone, Dec. 2, 1863; Banks to Herron, Dec. 25, 1863; Davis to E. O. C. Ord, Feb. 10, 1864, *OR* 1, XXVI (1), 830–31, 880–81; XXXIV (2), 287–89; Marten, *Texas Divided,* 116, 126.

26. Herron to Lincoln, May 25, 1864; J. B. Fry to E. R. S. Canby, July 6, 1864, *OR* 3, IV, 409, 474–75; Marten, *Texas Divided,* 71.

27. Carleton to Banks, Dec. 25, 1863; Banks to Herron, Dec. 25, 1863; McCulloch to J. B. Magruder, Jan. 23, 1864, and to Kirby Smith, Feb. 5, 1864, *OR* 1, XXVI (1), 879–81; XXXIV (2), 909, 945.

28. *OR* 3, IV, 1269; Marten, *Texas Divided,* 75; Elliott, "Union Sentiment in Texas," 450.

29. R. P. Blount to Benjamin, Jan. 19, 1862, and B. R. Johnson to T. Jordan, Apr. 21, 1862, *OR* 1, VII, 840; X (2), 431.

30. J. B. Fry to G. H. Thomas, July 11, 1862, and to T. J. Wood, July 11, 1862; O. P. Morton to E. M. Stanton, May 11, 1863, *OR* 1, XVI (2), 124–25; *OR* 2, V, 589.

31. Buell, Special Orders No. 106, July 18, 1862; Buell to Stanton, July 19, 1862; Stanton to Buell, July 21, 1862; J. M. Wright to Major Sidell, Aug. 8, 1862, *OR* 1, XVI (2), 182, 288; *OR* 3, II, 233, 235.

32. E. M. McCook to W. H. Sinclair, Aug. 26, 1863; J. A. Garfield to J. H. King, Sept. 4, 1863; Rosecrans to E. D. Townsend, Sept. 11, 1863, *OR* 1, XXX (3), 179, 343, 529.

33. Dodge to Stanton, Jan. 9, 1864; to W. T. Sherman, Jan. 12, 1864; to T. S. Bowers, Jan. 29, 1864; and to J. B. McPherson, Apr. 6, 1864, *OR* 1, XXXII (2), 74, 255–56; XXXII (3), 274; *OR* 3, IV, 16–17.

34. M. L. Smith to R. R. Townes, Feb. 5, 1864, *OR* 1, XXXII (1), 128–29.

35. Lincoln to Stanton, Nov. 16, 1864, *Works of Lincoln,* VIII, 112.

36. Provost marshal general's report, Apr. 1865, *OR* 3, IV, 1269; D. M. Emerson to J. Peetz, Jan. 28, 1863; E. F. Winslow to Lieut. Noyes, Nov. 29, 1864; organization of troops, Department of Mississippi, Dec. 31, 1864; District of East Tennessee, Apr. 30, 1865, *OR* 1, XXIV (1), 331–32; XLI (4), 987–88; XLV (1), 1147; XLIX (2), 540; William S. Hoole, *Alabama Tories: The First Alabama Cavalry, U.S.A., 1862–1865* (Tuscaloosa, Ala.: Confederate Publishing Co., 1960), 14–18.

37. H. Brown to E. D. Townsend, Sept. 10, 1861; H. G. Wright to A. B. Ely, Apr. 13, 1862; J. Milton to J. Davis, Sept. 23, 1862, *OR* 1, VI, 124–25, 666; *OR* 4, II, 92–93; William H. Nulty, *Confederate Florida: The Road to Olustee* (Tuscaloosa: University of Alabama Press, 1990), 36–37 and *passim.*

38. C. P. Stone to Asboth, Oct. 29, 1863; Asboth to Stone, Dec. 27, 1863; S. M. Eaton to C. T. Christensen, Jan. 13, 1865; organization of troops, Dec. 31, 1863, *OR* 1, XXVI (1), 780–81, 886–87, 896; XLVIII (1), 508.

39. Saxton to Stanton, Mar. 14, 1863, *OR* 1, XIV, 226. In April 1865 the U.S. provost marshal general credited Florida with 1,290 white and 1,044 black troops. *OR* 3, IV, 1269–70.

40. H. D. Capers to J. L. Cross, Mar. 27, 1864; W. G. Barth to W. M. Gardner, Mar. 30, 1864, *OR* 1, XXXV (2), 390–91; LIII, supplement, 316–21.

41. J. P. Hatch to J. W. Turner, Apr. 3, 1864; J. G. Foster, General Orders No. 82, June 6, 1864, *OR* 3, IV, 212–13, 419–20.

42. Organization of troops, Apr. 30, 1865; provost marshal general's report, Apr. 1865, *OR* 1, XLVIII (2), 260; *OR* 3, IV, 1269.

5. Galvanized Yankees

1. Coulter, *Confederate States,* 479–80; McPherson, *Battle Cry of Freedom,* 791–92; Randall, *Civil War and Reconstruction,* 437–39.

2. Halleck to Lorenzo Thomas, Mar. 1, 1862; W. Hoffman to Thomas, Oct. 11, 1862, with endorsement by J. C. Kelton, Oct. 27, 1862, OR 2, I, 170; IV, 615–16.

3. Stanton to R. Murray, July 10, 1862; O. P. Morton to Halleck, Aug. 5, 1862, OR 2, IV, 162–63, 343.

4. W. F. Lynch to N. H. McLean, Feb. 4, 1863; G. Sawin to McLean, Feb. 4, 1863; Thielemann to W. Hoffman, Feb. 19, 1863; Hoffman to Thielemann, Feb. 25, 1863, OR 2, V, 240–41, 297.

5. H. W. Freedley to W. Hoffman, Mar. 11, 1863; W. H. Ludlow to Stanton, Apr. 7, 1863; P. H. Watson to Ludlow, Apr. 7, 1863; Hoffman to A. E. Burnside, June 20, 1863; Burnside to S. P. Carter, June 20, 1863; Hoffman to J. M. Schofield, Aug. 5, 1863, and to W. S. Rosecrans, Aug. 7, 1863; J. B. Fry to Stanton, Feb. 27, 1865; OR 2, V, 395, 446; VI, 31, 178, 186; OR 3, IV, 1202–4; D. Alexander Brown, *The Galvanized Yankees* (Urbana: University of Illinois Press, 1963), 64–65.

6. C. Goddard to J. P. Brownlow, Aug. 30, 1863, OR 1, XXX (3), 230–31; Brown, *Galvanized Yankees,* 65.

7. G. Marston to W. Hoffman, Oct. 7, 1863; Butler to Stanton, Dec. 27, 1863, OR 2, VI, 356–57, 768; Butler, *Butler's Book* (Boston: A. M. Thayer & Co., 1892), 584.

8. Lincoln to Butler, Jan. 2, 1864; Stanton to Butler, Jan. 2, 1864; Butler to G. Marston, Jan. 9, 1864; Butler, Special Orders No. 11, Jan. 11, 1864; Butler to W. Hoffman, Mar. 11, 1864; J. B. Fry to Butler, Mar. 24, 1864, OR 2, VI, 808, 823, 826, 1033–34, 1090; Brown, *Galvanized Yankees,* 67.

9. Clark to Benjamin, Sept. 25, 1861; E. C. Sanders to J. G. Foster, Apr. 24, 1863, OR 1, IV, 649–50; OR 2, VI, 518–20.

10. Shorter to Seddon, May 8, 1863; Morton to Stanton, May 11, 1863; Hitchcock to Stanton, May 21, 1863; Seddon to Shorter, May 23, June 8, 1863; Yates to Stanton, May 29, 1863; Hitchcock to Stanton, June 8, 1863; Streight, report, Dec. 10, 1864, OR 1, XXIII (1), 284–95; OR 2, V, 589–90, 716, 946–47, 955–56, 969.

11. Coulter, *Confederate States,* 467–68.

12. Diaries of Lieut. William T. Mumford, Mar. 6, 1863, Mobile Museum Department, Mobile, Ala.; George N. Carpenter, *History of the Eighth Regiment Vermont Volunteers* (Boston: Deland & Barta, 1886), 66; Winters, *Civil War in Louisiana,* 155–56. Notes courtesy of Art Bergeron.

13. Boatner, *Civil War Dictionary,* 651–52.

14. Peck to Pickett, Feb. 11, 13, 20, 27, 1864; Pickett to Peck, Feb. 16, 17, 1864; Butler to Grant, Apr. 14, 1864, OR 1, XXXIII, 865–70.

15. Grant to Johnston, Feb. 26, 1864, and to Pickett, July 18, 1864; Pickett to Grant, Mar. 12, 1866; Grant to Johnson, Mar. 1, 16, 1866, *Grant Papers,* X, 155–56; XI, 448; XVI, 85–86; Pickett to Johnson, June 1, 1865, *Johnson Papers,* VIII, 164–65; E. D. Townsend to Stanton, May 1, 1866; Stanton to S. Colfax, May 2, 1866, OR 2, VIII, 903–4; Rush C. Hawkins, *An Account of the Assassination of Loyal Citizens of North Carolina* (New York: J. H. Folan, 1897), 13, 16, 21–23. The relevant documents were published in 31st Congress,

1st session, *House Executive Document No. 98* (Washington, D.C.: Government Printing Office, 1866), 10–89.

16. I. Vogdes to J. W. Shaffer, Aug. 4, 1864; Grant to Halleck, Aug. 9, 1864, *OR* 1, XL (1), 820–21; XLI (2), 619; *Grant Papers*, XI, 385–86; Brown, *Galvanized Yankees*, 72.

17. Lincoln to Huidekoper, Sept. 1, 1864; to Stanton, Sept. 20, 1864; to Grant, Sept. 22, 1864; and to J. B. Fry, Oct. 8, 1864; S. N. Pettis to Lincoln, Sept. 26, 1864, *Works of Lincoln*, VII, 530–31.

18. Halleck to Pope, Aug. 11, 1864; Pope to Sibley, Aug. 23, 1864; Pope to Halleck, Sept. 17, 1864; Butler to Stanton, Sept. 20, 1864; Grant to Stanton, Sept. 25, 1864; Sibley to J. F. Meline, Oct. 6, 1864; Pope to Halleck, Oct. 12, 1864; Halleck to Grant, Oct. 15, 1864, *OR* 1, XXXII, 948; XLI (2), 662, 831; XLI (3), 236, 677; *Grant Papers*, XI, 385–86.

19. A. J. Johnson to J. B. Fry, Nov. 18, 1864; Pope to Halleck, Feb. 6, 1865; Halleck to Pope, Feb. 6, 1865, *OR* 1, XLVIII (1), 760–61; *OR* 3, IV, 940–41.

20. Grant to Halleck, Dec. 7, 1864; Halleck to Grant, Dec. 8, 1864, *Grant Papers*, XIII, 79; A. J. Bahney to H. W. Wessells, Jan. 5, 1865; E. A. Hitchcock endorsement, Jan. 14, 1865, *OR* 3, IV, 1037.

21. Dodge to J. M. Bell, Mar. 5, 1865; Pope to Halleck, Mar. 11, 1865; T. M. Vincent to Pope, Mar. 23, 1865, *OR* 1, XLVIII (1), 1151; *OR* 2, VIII, 358–59, *OR* 3, IV, 1252. A sixth regiment of U.S. Volunteers was raised and sent to the West after the Civil War had ended.

22. Seddon to Pemberton, Mar. 7, 1863; S. Jones to B. Bragg, Sept. 13, 1864, and to Seddon, Sept. 30, 1864; Seddon to M. J. Wright, Sept. 30, 1864; *OR* 2, V, 845; VII, 821–22; *OR* 4, III, 694.

23. W. D. Pickett to W. J. Hardee, Oct. 12, 1864; W. M. Gardner to S. Cooper, Nov. 2, 1864; D. W. Vowles, report, Nov. 8, 1864; J. G. Foster to Halleck, Nov. 11, 12, 1864, *OR* 2, VII, 972–74, 1086, 1120–23.

24. Lee to Seddon, Nov. 14, 1864; Seddon to Lee, Nov. 17, 1864, *OR* 4, III, 822–25.

25. Hardee to S. Cooper, Dec. 24, 1864, *OR* 2, VII, 1268. See also *Battles and Leaders*, IV, 669n.

26. J. W. Noble to J. S. Little, Jan. 13, 1865; Grierson, report, Jan. 14, 1865; Dodge to J. M. Bell, Mar. 5, 1865; Pope to Halleck, Mar. 11, 1865, *OR* 1, XLV (1), 847; XLVIII (1), 1151; *OR* 2, VIII, 124–26, 358–59; Brown, *Galvanized Yankees*, 122.

27. J. B. Hoge to D. H. Maury, Jan. 10, 1865; York to Lee, Jan. 17, 1865; Hardee, Special Orders No. 38, Feb. 14, 1865, *OR* 4, III, 1011–12, 1029–30, 1083.

6. What Manner of Men

1. Brownlow, *Sketches of the Rise, Progress, and Decline of Secession*, 273–74.

2. J. Pool to Z. Vance, Sept. 18, 1862, *Vance Papers*, I, 199–200; R. S. Garnett to G. Deas, July 1, 1861; S. A. M. Wood to B. Bragg, Nov. 17, 1861; D. Leadbetter to S. Cooper, Dec. 8, 1861, *OR* 1, II, 239; IV, 249; VII, 747.

3. Beth G. Crabtree and James W. Patton, *"Journal of a Secesh Lady": The Diary of Catherine Ann Devereux Edmondston, 1860–1866* (Raleigh: N.C. Division of Archives and History, 1979), 242–43, 290–91n.

4. Durrill, *War of Another Kind,* 229–30, 235–40.

5. Burnside to Stanton, May 5, 1862, OR 1, IX, 385; Reader, *History of the . . . Second Virginia Infantry,* 26–39; Smyrl, "Texans in the Federal Army," 235.

6. Peirpoint to Cameron, June 28, 1861, and W. B. Wood to J. P. Benjamin, Nov. 20, 1861, OR 1, II, 731; IV, 250.

7. Butler to Stanton, May 16, 1862, OR 1, XV, 424; J. S. Denison to S. P. Chase, Aug. 26, 1862, *Diary and Correspondence of Samuel P. Chase,* 311; Winters, *Civil War in Louisiana,* 142–43.

8. E. J. Davis to E. O. C. Ord, Feb. 10, 1864, OR 1, XXXIV, 287; Marten, *Texas Divided,* 77–78, 122–24.

9. J. A. Seddon to Lee, Nov. 17, 1864, and W. J. Hardee, Special Orders No. 38, Feb. 14, 1865, OR 4, III, 824, 1083; Coulter, *Confederate States,* 443.

10. Durrill, *War of Another Kind,* 3–7, 108–9, 166, 173.

11. Auman and Scarborough, "Heroes of America," 345.

12. John R. Phillips, "An Alabama Bluecoat," *Civil War Times Illustrated,* IX (November 1970), 17.

13. C. Bussey to M. L. Harrison, Feb. 28, 1865, OR 1, XLVIII (1), 1008.

14. This account is based primarily on the reports of Lieutenant Colonel Thomas H. Harris, Apr. 26, 1864, and Lieutenant Mack J. Leaming, Jan. 17, 1865, OR 1, XXXII (1), 556–57, 559–63, and on Forrest's reports cited below. For a balanced and reliable study, see Albert Castel, "The Fort Pillow Massacre: A Fresh Examination of the Evidence," *Civil War History,* IV (1958), 37–50.

15. Sworn statement of W. R. McLagan, Apr. 25, 1864; see also C. C. Washburn to Forrest, July 2, 1864, OR 1, XXXII (1), 609–13, 622–23.

16. Forrest to L. Polk, to T. M. Jack, and to J. Davis, all Apr. 15, 1864; Chalmers to his soldiers, Apr. 20, 1864, OR 1, XXXII (1), 609–13, 622–23.

17. Lincoln, Sanitary Fair speech, Apr. 18, 1864, and Lincoln to Stanton, May 17, 1864, *Works of Lincoln,* VII, 302–3, 345–46; McPherson, *Battle Cry of Freedom,* 794.

18. Davis to Secretary of War, Aug. 10, 1864, OR 1, XXXII (1), 617.

19. Opinion on the draft [Sept. 14?] 1863, *Works of Lincoln,* VI, 445–46.

20. J. J. Peck to R. S. Davis, Apr. 14, 1864, OR 1, XXXIII, 870–71. For boards of enrollment, see OR 3, V, 891–911.

21. H. Maynard to G. H. Thomas, Dec. 8, 1861; Rosecrans to Stanton, Sept. 11, 1863; J. C. Kelton to W. R. Price, OR 1, VII, 484–85; XXX (3), 529; OR 3, IV, 925; Carter, *First Regiment of Tennessee Volunteer Cavalry,* 264.

22. Phillips, "An Alabama Bluecoat," 18; G. G. Garner, General Orders No. 124, Aug. 25, 1862; Forrest, report, Nov. 6, 1862, OR 1, XVI (1), 958; XX (1), 6–7; Bishop, *Loyalty on the Frontier,* 7; Hedrick to Lincoln, Sept. 23, 1862, Robert Todd Lincoln Collection, Library of Congress.

23. Carter, *First Regiment of Tennessee Volunteer Cavalry,* 12; Phillips, "An Alabama Bluecoat," 16. See also Temple, *East Tennessee,* 544.

24. J. R. Matthews to A. Johnson, June 12, 1865, *Johnson Papers,* VIII, 224–25.

25. Temple, *East Tennessee*, 551; [Demby], *Mysteries and Miseries of Arkansas*, 7–8.

26. F. H. Hamilton to A. Johnson, June 9, 1863, *Johnson Papers*, VI, 241–42 and n; Butler to Halleck, Aug. 27, 1862, and J. J. Peck to J. G. Foster, Aug. 25, 1863, *OR* 1, XV, 556; XXIX (2), 100–101; Smyrl, "Texans in the Federal Army," 248.

27. Banks to Halleck, Oct. 16, 1863, *OR* 1, XXVI (1), 767; Report, Provost Marshal General's Bureau, Mar. 17, 1866, *OR* 3, V, 607–8; Lincoln to Johnson, July 3, 1862, *Works of Lincoln*, V, 302–3; J. A. Rogers to Johnson, Aug. 20, 1862, *Johnson Papers*, V, 626–27.

28. Peirpoint to Cameron, June 28, 1861, and H. J. Fisher to G. W. Munford, Oct. 23, 1861, *OR* 1, II, 730; V, 915.

29. Butler to Stanton, May 16, 1862; J. G. Blunt to Schofield, Nov. 9, 1862; J. A. Logan to Rawlins, Feb. 6, 1864, *OR* 1, XIII, 786; XV, 424; XXXII (1), 128.

30. Banks, Special Orders No. 209, Aug. 24, 1863; J. Y. Smith to Stanton, Sept. 4, Nov. 7, 1863; H. Robinson, testimony before a military commission, Sept. 5, 1863; Banks to T. M. Vincent, Oct. 16, 1863, *OR* 1, XXVI (1), 262–73.

31. H. A. Crane to H. W. Bowers, Sept. 4, 1864, *OR* 1, LII (1), 614.

32. *Knoxville Whig*, Aug. 30, 1865, and Brownlow to Johnson, Aug. 31, 1865, *Johnson Papers*, 686 and n.

33. S. Crane to J. Darr, May 27, 1863, *OR* 3, III, 237.

34. C. P. Stone to W. B. Franklin, Oct. 28, 1863, *OR* 1, XXVI (1), 778; J. B. Mitchell to Johnson, July 2, 1864, *Johnson Papers*, VII, 5–6 and 6n.

35. F. Clarkson to A. A. Neal, Dec. 18, 1863; I. N. Palmer to B. F. Butler, Apr. 23, 1864, and to R. S. Davis, Apr. 28, 1864, *OR* 1, XXIX (1), 979–80; XXX, 959–60, 1010.

36. A. W. Bishop to C. W. Marsh, Nov. 17, 1862, and J. I. Worthington, report, Jan. 8, 1864, *OR* 1, XIII, 800; XXII (1), 781.

37. O. Adair "and 85 others" to C. C. Andrews, Mar. 16, 1864, and J. Brown to F. Steele, June 26, 1864, *OR* 1, XXXIV (2), 631; (4), 561.

38. C. Bussey to J. Levering, Mar. 11, 1865, *OR* 1, XLVIII (1), 1150–51.

39. Butler to Stanton, May 16, July 16, 1862, *OR* 1, XV, 424, 521.

40. E. J. Davis to E. O. C. Ord, Feb. 10, 1864; McClernand to R. B. Irwin, Apr. 9, 1864; H. M. Day to W. H. Clark, Aug. 3, 1864, *OR* 1, XXXIV (2), 288; (3), 102; XLV (2), 532.

41. Marten, *Texas Divided*, 124–26.

42. Johnson to Thomas, Aug. 16, 1864, *Johnson Papers*, VII, 98; Phelps to J. B. Sanborn, Dec. 4, 1864, and Sanborn endorsement, Dec. 8, 1864, *OR* 1, XLI (4), 764.

43. Marten, *Texas Divided*, 78; Hoole, *Alabama Tories*, 18; *Report of the Adjutant General of Arkansas*, 256; Richard N. Current, *The History of Wisconsin: The Civil War Era, 1848–1873* (Madison: State Historical Society of Wisconsin, 1976), 353, 355; J. B. Fry to Stanton, Sept. 11, 1865, and report of the Provost Marshal General's Bureau, Mar. 17, 1866, *OR* 3, V, 109, 688–89.

44. Eaton, *Southern Confederacy*, 271; Coulter, *Confederate States*, 463–64.

7. Fighting by Southern Federals

1. R. E. Holcomb to R. B. Irwin, Jan. 5, 1863, and to W. B. Hunt, Apr. 28, 1863; W. Dwight to J. Hibbert, Apr. 27, 1863, OR 1, XV, 198, 373, 378.

2. Banks, General Order No. 49, June 15, 1863, and No. 25, Feb. 19, 1864, OR 1 XXVI (1), 56–59, and (2), 21–23.

3. Lincoln to James C. Conkling, Aug. 26, 1863, *Works of Lincoln,* VI, 409.

4. T. J. Lucas to F. W. Emery, Mar. 23, 1864, and A. L. Lee to G. B. Drake, Apr. 5, 1864, OR 1, XXXIV (1), 448–49, 463.

5. J. M. Neil to B. B. Campbell, Feb. 1, 1865, with endorsement by T. W. Sherman, Feb. 3, 1865, OR 1, XLI (2), 259; XLVIII (1), 82–83.

6. F. Steele, report, Apr. 12, 1865, and P. A. Willis, report, Apr. 15, 1865, OR 1, XLIX (1), 279–80, 284–85.

7. B. F. Morey to N. P. Banks, Sept. 14, 1864, and Banks, Special Orders No. 248, Sept. 14, 1864, OR 1, XLI (3), 183–84.

8. T. W. Sherman, report, May 18, 1863, OR 1, XV, 406; Smyrl, "Texans in the Federal Army," 238–39.

9. Banks to F. J. Herron, Dec. 25, 1863; Herron to W. Dwight, June 26, 1864; H. M. Day to G. B. Drake, Aug. 15, 1864; OR 1, XXXIV (4), 599; XXVI (1), 880–81; XLI (1), 212; Smyrl, "Texans in the Federal Army," 243.

10. Wallace to Grant, Feb. 22, 1865, OR 1, XLVIII (1), 938.

11. Organization of troops, Department of the Gulf, June 9, 1864; Asboth to J. Hibbert, Feb. 10, 1865, and G. B. Drake to Asboth, Feb. 13, 1865, OR 1, XXXIV (4), 277; XLIX (1), 687, 707.

12. E. H. Newton to M. D. McAlester, Oct. 17, 1864; A. B. Spurling, report, Mar. 27, 1865; Spurling to F. Steele, Apr. 8, 1865, OR 1, XLV (4), 26; XLIX (1), 309; XLIX (2), 288.

13. E. C. Weeks, report, Feb. 16, 1865; Weeks to J. S. Ransom, May 30, 1865, OR 1, XLIX (1), 40–41; XLIX (2), 984.

14. D. W. Emerson, report, Jan. 28, 1863, OR 1, XXIV (1), 331–32.

15. B. H. Grierson to T. H. Harris, Apr. 2, 1864; J. Kargé, report, July 24, 1864; J. C. Hess, report, Aug. 27, 1864, OR 1, XXXII (3), 235–36; XXXIX (1), 247, 392–94.

16. Grierson, report, Jan. 14, 1865; E. D. Osband to H. Davis, Mar. 28, 1865; organization of troops, District of the Etowah, Apr. 30, 1865; L. Merrill to G. H. Thomas, May 4, 1865, OR 1, XLV (1), 845–47; XLIX (2), 120, 540, 606.

17. S. G. French to S. Cooper, Dec. 12, 1862; J. T. Mizell, report, Dec. 16, 1862; C. W. Flusser to J. G. Foster, Dec. 30, 1862, OR 1, XVIII, 48–49.

18. J. J. Peck, General Orders No. 34, Nov. 10, 1863; No. 39, Nov. 28, 1863; No. 2, Jan. 2, 1864, OR 1, XXIX (1), 496, 661, 995–96.

19. Wessells to Peck, Aug. 18, 1864; Ripley to Peck, Apr. 22, 1864; Palmer to B. F. Butler, Apr. 23, 1864, OR 1, XXXIII, 299, 948–49, 959–60.

20. Schofield to S. R. Curtis, Nov. 9, 1862; A. W. Bishop to C. W. Marsh, Nov. 19, 1862; Herron to Curtis, Dec. 12, 1862, OR 1, XIII, 784, 805–6; XXII (1), 102–3.

21. M. L. Harrison, report, Jan. 27, 1863, and J. Stuart, report, Jan. 28, 1863, *OR* 1, XXII (1), 220–21.

22. W. A. Phillips to Curtis, Feb. 17, 1863; Harrison to Curtis, Apr. 1, 1863, and to Herron, Apr. 3, 1863, *OR* 1, XXII (2), 114, 192–93.

23. Harrison, reports, Apr. 18, 19, 1863; Curtis to Harrison, Apr. 20, 1863; Cabell, report, Apr. 25, 1863; J. McNeil to Harrison, Sept. 8, 1863, *OR* 1, XXII (1), 305–13; XXII (2), 517–18.

24. Harrison to Curtis, Oct. 28, 1864, and to J. B. Sanborn, Nov. 20, 1864; Sanborn to A. Pleasonton, Nov. 12, 1864, *OR* 1, XLI (1), 397; XLI (4), 544–45, 631.

25. R. R. Livingston to W. D. Green, Feb. 26, 1864; H. C. Fillebrown to J. W. Stephens, May 5, 1864; J. M. Wilson to C. T. Christensen, Nov. 15, 1864, and Jan. 21, 1865, *OR* 1, XXIX (2), 426; XXIV (3), 460; XLI (4), 570; XLVIII (1), 600–1.

26. D. Provence to E. P. Turner, Feb. 16, 1865; L. N. C. Swagerty to J. J. Fagan, Mar. 8, 1865; M. J. Thompson to J. J. Reynolds, Apr. 12, 1865, *OR* 1, XLVIII (2), 78–79.

27. Hoole, *Alabama Tories*, 24–27.

28. H. Binmore to Spencer, Oct. 3, 1863; Hurlbut to J. C. Kelton, Oct. 6, 1863; Ferguson, report, Oct. 31, 1863, *OR* 1, XXX (4), 118–19; XXXI (1), 38; Hoole, *Alabama Tories*, 29–31.

29. Hoole, *Alabama Tories*, 32–33, 35, 37–42.

30. Spencer, report, Mar. 30, 1865; Kirkpatrick, report, Apr. 5, 1865, *OR* 1, XLVII (1), 857–63, 891–95; Hoole, *Alabama Tories*, 43–47.

31. McClellan, address, May 26, 1861; to E. D. Townsend, June 3, 10, 1861; and "To the Inhabitants of Western Virginia," June 23, 1861, *OR* 1, II, 49, 64–65, 196.

32. Kelley to Scott, Oct. 28, 1861; Scott to Kelley, Oct. 30, 1861, *OR* 1, V, 378–80.

33. J. C. Wheeler to W. S. Rosecrans, Nov. 13, 1861; "Record of Events," Department of Western Virginia, Dec. 1861, *OR* 1, V, 411–12, 496.

34. R. H. Milroy, reports, May 14, Sept. 12, 1862; H. Haupt to H. W. Halleck, Aug. 28, 1862, *OR* 1, XII (1), 465–67; XII (2), 318–20; XII (3), 719.

35. J. Snider, report, Sept. 20, 1862; McClellan, report, Oct. 15, 1862; J. H. Lockwood, report, Dec. 16, 1862, *OR* 1, XIX (1), 58, 322; XXI, 131, 299.

36. J. H. Lockwood, report, July 5, 1863; C. E. Capehart, report, Aug. 17, 1863; N. P. Richmond, report, Sept. 5, 1863, *OR* 1, XXVII (1), 463–64, 1005–7, 1018–20.

37. Averell, reports, Aug. 30, Sept. 1, 1863; B. F. Kelley to A. I. Boreman, Nov. 8, Dec. 23, 1863, *OR* 1, XXIX (1), 32–41, 503; XXIX (2), 438, 580.

38. Thoburn, report, Sept. 19, 1864; T. M. Harris, report, Sept. 27, 1864; Army of the Potomac, General Orders No. 10, Mar. 7, 1865; Appomattox campaign, Mar. 29–Apr. 9, 1865, *OR* 1, XLIII (1), 369, 389; XLVI (1), 564; XLVI (2), 876.

39. Goodheart, *History of the Independent Loudoun Virginia Rangers*, 1, 26–27.

40. Means to Miles, Aug. 27, 1862; Miles to W. D. Whipple (two communications), Aug. 27, 1862, *OR* 1, LI (1), 744–46.

41. Munford, report of operations, Aug. 26–Sept. 3, 1862; Miles to Halleck, Sept. 2, 1862; Wool to Stanton, Sept. 3, 1862; Stuart to R. H. Chilton, Oct. 13, 1862, *OR* 1, XII (2), 745, 747–49, 805; XIX (2), 174.

42. Proceedings of a Military Commission Held at Washington City, D.C., Sept. 23, 1862, *OR* 1, XIX (1), 749, 752–55, 799–800.

43. Kelley to Means, Feb. 27, 1863; McReynolds, report, May 14, 1863; Schenck to W. H. Morris, May 14, 1863; J. W. Garrett to Stanton, June 18, 1863; White to W. E. Jones, June 20, 1863, *OR* 1, XXV (1), 1108; XXV (2), 109; XXVII (2), 771; XXVII (3), 200–201; LI (1), 1041.

44. Halleck to Means, June 25, July 2, 1863; W. H. Chesebrough to Captain Cannon, July 1, 1863, *OR* 1, XXVII (3), 317–18, 492; LI (1), 1067–68.

45. Means to Schenck, July 23, 1863; Schenck to Halleck, July 23, 1863; Lockwood to D. N. Couch, Aug. 1, 1863; Means to Heintzelman, Aug. 8, 1863; and to Stanton, Aug. 15, 1863; Taylor to Lowell, Aug. 15, 1863, *OR* 1, XXVII (3), 757, 826–27; XXIX (1), 67; XXIX (2), 52–53.

46. White, report, Oct. 2, 1863; Imboden, report, Oct. 19, 1863; Means, report, Oct. 20, 1863, *OR* 1, XXIX (1), 203–4, 490–91.

47. W. Rumsey to R. F. Taylor, Apr. 1, 1864; Weber to Averell, Apr. 13, 1864, and to T. Melvin, Apr. 19, 1864; Sigel to Weber, Apr. 19, 1864; H. M. Burleigh to Captain Bamford, Apr. 24, 1864; S. F. Woods to Bamford, Apr. 25, 1864; Melvin to Crook, Apr. 26, 1864, *OR* 1, XXXIII, 789, 859–60, 912, 974, 989.

48. Means to Stanton, Aug. 15, 1864; Mosby, report, Sept. 11, 1864; S. F. Adams to Keyes, Sept. 23, 1864; J. D. Stevenson to P. H. Sheridan, Oct. 16, 1864, and to Captain Chamberlain, Mar. 29, 1865; Hancock, report, Feb. 18, 1867, *OR* 1, XLIII (1), 633–35, 799; XLIII (2), 160, 391; XLVI (2), 526; XLVI (3), 279.

49. Carter to G. H. Thomas, Nov. 25, 1861, and to C. O. Joline, June 23, 1862; Morgan to Halleck, Aug. 23, 1862, and to H. G. Wright, Oct. 3, 12, 1862, *OR* 1, VII, 948; X, 67–69; XVI (1), 861, 991; XVI (2), 609–10.

50. Reports of L. Zahm, Jan. 2, 1863; R. H. G. Minty, Jan. 7, 1863; W. S. Hall, Jan. 9, 1863; and J. G. Spears, Jan. 9, 1863, *OR* 1, XX (1), 416–19, 623–26, 634, 647–48.

51. H. C. Gilbert to J. Coburn, Oct. 28, 1863; A. P. Campbell, report, Dec. 28, 1863; T. T. Garrard to E. E. Potter, Jan. 27, 1864, and to J. A. Campbell, Mar. 15, 1864; D. A. Carpenter, report, Sept. 14, 1864, *OR* 1, XXXI (1), 551, 554, 687, 847–48; XXXII (2), 232–33; XXXII (3), 73–74.

52. Reports of G. H. Thomas, Jan. 15, 1864; J. W. Beatty, Mar. 24, 1864; and G. Spalding, Sept. 21–28, 1864, *OR* 1, XXIX (1), 538; XXXI (2), 125; XXXII (1), 542–44.

53. Cox journal, No. 14, 1864; E. B. Beaumont to J. H. Wilson, Nov. 26, 1864, *OR* 1, XLV (1), 356, 1061–62.

54. Reports of J. W. Berry, Dec. 22, 1864; R. H. Dunn, Dec. 22, 1864; and J. A. Cooper, Dec. 23, 1864; J. T. Croxton to A. J. Alexander, Dec. 25, 1864, *OR* 1, XLV (1), 123, 372, 376–77, 574.

55. Reports of E. Hatch, Dec. 16, 1864; J. Wilson, Dec. 21, 1864; G. H. Thomas, Jan. 20, 1865; and D. E. Coon, Jan. 20, 1865, *OR* 1, XLV (1), 40, 551, 578, 591–92; Stanley F. Horn, *The Decisive Battle of Nashville* (Baton Rouge: Louisiana State University Press, 1956), 181.

56. Gillem to A. Johnson, Nov. 8, 16, 1864, *OR* 1, XXXIX (1), 844–46, 888–92.

57. Stoneman to Schofield, Nov. 26, 1864; Gillem, report, Dec. 30, 1864; Stoneman, report, Jan. 6, 1865, *OR* 1, XLV (1), 808–15, 819–24, 1073–74.

58. Reports of W. C. Bartlett, Jan. 28, 1865; J. C. Vaughn, Feb. 5, 1865; D. Tillson, Apr. 9, 1865; and Gillem, Apr. 25, 1865; Stoneman to Tillson, Apr. 27, 1865, *OR* 1, XLIX (1), 9, 330–38, 546, 961.

59. These calculations are based on statistics in Dyer, *Compendium,* 11–12, 40–45.

8. The Unknown Soldiers

1. Lee to J. A. Seddon, Jan. 10, 1863, *OR* 1, XXI, 1085–86.

2. Lincoln to Johnson, Mar. 26, 1863, and to Sherman, July 18, 1864, *Works of Lincoln,* VI, 149–50; VII, 449–50.

3. Thomas W. Humes, *The Loyal Mountaineers of Tennessee* (Knoxville: Ogden Brothers & Co., 1888), 9–10; Scott and Angel, *Thirteenth Regiment,* 51.

4. Ezra J. Warner, *Generals in Gray: Lives of the Confederate Commanders* (Baton Rouge: Louisiana State University Press, 1959), xxiii and *passim.* My count of twenty-six Northern-born-and-bred Confederate generals is derived from Warner's biographical sketches.

5. For the numbers of loyalist and rebel soldiers, see the Appendix.

6. J. T. Peirce to Grant, Sept. 14, 1865, *Grant Papers,* XV, 588; Hoole, *Alabama Tories,* 49–51.

7. Merrill to Thomas, May 4, 1865; Palmer, report, May 6, 1865; Asboth to Christensen, May 15, 1865; A. J. Smith to J. Hough, June 27, 1865, *OR* 1, XLIX (1), 550; XLIX (2), 606, 797, 1044–45.

8. J. W. Scully to Johnson, May 14, 1865; R. Johnson to Johnson, May 31, 1865, *Johnson Papers,* VIII, 70–71, 155.

9. Letters to Johnson from J. D. Parkinson, May 29, 1865; R. H. Northrop, May 30, 1865; and B. W. Huntington, June 9, 1865, *Johnson Papers,* VIII, 135–36, 147, 207.

10. W. Dils to Johnson, May 15, 1865, *Johnson Papers,* VIII, 72; W. J. McNemar et al. to Grant, Aug. 29, 1865; J. T. Peirce to Grant, Sept. 14, 1865, *Grant Papers,* XV, 577–78, 588.

11. A. W. Dillard to Johnson, Aug. 14, 1865, *Johnson Papers,* VIII, 582–83; G. W. Welker to Stevens, Dec. 2, 1865, Thaddeus Stevens Papers, Library of Congress.

12. Grant to A. W. Randall, Aug. 4, 1866, *Grant Papers,* XVI, 278–79.

13. Grant to Johnson, Feb. 9, 1866, *Grant Papers,* XVI, 52.

14. Foster to Morrill, Feb. 28, Mar. 1, 1866, Justin S. Morrill Papers, Library of Congress.

15. M. Roberts to Stevens, May 15, 1866, Stevens Papers.

16. James G. Blaine, *Twenty Years of Congress: From Lincoln to Garfield*, 2 vols. (Norwich, Conn.: Henry Hill Publishing Co., 1884), II, 90, 227; B. W. Hunter to Grant, Aug. 7, 1866, *Grant Papers*, XVI, 536–37; *New York Times*, Sept. 8, 1866.

17. Tourgee, "notes of a speech in 1866," Albion W. Tourgée Papers, Chautauqua County Historical Society, Westfield, N.Y.; Blaine, *Twenty Years of Congress*, II, 230.

18. Grant to H. B. Anthony, Jan. 29, 1867, *Grant Papers*, XVII, 389; *Report of the Adjutant General of Arkansas*, 1. Incomplete muster rolls for thirty-three white Federal regiments are in *Report of the Adjutant General of the State of Tennessee, of the Military Forces of the State, from 1861 to 1866* (Nashville: S. C. Mercer, Printer to the State, 1866).

19. W. H. Hampton to Grant, May 14, 1867; Grant to H. Stanbery, Aug. 31, Sept. 4, 1867; J. M. Binckley to Grant, Sept. 7, 1867, *Grant Papers*, XVII, 311–13.

20. Marten, *Texas Divided*, 129–31, 140–41.

21. O. O. Howard to Grant, Mar. 10, 1868, *Grant Papers*, XVIII, 523–25.

22. Forrest interview with *Cincinnati Commercial* reporter in Memphis, Aug. 28, 1868, quoted in Richard N. Current, ed., *Reconstruction, 1865–1877* (New York: Prentice-Hall, 1965), 93.

23. Mary R. Dearing, *Veterans in Politics: The Story of the G.A.R.* (Baton Rouge: Louisiana State University Press, 1952), 114–15, 420.

24. Allen W. Trelease, *White Terror: The Ku Klux Klan Conspiracy and Southern Reconstruction* (New York: Harper & Row, 1971), 19, 76; Meade to Grant, July 21, 1868, *Grant Papers*, XVIII, 232.

25. Richard N. Current, *Those Terrible Carpetbaggers* (New York: Oxford University Press, 1988), 109, 205–6.

26. Tourgee, *A Fool's Errand*, ed. by John Hope Franklin (Cambridge: Harvard University Press, 1961), 144. On the reimbursement of Unionists for property losses, see Frank W. Klingberg, *The Southern Claims Commission* (Berkeley: University of California Press, 1955), *passim*.

27. Dearing, *Veterans in Politics*, 419; Blaine, *Twenty Years of Congress*, II, 473.

28. Dearing, *Veterans in Politics*, 421; Oliver P. Temple, *East Tennessee and the Civil War* (Cincinnati: R. Clarke Co., 1899), 531.

29. For regimental and other histories of Southern Federals, see Allan Nevins, James I. Robertson, and Bell I. Wiley, eds., *Civil War Books: A Critical Bibliography*, 2 vols. (Baton Rouge: Louisiana State University Press, 1967–69). On Alabama recollections, see Hoole, *Alabama Tories*, 19n, and *Civil War Times Illustrated*, IX (November 1970), 15–20.

30. Sherman, *Memoirs*, II, 152, 269, 294, 340, 342; Johnson and Buel, *Battles and Leaders*, I, 652–59; II, 701–8.

31. Nicolay and Hay, *Abraham Lincoln*, IV, 235, 329–32; V, 61–62, 71, and *passim*.

32. *Autobiography and Personal Reminiscences of Major-General Benj. F. Butler: Butler's Book* (Boston: A. M. Thayer & Co., 1892), 491–95. Butler re-

fers to recruiting prisoners at Point Lookout on page 587 and reprints some of the correspondence concerning the execution of North Carolina loyalists on pages 1048–50.

33. Thomas L. Livermore, *Numbers and Losses in the Civil War in America, 1861–65,* with an introduction by Edward E. Bartell, Jr. (Bloomington: Indiana University Press, 1957), 19.

Appendix

1. Classification of the forces credited, *OR* 3, IV, 1270. Essentially the same statistics on "troops furnished by the several states" can be found in Dyer, *Compendium,* 11.

2. Charles C. Anderson, *Fighting by Southern Federals* (New York: Neale Publishing Co., 1912), 9–11 and *passim.*

3. *Tennessee in the Civil War,* II, 453–608; Scott and Angel, *Thirteenth Regiment,* 49–50; *Johnson Papers,* VII, 388.

4. The quotation is from Curry, *House Divided,* 167–68, citing *Third Biennial Report of the Department of Archives and History of the State of West Virginia* (Charleston, W.Va., 1909) and Charles H. Ambler and Festus P. Summers, *West Virginia, the Mountain State* (New York, 1958), without giving page references. The U.S. provost marshal general credited West Virginia with 27,714 as the "aggregate reduced to a 3-years' standard"; *OR* 3, IV, 1269.

5. *Report of the Adjutant General of Arkansas,* 1, 256; [Demby], *Mysteries and Miseries of Arkansas,* 35.

6. Butler to Stanton, Sept. 1862, *OR* 1, XV, 559.

7. Paludan, *Victims,* 58–59; M. Roberts to Thaddeus Stevens, May 15, 1866, Stevens Papers.

8. Hoole, *Alabama Tories,* 14–18; O. P. Morton to E. M. Stanton, May 11, 1863; E. M. McCook to W. H. Sinclair, Aug. 26, 1863, *OR* 1, XXX (3), 179; *OR* 2, V, 589.

9. Compiled Service Records, cited in Marten, *Texas Divided,* 75.

10. Livermore, *Numbers and Losses,* 10, 18–19, 63.

11. Albert B. Moore, *Conscription and Conflict in the Confederacy* (New York: Macmillan, 1924), 357–58; McPherson, *Battle Cry of Freedom,* 306–7n.

12. One could assume that the loyalists numbered only 90,000 and the rebels 850,000. The loss would then be 9.5 percent of the Confederacy's military manpower. Or one could assume that the loyalists numbered 90,000 and the rebels as many as 900,000. The loss would still be 9 percent. Even this, when considered a double loss, that is, 18 percent, amounts to a very serious shortfall for the Confederacy. Whatever the precise numbers, there can be no doubt that the loyalist defection had a significant bearing on the outcome of the war.

Bibliography

*T*HE BASIC SOURCE for this book is that great
and wonderful storehouse of information *The War of the Rebellion: A
Compilation of the Official Records of the Union and Confederate Armies*, 128 vols. (Washington, D.C.: Government Printing Office,
1880–1901), commonly referred to simply as the *Official Records* and
cited herein as *OR*.

"Nothing is printed in these volumes except duly authenticated contemporaneous records of the war," the compiler declared in the penultimate volume, and there is no reason for hesitating to take him at
his word. But he went on to say that part of the compiler's task had
been "to correct and verify the orthography of the papers used." In
fact, he and his predecessors had corrected not only the spelling but
also the punctuation and grammar. Consequently the hundreds of authors of the correspondence and reports appear to have been uniformly careful and even polished as writers.

Such a very skillful writer as Ulysses S. Grant could not always take
time in the press of military duties to be fastidious about his composition. Here is one of his communications as he actually wrote it and as
it is reproduced in the *Grant Papers*, XI, 385:

The 7th Regt US Vols composed of deserters and prisoners from the
rebel ranks is now on duty at Norfolk—

I have ordered it to the Dept of the North West—Please direct
Pope to send an equal amount of troops to Genl Sherman and if he
can send more to do it. My own opinion is that two or three Regts
can be sent from the Dept of the NW. without danger.

The 1st Regt. US Vols. number 1000 for duty and is a first class
Regiment but it is not right to expose them as where to be taken
Prisoners they must suffer as deserters.

That letter is perfectly clear and needed no editing except for the correction of the slip at the beginning where Grant wrote "7th" when he meant "1st." Following is the edited version as it appears in *OR* 1, XLI (2), 619 (series 1, volume XLI, part 2, page 619):

> The First Regiment of U.S. Volunteers, composed of deserters and prisoners from the rebel ranks, is now on duty at Norfolk. I have ordered it to the Department of the Northwest. Please direct Pope to send an equal amount of troops to General Sherman, and if he can send more to do it. My own opinion is that two or three regiments can be sent from the Department of the Northwest without danger. The First Regiment U.S. Volunteers numbers 1,000 for duty, and is a first-class regiment, but it is not right to expose them where, to be taken prisoners, they must surely suffer as deserters.

Note especially the added word "surely" in the last sentence. One can only imagine what some of the letters and reports, written by men far less literate than Grant, must have looked like before the compilers cleaned them up.

Ever since their publication the *Official Records,* as edited, have constituted a treasure trove for historians of the Civil War. Researchers using them seldom find what they are *not* looking for. They have not previously looked for all the items having to do with Lincoln's loyalists. There are a great many such documents in the compilation, as the endnotes of the present book attest. There are also a few relevant items in *Official Records of the Union and Confederate Navies in the War of the Rebellion,* 30 vols. (Washington, D.C.: Government Printing Office, 1894–1922), cited herein as *ORN.*

Other important contemporary sources are the published works of Abraham Lincoln and papers of Andrew Johnson and Ulysses S. Grant. The Robert Todd Lincoln Collection of manuscripts in the Library of Congress, consisting mostly of President Lincoln's incoming mail, contains relevant material, as do a few other Library of Congress collections, which are identified in Sellers, *Civil War Manuscripts.*

Noteworthy books by contemporaries are listed below under the names of Barton, Blaine, Brownlow, Carter, Chase, Demby, Edmondston, Goodheart, Hawkins, Humes, Reader, Scott, Sutton, and Temple. The most helpful scholarly studies are those by Auman, D. A. Brown, Curry, Durrill, Elliott, Hoole, Marten, and Smyrl. Indispensable references are Dyer's *Compendium* and Boatner's *Civil War Dic-*

tionary, the latter a vade mecum that deserves many more specific acknowledgments than it has received in my notes.

The following list, alphabetical by author, consists of published primary and secondary sources that have been found relevant to the present work.

Adkins, John R. "The Public Career of Andrew Jackson Hamilton." M.A. thesis, University of Texas, Austin, 1947.

Ambler, Charles H. *Francis H. Pierpont, Union War Governor of Virginia and Father of West Virginia.* Chapel Hill: University of North Carolina Press, 1937.

Anderson, Charles C. *Fighting by Southern Federals.* New York: Neale Publishing Co., 1912.

Arkansas. *Report of the Adjutant General of Arkansas, for the Period of the Late Rebellion, and to November 1, 1866.* Washington, D.C.: Government Printing Office, 1867.

Auman, William T. "Neighbor against Neighbor: The Inner Civil War in the Randolph County Area of Confederate North Carolina." *North Carolina Historical Review,* LXI (January 1984), 59–92.

Auman, William T., and David D. Scarboro. "The Heroes of America in Civil War North Carolina." *North Carolina Historical Review,* LVIII (October 1981), 327–63.

Baker, D. W. C., comp. *A Texas Scrap-Book, Made Up of the History, Biography, and Miscellany of Texas and Its People.* New York: A. S. Barnes & Co., 1875.

Barrett, John G. *The Civil War in North Carolina.* Chapel Hill: University of North Carolina Press, 1963.

Barton, Thomas H. *Autobiography, Including a History of the Fourth Regt. West Va. Vol. Inf'y. . . .* Charleston, W.Va.: Print Co., 1890.

Bishop, Albert W. *Loyalty on the Frontier, or Sketches of Union Men of the South-West; with Incidents and Adventures in Rebellion on the Border.* St. Louis: R. P. Studley and Co., 1863.

Blaine, James G. *Twenty Years of Congress, from Lincoln to Garfield.* 2 vols. Norwich, Conn.: Henry Hill Publishing Co., 1884.

Boatner, Mark M., III. *The Civil War Dictionary.* New York: David McKay, 1959.

Brown, Dee Alexander. *The Galvanized Yankees.* Urbana: University of Illinois Press, 1963.

Brown, Norman D. *Edward Stanly: Whiggery's Tarheel "Conqueror."* University: University of Alabama Press, 1974.

Brownlow, William G. *Sketches of the Rise, Progress, and Decline of Secession; with a Narrative of Personal Adventures Among the Rebels.* Philadelphia: George W. Childs, 1862.

Butler, Benjamin F. *Autobiography and Personal Reminiscences of Major-General Benj. F. Butler: Butler's Book.* Boston: A. M. Thayer & Co., 1892.

Carter, William R. *History of the First Regiment of Tennessee Volunteer Cavalry in the Great War of the Rebellion. . . .* Knoxville: Gaut-Ogden Co., 1902.

Chase, Salmon P. *Diary and Correspondence of Salmon P. Chase. (Annual Report of the American Historical Association for the Year 1902,* Vol. II.) Washington, D.C.: Government Printing Office, 1903.

Coulter, E. Merton. *The Confederate States of America, 1861–1865.* Baton Rouge: Louisiana State University Press, 1950.

Curry, Richard O. *A House Divided: A Study of Statehood Politics and the Copperhead Movement in West Virginia.* Pittsburgh: University of Pittsburgh Press, 1964.

Dearing, Mary R. *Veterans in Politics: The Story of the G.A.R.* Baton Rouge: Louisiana State University Press, 1952.

Delaney, N. C. "Charles Henry Foster and the Unionists of Eastern North Carolina." *North Carolina Historical Review,* XXXVII (July 1960).

[Demby, James W.] *Mysteries and Miseries of Arkansas; or, a Defence of the Loyalty of the State.* By a Refugee. St. Louis: the Author, 1863.

Durrill, Wayne K. *War of Another Kind: A Southern Community in the Great Rebellion.* New York: Oxford University Press, 1990.

Dyer, Frederick H. *Compendium of the War of the Rebellion.* [1908.] Dayton, Ohio: National Historical Society, 1979.

Eaton, Clement. *A History of the Southern Confederacy.* New York: Macmillan, 1954.

Edmondston, Catherine. *"Journal of a Secesh Lady": The Diary of Catherine Ann Devereux Edmondston, 1860–1866.* Raleigh: North Carolina Division of Archives and History, 1979.

Elliott, Claude. "Union Sentiment in Texas, 1861–1865." *Southwestern Historical Quarterly,* L (April 1947), 449–77.

Escott, Paul D. *Many Excellent People: Power and Privilege in North Carolina, 1850–1900.* Chapel Hill: University of North Carolina Press, 1985.

Goodheart, Briscoe. *History of the Independent Loudoun Virginia Rangers, U.S. Vol. Cav. (Scouts) 1862–65.* Washington, D.C.: Press of McGill & Wallace, 1896.

Grant, Ulysses S. *The Papers of Ulysses S. Grant.* Edited by John Y. Simon. 18 vols. Carbondale: Southern Illinois University Press, 1967–1991.

Gray, Ronald N. "Edmund J. Davis, Radical Republican and Reconstruction Governor of Texas." Ph.D. diss., Texas Tech University, 1976.

Hamand, Lavern M. "Ward Hill Lamon, Lincoln's 'Particular Friend.'" Ph.D. diss., University of Illinois, 1949.

Harrington, Fred H. *Fighting Politician: Major General N. P. Banks.* Philadelphia: University of Pennsylvania Press, 1948.

Hassler, Warren W., Jr. *General George B. McClellan: Shield of the Union.* Baton Rouge: Louisiana State University Press, 1957.

Hawkins, Rush C. *An Account of the Assassination of Loyal Citizens of North Carolina, for Having Served in the Union Army, Which Took Place at Kingston* [sic] *in the Months of February and March, 1864.* New York: J. H. Folan, 1897.

Hoole, William S. *Alabama Tories: The First Alabama Cavalry, U.S.A., 1862–1865.* Tuscaloosa, Ala.: Confederate Publishing Co., 1960.

Humes, Thomas W. *The Loyal Mountaineers of Tennessee.* Knoxville: Ogden Brothers & Co., 1888.

Johnson, Andrew. *The Papers of Andrew Johnson.* Edited by Leroy P. Graf, Ralph W. Haskins, and Paul Bergeron. 8 vols. Knoxville: University of Tennessee Press, 1967–1989.

Johnson, Ludwell H. *Red River Campaign: Politics and Cotton in the Civil War.* Baltimore: Johns Hopkins Press, 1958.

Johnson, R. U., and C. C. Buel. *Battles and Leaders of the Civil War.* 4 vols. New York: The Century Co., 1887–1888.

Klingberg, Frank W. *The Southern Claims Commission.* Berkeley: University of California Press, 1955.

Lincoln, Abraham. *The Collected Works of Abraham Lincoln.* Edited by Roy P. Basler. 9 vols. New Brunswick, N.J.: Rutgers University Press, 1953–1955.

Livermore, Thomas L. *Numbers and Losses in the Civil War in America: 1861–65.* [1900.] With an introduction by Edward E. Barthell, Jr. Bloomington: Indiana University Press, 1957.

McPherson, James M. *Battle Cry of Freedom: The Civil War Era.* New York: Oxford University Press, 1988.

Marten, James. *Texas Divided: Loyalty and Dissent in the Lone Star State, 1856–1874.* Lexington: University Press of Kentucky, 1990.

Moore, Albert B. *Conscription and Conflict in the Confederacy.* New York: Macmillan, 1924.

Nevins, Allan, James I. Robertson, and Bell I. Wiley, eds. *Civil War Books: A Critical Bibliography.* 2 vols. Baton Rouge: Louisiana State University Press, 1967–1969.

Nicolay, John G., and John Hay. *Abraham Lincoln: A History.* 10 vols. New York: The Century Co., 1890.

Nulty, William H. *Confederate Florida: The Road to Olustee.* Tuscaloosa: University of Alabama Press, 1990.

Paludan, Philip S. *Victims: A True Story of the Civil War.* Knoxville: University of Tennessee Press, 1981.

Phillips, John R. "An Alabama Bluecoat." With an introduction by Donald B. Dodd. *Civil War Times Illustrated,* IX (November 1970), 15–20.

Quarles, Benjamin. *The Negro in the Civil War.* Boston: Little, Brown, 1953.

Randall, J. G. *The Civil War and Reconstruction.* Boston: D. C. Heath, 1937.

Reader, Francis S. *History of the Fifth West Virginia Cavalry, Formerly the Second Virginia Infantry, and of Battery G, First West Va. Light Artillery.* New Brighton, Pa.: F. S. Reader. 1890.

Scott, Samuel W., and Samuel P. Angel. *History of the Thirteenth Regiment, Tennessee Volunteer Cavalry, U.S.A. . . .* Knoxville, 1903.

Sellers, John R., comp. *Civil War Manuscripts: A Guide to the Collections in the Manuscript Division of the Library of Congress.* Washington, D.C.: Library of Congress, 1986.

Smyrl, Frank H. "Texans in the Federal Army, 1861–1865." *Southwestern Historical Quarterly,* LXV (October 1961), 234–50.

Sutton, Joseph J. *History of the Second Regiment West Virginia Cavalry Volunteers, During the War of the Rebellion.* Portsmouth, Ohio, 1892.

Temple, Oliver P. *East Tennessee and the Civil War*. Cincinnati: R. Clarke Co., 1899.

Tennessee. Adjutant General's Office. *Report of the Adjutant General of the State of Tennessee, of the Military Forces of the State, from 1861 to 1866*. Nashville: S. C. Mercer, Printer to the State, 1866.

Tennessee. Civil War Centennial Commission. *Tennessee in the Civil War: A Military History of Confederate and Union Units with Available Rosters of Personnel*. 2 vols. Nashville, 1964.

Tourgee, Albion W. *A Fool's Errand*. Edited by John Hope Franklin. Cambridge: Harvard University Press, 1961.

Trefousse, Hans L. *Andrew Johnson: A Biography*. New York: W. W. Norton, 1989.

Trelease, Allen W. *White Terror: The Ku Klux Klan Conspiracy and Southern Reconstruction*. New York: Harper & Row, 1971.

U.S. Congress. 39th Congress, 1st session. *House of Representatives Executive Document No. 98*. Washington, D.C.: Government Printing Office, 1866.

U.S. Congress. 41st Congress, 2d session. *House of Representatives Executive Document No. 244*. Washington, D.C.: Government Printing Office, 1870.

Vance, Z. B. *The Papers of Zebulon Baird Vance, Vol. I, 1843–1862*. Edited by Frontis W. Johnston. Raleigh: North Carolina Department of Archives and History, 1963.

Warner, Ezra J. *Generals in Gray: Lives of the Confederate Commanders*. Baton Rouge: Louisiana State University Press, 1959.

Winters, John D. *The Civil War in Louisiana*. Baton Rouge: Louisiana State University Press, 1963.

Index

ILLINOIS
INDIANA
St. Louis
MISSOURI
Louisvil
Springfield
Ozark Mts.
Nashvill
Fayetteville
Chattano
INDIAN TERRITORY
ARKANSAS
Fort Pillow
Memphis
Helena
Tennessee R.
Little Rock
Decatur
MISSISSIPPI
ALABAMA
Montgome
Shreveport
Vicksburg
Corinth
TEXAS
LOUISIANA
Port Hudson
New Orleans
Galveston
Fort St. Philip
Fort Jackson
Mississippi Delta
Gulf of Mexico
Brazos Santiago
Rio Grande
Brownsville
Matamoros
MEXICO